101 Things You Need to Know

... and Some You Don't!

* Write your own dedications in here

Richard dedicates this book to

Helen * and Ruby *

Tracey dedicates this book to

Tom * and Toby *

Published in the United States of America in 2007 by
Walker Publishing Company, Inc.
Distributed to the trade by Holtzbrinck Publishers

Published in Great Britain in 2006 by Bloomsbury Publishing Plc

For information about permission to reproduce selections from this book, write to Permissions, Walker & Company, 104 Fifth Avenue, New York, New York 10011

Library of Congress Catalog-in-Publication Data available upon request
ISBN-13: 978-0-8027-9674-5 • ISBN-10: 0-8027-9674-5 (paperback)

Visit Walker & Company's Web site at www.walkeryoungreaders.com

Printed in Malaysia by Tien Wah Press

2 4 6 8 10 9 7 5 3 1

All papers used by Walker & Company are natural, recyclable products made from wood grown in well-managed forests. The manufacturing processes conform to the environmental regulations of the country of origin.

www.101thingstodobook.com

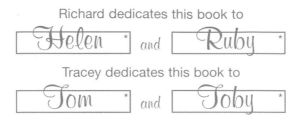

101 Things You Need to Know

. . . and Some You Don't!

Designed and illustrated by Richard Horne
Written by Tracey Turner and Richard Horne

Walker & Company
New York

Introduction

Ever wonder where things you take for granted in your daily life actually come from? Or ponder how things in nature ended up the way they are—like, why isn't the ocean purple and sweet tasting rather than salty? The world is full of weird and fascinating things, far too many to learn about them all, but this is a great place to start and a fun way to make sure you don't end up old and boring.

Master

Why do stars twinkle? How would you survive an avalanche? Can you sneeze with your eyes open? What's the scariest thing in the world? The answers lie inside, so sharpen your curiosity and prepare to be amazed. . . .

Complete

Keep track of what you have mastered by filling in the easy-to-follow forms.

Bask in the Glory

When you have finished, you will be wise and knowledgeable and the envy of all your less-interesting friends.

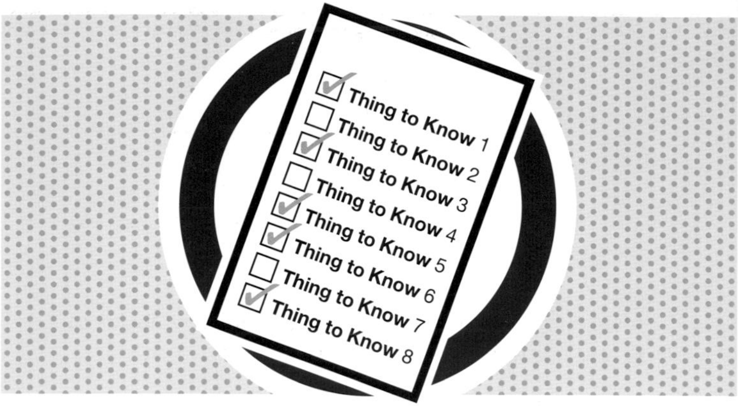

How to Use This Book

The idea is simple. Master the **101 Things You Need to Know**, check the boxes, fill in the forms, and stick in the colored stars as you go.

About the Forms

- Be honest with the information you enter in the forms.
- There may be a few tricky questions on some of the forms. Don't worry if you get stuck—you'll find the answers at the back of the book.
- You may find some of the forms too small for all the information you'd like to enter. To solve this problem, you can copy the extra pages at the back of the book or visit the Web site for extra or duplicate pages at **www.101thingstodobook.com**.

Your **Things to Know**

If there are **Things You Need to Know** that aren't mentioned in the book, add your top ten **Things to Know** on the pages provided at the back.

Helpful Tips

The tips on the opposite page offer some guidelines to completing the **Things to Know**.

101 Things You Need to Know . . . and Some You Don't!

Tips

- Master as many **Things to Know** as possible before it's too late and you become old and boring.
- Always carry this book with you (you may **Need to Know** something at an unexpected moment).
- As you learn more amazing **Things to Know**, be aware that friends may envy how interesting and knowledgeable you've become.
- You don't have to do it alone. Many of the **Things to Know** will be more fun if you master them with the help of your friends (and stop them from being envious too).
- Push yourself. This book is crammed with fascinating **Things to Know,** but there's always more to discover.
- Think outside the box. If you find some **Things to Know** that really interest you, don't stop here—do your own research and find out even more.
- Above all, have fun. The **Things to Know** are something to enhance your daily life and make the world more interesting.

101 Things You Need to Know . . . and Some You Don't!

Some Things You Will Need

Here is a list of some of the items you will need to complete the **101 Things You Need to Know**. You don't need to have them all before you start, but it's advisable to at least have a pen, a pair of scissors, glue, a camera, access to a computer, and some money. You can get hold of the other items as you continue through the list, but the willingness to learn, a sense of adventure, spontaneity, a mischievous spirit, a sense of humor, a good imagination, and optimism are all up to you.

- ☐ A secret hiding place for this book!
- ☐ A brain like a sponge
- ☐ A good imagination
- ☐ Neat handwriting
- ☐ A pen
- ☐ Paper
- ☐ Glue
- ☐ A camera
- ☐ A computer
- ☐ A photocopier
- ☐ A pair of scissors
- ☐ Skills to trade
- ☐ A little help from your parents
- ☐ A little help from your friends
- ☐ A willing assistant
- ☐ The Sun
- ☐ The Moon
- ☐ The stars
- ☐ A rainbow
- ☐ A waterfall
- ☐ A mountain
- ☐ An earthquake
- ☐ Thunder and lightning
- ☐ Various cloudy days
- ☐ A hot country
- ☐ A cold country
- ☐ Various nocturnal creatures
- ☐ Various camouflaged creatures
- ☐ A pet
- ☐ Salt
- ☐ Water
- ☐ Two grains of sand
- ☐ A lot of sand
- ☐ A spade
- ☐ A pirate outfit
- ☐ A newspaper
- ☐ A magnifying glass
- ☐ Fireworks
- ☐ A balloon
- ☐ A wool sweater
- ☐ Snow
- ☐ A stopwatch
- ☐ A haunted house
- ☐ A fast pair of legs
- ☐ A bike
- ☐ A skateboard
- ☐ A golf ball
- ☐ A Ping-Pong ball
- ☐ A football
- ☐ Various fish
- ☐ A strong stomach
- ☐ A grain of rice
- ☐ Two peas
- ☐ Two grapes
- ☐ Three crackers
- ☐ Chocolate
- ☐ Lots of honey
- ☐ Dog poop
- ☐ Basic cooking skills
- ☐ A calendar
- ☐ A set of scales
- ☐ A sixth sense
- ☐ A feather
- ☐ A stone
- ☐ A jumbo jet
- ☐ A sense of humor

101 Things You Need To Know and Some You Don't!

Important Information

WARNING:

WHEN EMBARKING ON THE **101 THINGS YOU NEED TO KNOW AND SOME YOU DON'T,** PLEASE PROCEED WITH CARE.

FOR SOME OF THE **THINGS TO KNOW** YOU WILL NEED THE SUPERVISION OF AN ADULT. IF IN DOUBT, CONSULT AN ADULT ANYWAY.

ONLY THE BEST OF EFFORTS HAVE BEEN MADE TO ASSURE THE ACCURACY, COMPLETENESS, AND USEFULNESS OF THE INFORMATION CONTAINED WITHIN THESE PAGES.

THE PUBLISHER AND AUTHORS, HOWEVER, CANNOT ASSUME RESPONSIBILITY FOR ANY ACCIDENTS THAT OCCUR AS A RESULT OF USING THIS BOOK.

101 Things You Need to Know and Some You Don't!

The List

1. ☐ What Was the Biggest Bang Ever?
2. ☐ What Is DNA (and Are We All That Different from Chimps)?
3. ☐ Why Don't Fish Drown?
4. ☐ What Were the Seven Wonders of the World?
5. ☐ Why Is Our Blood Red?
6. ☐ What Is the Oldest Living Thing in the World?
7. ☐ What Is the Difference Between a Fruit and a Vegetable?
8. ☐ Is Time Travel Possible?
9. ☐ Who Would Win the Animal Olympic 100-Meter Race?
10. ☐ How Do You Do an Ollie on a Skateboard?
11. ☐ Who Were the First Chocoholics?
12. ☐ How Big Is the Universe?
13. ☐ Did Cannibals Really Exist?
14. ☐ Will Your Stomach Explode if You Eat Too Much?
15. ☐ When Was It Possible to Walk from London to New York?
16. ☐ How Do Mountains Grow?
17. ☐ Is Your Teacher an Alien?
18. ☐ What Are the Biggest and Smallest Animals in the World?
19. ☐ How Much Does the Earth Weigh?
20. ☐ Which Way Is North?
21. ☐ What Is the Solar System (and Could It Fit in Your Yard)?
22. ☐ Why Don't We Fall Off the Earth?
23. ☐ How Does a Snake Swallow Things Bigger Than Its Own Head?
24. ☐ When Did Money Start Making the World Go Around?
25. ☐ If Light Is Invisible, How Can We See?
26. ☐ How Do You Avoid Being Struck by Lightning?
27. ☐ What Is the Deadliest Martial Art?
28. ☐ When Should You Use the Heimlich Maneuver?
29. ☐ How Long Is a Light-Year?
30. ☐ What Is at the Bottom of the Ocean?
31. ☐ Can a Cockroach Really Live for a Week Without Its Head?
32. ☐ What Is an Ice Age (and When Are We Due for Another One)?
33. ☐ How Do You Survive Falling over a Waterfall?
34. ☐ What Is the World's Favorite Pet?
35. ☐ Why Is the Sky Blue?
36. ☐ How Many Stars Are There in the Milky Way?
37. ☐ Can You Sneeze with Your Eyes Open?
38. ☐ Why Is the Ocean Salty?
39. ☐ What Is the Worst Smell Ever?
40. ☐ How Did the Ancient Egyptians Make the Pyramids?
41. ☐ What Is the World's Most Dangerous Shark?
42. ☐ How Big Is an Atom?
43. ☐ How Do Clouds Stay Up?
44. ☐ What Happens in the Bermuda Triangle?
45. ☐ Why Do Some Animals Shed Their Skin?
46. ☐ Who Built Stonehenge, How and Why?
47. ☐ Who Is the Richest Person in the World?
48. ☐ What Makes Farts So Smelly?
49. ☐ Does One Dog Year Equal Seven Human Years?
50. ☐ Where on Earth Is the Coldest Place?
51. ☐ How Do You Survive on a Desert Island?

101 Things You Need to Know and Some You Don't!

The List

What Was the Biggest Bang Ever?

The big bang theory is one way of explaining how the universe began. Other theories have been put forward, but none as popular. Most scientists accept it as the most probable theory, even though it's been pretty impossible to prove

Ka-Boom!

A priest named George Lemaître first came up with the big bang theory in 1927. He proposed that the universe began when a single atom exploded. Later experiments suggest that his theory was correct. According to the standard big bang theory . . .

- First, about 13.7 billion years ago, there was a "singularity." A singularity isn't fully understood, but it's an area where the pressure of gravity squashe matter into an infinitely small point of infinite density (singularities lie at the center of black holes). No one knows where the singularity came from in the first place, of course.
- Then, the singularity began to expand. This is the "big bang"—except scientists say that it's wrong to think of it as an explosion (so it's really not a very good name). The singularity went from being absolutely tiny and incredibly hot to extremely large (i.e., the size of the universe) and the sort of temperature it is today.
- Experiments support the big bang theory: Edwin Hubble discovered that galaxies seem to be moving away from us at speeds that are in proportion to how far away they are—suggesting that everything started out from the same point and is now expanding outward.

Big Balloon Theory? Scientists argue that it's more accurate to think of the big bang as a big expansion—instead of an explosion, think of an infinitely small balloon being blown up until it's the size of the universe.

What Was the Biggest Bang Ever? **Form**

Once you have mastered this **Thing to Know**, stick your Achieved Star here and fill in the form

Achieved

THE COSMIC CALENDAR

The history of the universe can be expressed as a calendar. According to Carl Sagan's Cosmic Calendar, if the big bang occurs on the very first second of January 1 and present day is represented as midnight on December 31, then the first humans won't appear until 1:30 p.m. on December 31! Write these facts on a calendar, and every time you reach a day with an event, educate those around you with your amazing knowledge of the universe.

01 January
January 1
The big bang

01 March
March 1
The Milky Way is formed

09 September
September 9
The solar system is formed

14 September
September 14
The Earth is formed

25 September
September 25
Oldest known single-celled life appears

02 October
October 2
Oldest known rocks are formed

09 October
October 9
Oldest known fossils (bacteria/algae) appear

12 November
November 12
Photosynthetic plants appear

15 November
November 15
First multicellular organisms appear

15 December
December 15
An explosion of life—many new forms appear

17 December
December 17
First vertebrates appear

18 December
December 18
Land plants appear

20 December
December 20
Four-legged animals appear

21 December
December 21
Insects appear

24 December
December 24
Dinosaurs appear

25 December
December 25
Mammals appear

27 December
December 27
Birds appear

29 December
December 29
Meteorite, asteroid, or comet wipes out the dinosaurs

31 December

The rest of Earth's history took place on December 31. The timescale for this period is measured in hours, minutes, and seconds, as a lot takes place in such a small period of time.

1:30:00 p.m.
First man

10:30:00 p.m.
Agriculture

11:59:20 p.m.
Egyptian civilizations

11:59:50 p.m.
Birth of Christ

11:59:56 p.m.
Crusades

11:59:58 p.m.
Renaissance

11:59:59 p.m.
Space travel

00.00.00
Present day

At the same time you could master these **Things to Know**:
12: How Big Is the Universe? • 21: What Is the Solar System (and Could It Fit in Your Yard)? • 101: What Would Happen to You in a Black Hole?

What Is DNA (and Are We All That Different from Chimps)?

The initials *DNA* save us from having to say "deoxyribonucleic acid"—which is the chemical that controls all life on Earth. DNA contains the instructions for making every living thing. It's like a teeny-weeny computer program.

Designer Genes

Your DNA is found inside each cell in your body, and it's unique to you (unless you have an identical twin). Inside cells, DNA forms chromosomes. Living things have different numbers of chromosomes: humans have 46, in 23 pairs. You get half of each of your chromosome pairs from your mother and the other half from your father. These 23 pairs are called your "genome" and contain about 35,000 genes. A gene is part of a DNA molecule and makes one of the many proteins you need to live. Your genes make proteins by putting together amino acids, and there are only four of them: adenine, guanine, cytosine, and thymine. Just one amino acid in the wrong place could mean a serious disease.

You're probably feeling pretty pleased with yourself, since you're such a unique and complex creature. But it might surprise you to know that we're not all that different from other animals: scientists used DNA from the blood of a male chimp named Clint and discovered that at least 96% of the genetic makeup of humans and chimps (our closest living relatives) is the same. So why don't we live in the trees and grunt a lot? Well, among the 3 billion DNA molecules in each genome, scientists also found 40 million differences.

Are you a monkey or a mouse? There are *ten times* fewer genetic differences between humans and chimps than there are between mice and rats! Having said that, human and mouse DNA is about 60% similar. Now, time for some cheese. . . .

What Is DNA (and Are We All That Different from Chimps)? **Form**

Once you have mastered this **Thing to Know,** stick your Achieved Star here and fill in the form

Achieved

HUMAN EVOLUTION

Below is a diagram showing the evolution of the human race over millions of years, beginning with single-celled organisms and ending with you! If your family and friends were a link in the evolutionary chain, which link would they be? Would your brother be a single-celled organism? Would your dad be the Missing Link? And would your best friend be Neanderthal man? Write their names in the boxes provided.

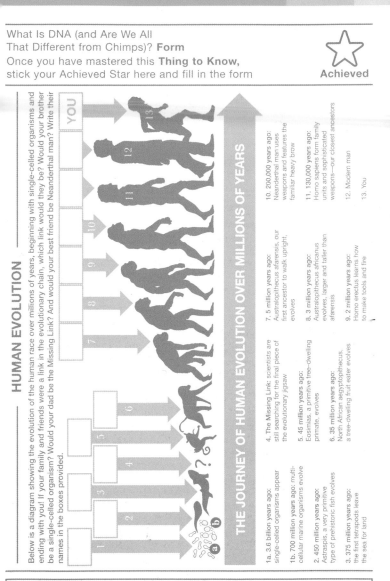

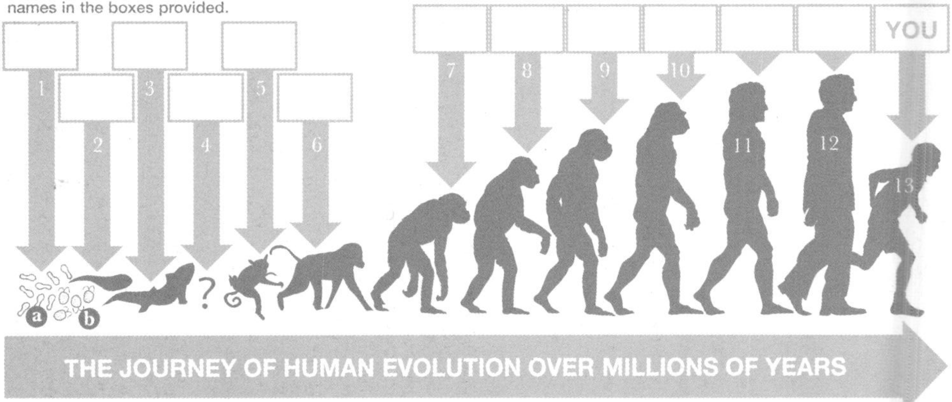

1a. **3.6 billion years ago:** single-celled organisms appear

1b. **700 million years ago:** multi-cellular marine organisms evolve

2. **450 million years ago:** Astraspis, a very primitive type of prehistoric fish evolves

3. **375 million years ago:** the first tetrapods leave the sea for land

4. **The Missing Link:** scientists are still searching for the final piece of the evolutionary jigsaw

5. **45 million years ago:** Eosimias, a primitive tree-dwelling primate, evolves

6. **35 million years ago:** North African aegyptopithecus, a tree-dwelling fruit eater evolves

7. **5 million years ago:** Australopithecus afarensis, our first ancestor to walk upright, evolves

8. **3 million years ago:** Australopithecus africanus evolves, larger and taller than afarensis

9. **2 million years ago:** Homo erectus learns how to make tools and fire

10. **200,000 years ago:** Neanderthal man uses weapons and features the familiar heavy brow

11. **130,000 years ago:** Homo sapiens form family units and sophisticated weapons—our closest ancestors

12. Modern man

13. You

At the same time you could master these **Things to Know:**
6: What Is the Oldest Living Thing in the World? • 17: Is Your Teacher an Alien? • 18: What Are the Biggest and Smallest Animals in the World? • 85: Why Do We Dream?

Why Don't Fish Drown?

Like us, fish need to breathe oxygen—so how do they do it underwater? It's a good trick, but evolution has a lot of work to do if we're ever to manage it.

Fishy Business

As you've probably guessed, the answer has to do with gills, which fish have developed in order to avoid inconvenient trips to the surface. (Marine mammals, such as whales and dolphins, need to visit the surface regularly for air.) Water contains some oxygen, but not nearly as much as the air. Here's how fish use their gills to take the oxygen they need out of the water:

- The fish opens and closes its mouth to pump water through its gills. (Some fish don't have a very good pumping system, which means they have to move constantly to keep water flowing through their gills.)
- Water moves through the fish's mouth and into its gill filter system, called gill rakers, to strain out anything floating in the water.
- The water continues through the gills, which contain tiny membranes. These membranes take the oxygen from the water and release carbon dioxide (just as our lungs take oxygen from the air when we breathe in and expel carbon dioxide when we breathe out).

Gills are very efficient at taking oxygen from water and putting it into the fish's bloodstream. But they don't work on land, because the gills collapse without the buoyancy of the water and the oxygen-rich air is too much for them.

Landing a fish: some fish can breathe on land. The walking catfish can move around on land, taking in air through specialized air-breathing structures attached to its gills. There are spines on its side fins that help it to "walk"—well, wriggle—along.

Why Don't Fish Drown? **Form**

Once you have mastered this **Thing to Know,**
stick your Achieved Star here and fill in the form

Achieved

SEAFOOD

It smells funny, it looks funny, sometimes it feels funny in your mouth too—but fish can be yummy, if only you can summon up the courage to try it! Which of the fish listed below have you tasted, and what did you think (on a scale of 1 to 10)?

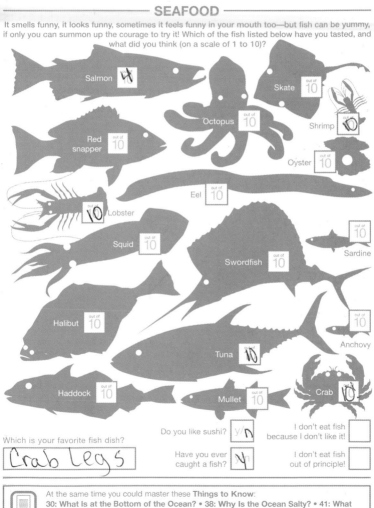

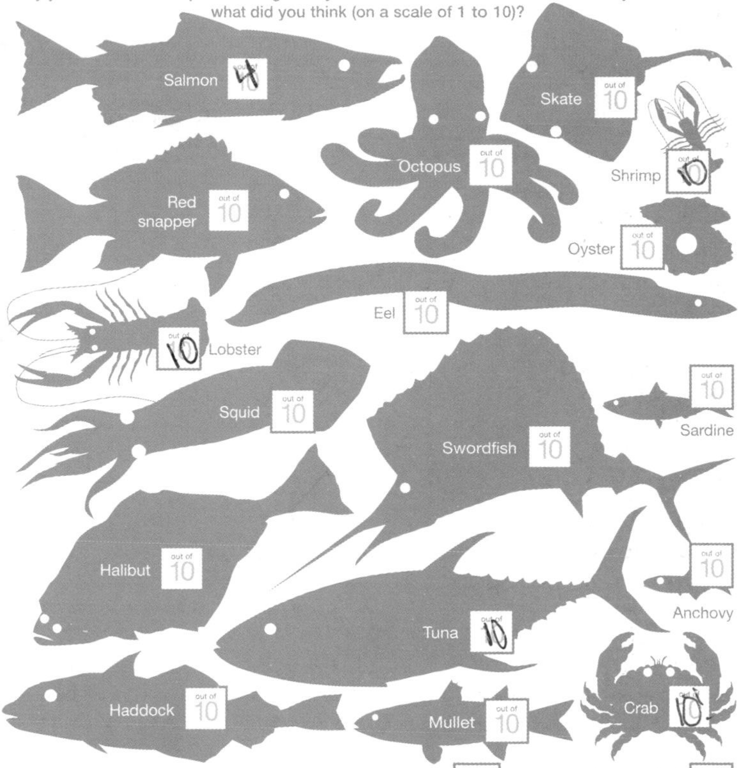

Which is your favorite fish dish?

Crab Legs

Do you like sushi? y/n n

Have you ever caught a fish? y/n y

I don't eat fish because I don't like it! ☐

I don't eat fish out of principle! ☐

At the same time you could master these **Things to Know**:
30: What Is at the Bottom of the Ocean? • 38: Why Is the Ocean Salty? • 41: What Is the World's Most Dangerous Shark? • 57: How Do Oysters Make Pearls?

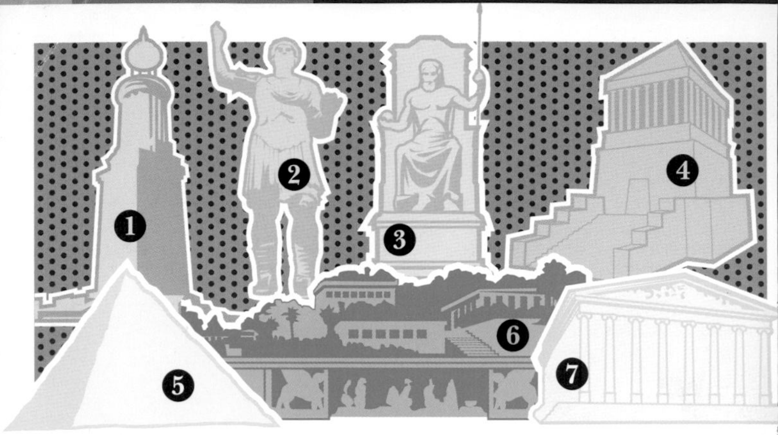

What Were the Seven Wonders of the World?

Most people have heard of the Seven Wonders of the World, but few people can say what they are. It's not surprising: the list was compiled in the Middle Ages, based on other lists made by various ancient Greeks, and even back then some of the wonders weren't around anymore. Now, only one survives.

Wonder Wall

1. Lighthouse of Alexandria (destroyed by earthquake, c. 1300s): at about 440 ft, this was one of the world's tallest buildings at the time it was built.
2. Colossus of Rhodes (destroyed by earthquake, c. 200 BC): this huge bronze statue of the sun god Helios stood in Rhodes harbor for 56 years.
3. Statue of Zeus at Olympia (destroyed by fire, c. AD 460): a 43-ft-tall gold-and-ivory statue of the king of the gods, whose head nearly touched the top of the Temple of Zeus (the site of the original Olympic Games).
4. Mausoleum at Halicarnassus (destroyed by earthquakes, c. 1400): this elaborate tomb for King Mausolus has given us the word *mausoleum*.
5. Great Pyramid of Giza, Egypt: the amazing stone tomb of Pharaoh Khufu has lasted more than 4,500 years. It's the only surviving Wonder!
6. Hanging Gardens of Babylon (disappeared): King Nebuchadnezzar is believed to have had a spectacular palace and gardens, with lush terraces supported on pillars, built as a gift for his homesick wife.
7. Temple of Artemis at Ephesus (destroyed by the Goths in AD 262): an ancient Greek marble temple built to honor the goddess of hunting.

Seven Natural Wonders? There's an unofficial list: Mt. Everest, Nepal; Victoria Falls, Zambia/Zimbabwe; Grand Canyon; Great Barrier Reef, Australia; Northern Lights; Paricutin Volcano, Mexico; & the harbor of Rio de Janeiro, Brazil.

What Were the Seven Wonders of the World? **Form**

Once you have mastered this **Thing to Know,** stick your Achieved Star here and fill in the form

Achieved

SEVEN ANCIENT WONDERS

1. Lighthouse of Alexandria, c. 282 BC • 2. Colossus of Rhodes, c. 250 BC • 3. Statue of Zeus at Olympia, c. 450 BC • 4. Mausoleum at Halicarnassus, c. 350 BC • 5. Great Pyramid of Giza, Egypt, c. 2560 BC • 6. Hanging Gardens of Babylon, c. 550 BC • 7. Temple of Artemis at Ephesus, c. 550 BC

SEVEN MODERN WONDERS

There's dispute over the definitive modern wonders list, but here are some of the main contenders. Check the boxes if you've visited the modern wonders below.

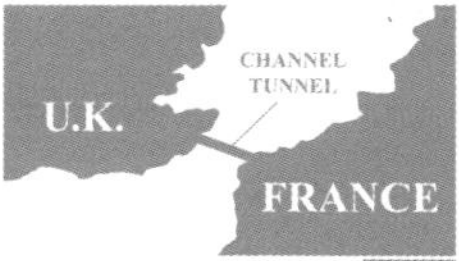

1. Channel Tunnel, English Channel ☐

2. Sydney Opera House, Sydney, Australia ☐

3. Golden Gate Bridge, San Francisco ☐

4. Taj Mahal, Agra, India ☐

5. Statue of Cristo Redentor, Rio, Brazil ☐

6. CN Tower, Toronto, Canada ☐

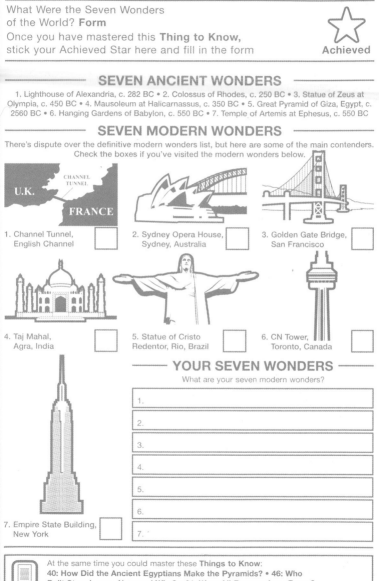

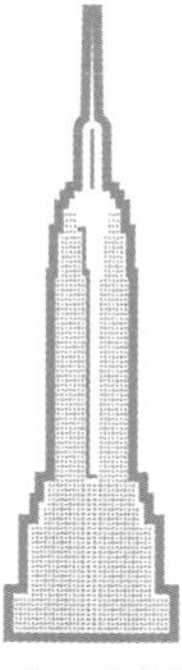

7. Empire State Building, New York ☐

YOUR SEVEN WONDERS

What are your seven modern wonders?

1.
2.
3.
4.
5.
6.
7.

At the same time you could master these **Things to Know**:
40: How Did the Ancient Egyptians Make the Pyramids? • 46: Who Built Stonehenge, How and Why? • 61: Were All Romans from Rome?

Aarrgh!!! Type O!
I didn't count on that!

Why Is Our Blood Red?

The short answer is that blood is red because of the red blood cells in human blood. There are millions of these tiny cells in a single drop of blood, and they get their red pigment from hemoglobin, the stuff that carries oxygen from your lungs to the rest of your body. Just over half your blood is made of plasma, which is a clear, yellowish liquid. But it's the red blood cells that give blood its overall color.

Seeing Red

Why should hemoglobin be red, rather than blue or green or pale lilac? It might be because it's easier to see. If it's foggy or hazy, we see the color red more easily than other colors because red light isn't scattered as easily—that's why stop signs and brake lights on cars are red. And our eyes are more sensitive to reds and yellows than other colors.

So it could be that we've evolved with red blood because it's easy to spot—after all, it's quite important if a person is bleeding that someone should know about it as quickly as possible.

Not All Blood Is Red . . .

Cockroaches have white blood.

Octopuses and lobsters have blue (or bluish white) blood.

A starfish's blood is a yellowish color.

Earthworms have green blood.

Some skinks—a type of lizard—have green blood too. (One of them is called the yellow-footed green-blooded skink—catchy, eh?)

Lots of insects have yellow or green blood.

Some creatures, such as coral and jellyfish, don't have blood at all.

Blood may be thicker than water, but it only makes up about 7% of your body's total weight, whereas water makes up about 60%. An average adult's body contains approximately 10 pints of blood, but about 95 pints of water.

Why Is Our Blood Red? **Form**

Once you have mastered this **Thing to Know,**
stick your Achieved Star here and fill in the form

Achieved

WHAT IS YOUR BLOOD GROUP?

Not everyone's blood is the same, but we all fall into one of four main blood groups: O, A, B, and AB. Your blood type is determined by your mother and father's blood groups. Look at the table below. If your father is blood type B and your mother is AB, your blood type will either be A, B, or AB. You can't figure out exactly what your blood type is—only a blood test by your doctor can do that—but the chart will give you some idea provided you know your parents' blood types.

MOTHER

FATHER	O	A	B	AB
O	O	O, A	O, B	A, B
A	O, A	O, A	O, A, B, AB	A, B, AB
B	O, B	O, A, B, AB	O, B	A, B, AB
AB	A, B	A, B, AB	A, B, AB	A, B, AB

BLOOD QUIZ

1. **What does almost every Peruvian have?**

(a) The same name
(b) The same blood group
(c) The same job
(d) The same parents

2. **What is the Rhesus blood type named after?**

(a) A scientist
(b) An experiment
(c) A monkey
(d) A surgical procedure

3. **What is the most common blood group in the world?**

(a) A (b) B (c) AB (d) O

4. **What is the rarest blood type in the world?**

(a) A (b) B (c) AB (d) O

5. **If you want to duel in Paraguay, what are you legally required to be?**

(a) Related to your opponent by blood
(b) Blood group AB
(c) A registered blood donor
(d) Male

6. **If you're described as having "blue blood," what does it mean?**

(a) You're a coward
(b) You belong to the royal family
(c) You're fashionable
(d) You're seriously ill

Answers at the back of the book.

At the same time you could master these **Things to Know**:
13: Did Cannibals Really Exist? • 72: Who Was the Most Bloodthirsty Pirate Ever?
73: Pus—What Is It Good For? • 98: Nails—What Are They Good For?

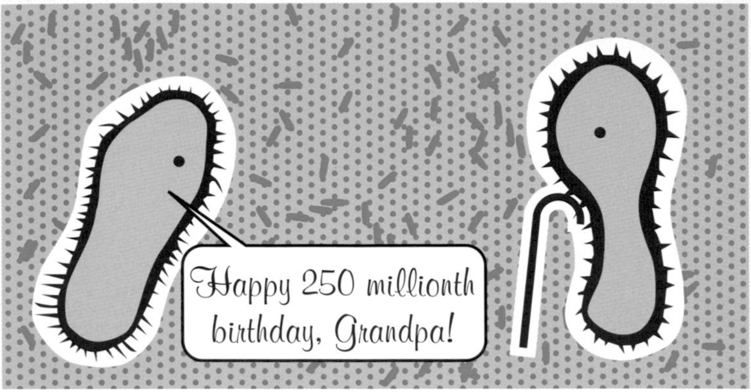
Happy 250 millionth birthday, Grandpa!

What Is the Oldest Living Thing in the World?

Rather disappointingly, the oldest living things that have been found so far are . . . bacteria. Well, at least they can boast about hanging out with the dinosaurs.

Once Upon a Germ

In 1999, bacteria discovered in sea salt in a state of suspended animation were reanimated in a laboratory—they were 250 *million* years old. If they could speak, they could tell us about life at the start of the Triassic period, when the very first dinosaurs appeared. Being bacteria, though, they've remained silent.

If you insist on your living thing being a bit more sophisticated than a bacterium, some plants have been around for a very long time indeed:

- King's Lomatia, a Tasmanian shrub, has been cloning itself for over 43,000 years. It doesn't reproduce sexually like most plants, so technically it's the same living thing that was around before we humans evolved.
- An Ice Age gum, a very rare type of eucalyptus tree found in Australia, is estimated to be 13,000 years old. And a box huckleberry bush colony in Pennsylvania is believed to be about the same age.

Compared to these gnarled old granddads (and a couple of other ancient plants you'll find on the time line opposite), even the oldest animal is a mere baby. The longest-living is probably a clam called the quahog—one has been found that's thought to be 220 years old.

The oldest land animal ever recorded was a tortoise named Tui Malia. It was given as a gift to the Tongan royal family by British explorer Captain Cook. It was 188 years old when it died.

What Is the Oldest Living Thing in the World? **Form**

Once you have mastered this **Thing to Know,** stick your Achieved Star here and fill in the form

Achieved

AS OLD AS TIME

Here is a time line of the oldest living things still alive today. (Bacteria from 250 million years ago have been omitted from the list due to the enormous scale that would be involved.)

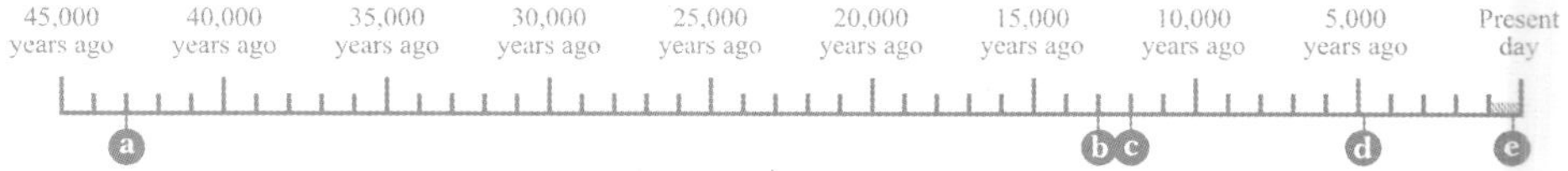

AS OLD AS TIME TIME LINE

a. King's Lomatia, Tasmania
43,000 years old

b. Ice Age gum Eucalyptus tree, Australia
13,000 years old

c. Creosote bush, California
12,000 years old

d. "Methuselah," Bristlecone pine, California
4,800 years old

e. Ocean quahog clam
220 years old

THE LAST 100 YEARS

Due to the scale of the time line above, the last 100 years is tiny! On this mini-time line, mark the oldest people you know and list them below.

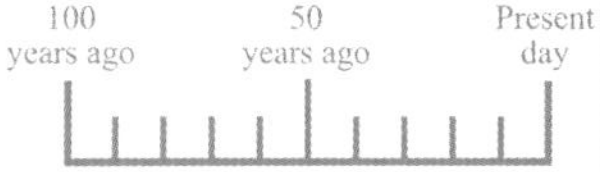

Person 1 and age	0 0
Person 2 and age	0 0
Person 3 and age	0 0
Person 4 and age	0 0
Person 5 and age	0 0

Who is your oldest living grandparent?

Is he/she the oldest person you know still alive? y/n

What is his/her date of birth? m m d d y y y y

What major historical events can he/she remember? List them below.

At the same time you could master these **Things to Know**:
2: What Is DNA (and Are We All That Different from Chimps)?
18: What Are the Biggest and Smallest Animals in the World?

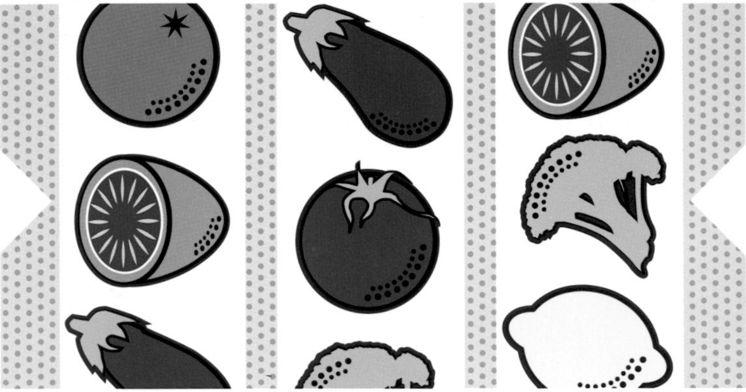

What Is the Difference Between a Fruit and a Vegetable?

Ever had an argument with someone about whether a tomato is a fruit or a vegetable? The trouble is, the technical answer isn't always the one that is used in practice. It really depends whether you're a botanist or a grocer!

I Say Tomato, You Say . . .

A fruit is the ripe ovary or ovaries (female reproductive organ) of a seed-bearing plant, which doesn't make it sound very appetizing. It contains the fertilized seed that would turn into a new plant or plants. Some nuts are fruits too—e.g., chestnuts and acorns—and so are grains. A vegetable, on the other hand, is used to describe any part of the plant that's grown to eat—this could be the seeds (e.g., peas), roots or tubers (e.g., potatoes), leaves (e.g., spinach), flowers (e.g., cauliflower), or stems (e.g., asparagus).

In practice, grocers (and most people) call tomatoes, cucumbers, and pumpkins vegetables, even though they're really fruit because they develop from the plant's reproductive parts. It seems that there's nothing wrong with this, since fruit-bearing plants *are* grown to eat. People tend to think of fruit as sweet and vegetables as savory. But you'd never catch a botanist referring to a cucumber as a vegetable. On the other hand, would you want to round off a meal with a cucumber, perhaps accompanied by a dollop of fresh cream? But surely it would be wrong to describe vegetables as fruits—unless they are, of course. Confused?

The world's most popular fruit is the tomato. It was introduced to Europe from South America in the 1500s. But in some parts of Europe, including Britain, it was thought to be poisonous and used as decoration instead of food.

What Is the Difference between a Fruit and a Vegetable? **Form**

Once you have mastered this **Thing to Know**, stick your Achieved Star here and fill in the form

Achieved

FRUITS AND VEGETABLES

Do you know your fruits from your veggies? Try this test below and see if you can guess which are fruits, which are vegetables, and which can be classed as both. Answers at the back of the book.

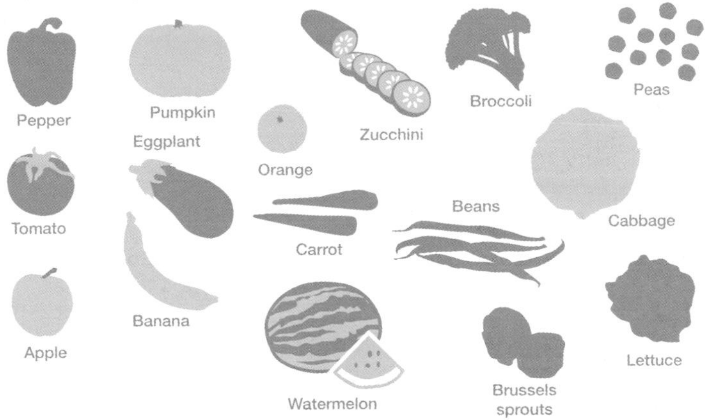

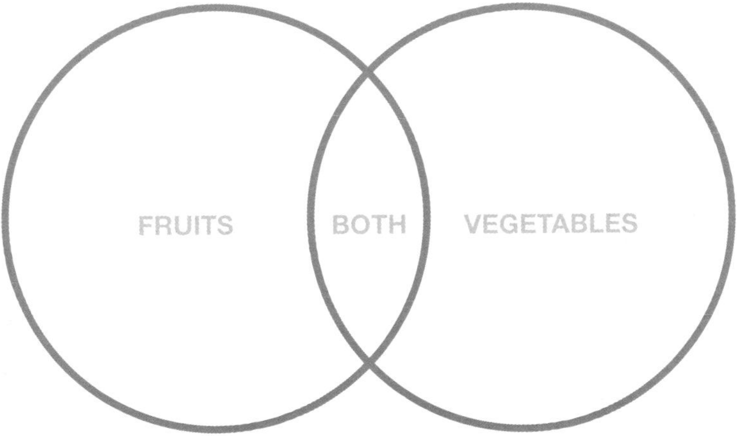

At the same time you could master these **Things to Know**:
6: What Is the Oldest Living Thing in the World? • 11: Who Were the First Chocoholics? • 13: Did Cannibals Really Exist?

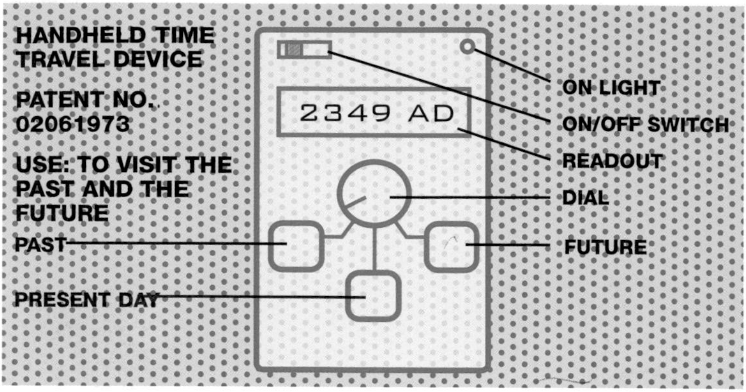

Is Time Travel Possible?

This is a very important question, because if it's possible to travel in time you can zip forward a few days and find out the winning lottery numbers.

Back to the Future

People have long been looking into the appealing possibility of time travel:

- Some scientists have come up with plans for time machines, which have to do with black holes, "wormholes," and the theory of relativity. But no one's actually built one because no one's developed the technology yet (and probably won't for a very long time).
- There are problems with traveling in time: it creates paradoxes. For instance, say you traveled back in time and accidentally stopped your parents from meeting. Then you would never have been born . . . and you would never have been able to go back in time and stop them from meeting . . . so you would have been born. . . . You get the idea.
- You could get around the time-travel paradox with a bit of quantum physics. One theory is that every time a subatomic particle (see **Thing to Know** No. 42) is faced with a choice, the universe splits to allow both choices. So there's an infinite number of different universes—including the one where your parents didn't meet.

So in answer to this question: not yet. Then again, perhaps. And maybe in a parallel universe someone's reading a book called **101 Things to Do on Your Time Travels**.

Doctor who? Probably the most famous example of a time machine is the one in the TV show *Dr. Who*—the TARDIS—which allows the doctor to travel in space and time. Its name stands for Time and Relative Dimension in Space.

Is Time Travel Possible? **Form**

Once you have mastered this **Thing to Know**, stick your Achieved Star here and fill in the form

Achieved

WAYS TO TIME TRAVEL

Don't get your hopes up. These experiments won't let you travel into the future to see how you've aged or help you visit prehistoric times, but they are a novel way of looking at time travel. . . .

EXPERIMENT 1

[x] Completed

EXPERIMENT 2

[x] Completed

EXPERIMENT 3

Andromeda galaxy

[ ] Completed

EXPERIMENT 1: Light moves at 186,282 miles per second. It takes 8.3 minutes for the light from the Sun to reach us, so if you look up at the sky on a sunny day (NEVER look directly at the Sun, as you will damage your eyes), you are seeing the Sun 8.3 minutes in the past.

EXPERIMENT 2: The same thing happens when you look up at the stars. The closest star to Earth is Alpha Centauri and it is 4.3 light-years away from us (which means that if you travel at the speed of light, you will reach it in 4.3 years). When we look at it from Earth, we see it 4.3 years in the past.

EXPERIMENT 3: If 4.3 years doesn't thrill you, take a look at the closest galaxy to us in the Milky Way. The light from the Andromeda galaxy has taken 2 million years to reach us. So if you were standing in this galaxy and looked at the Earth, you'd be looking at it around the time when humans first walked the Earth! Unfortunately, looking into space can only show us the past, not the future.

EXPERIMENT 4

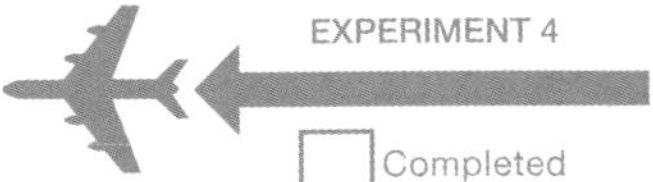

[ ] Completed

EXPERIMENT 4: Flying in a plane over different time zones means you can set off from one country and arrive many hours later or earlier than the time on your watch! If you fly east to west you will gain hours, and if you fly west to east you will lose hours—unless you fly over the international date line.

EXPERIMENT 5

[ ] Completed

EXPERIMENT 5: There is a place in the world where you can be in two days at once. Fiji, in the Pacific, stands on the international date line—an imaginary line that runs roughly at 180° longitude and shows where the beginning of one day and the end of another come together. We need it to offset the hours that are added or subtracted as one travels east or west. If you straddle the line, one foot will be in today, the other will be in yesterday or, if you prefer, today and tomorrow!

At the same time you could master these **Things to Know**:
20: Which Way Is North? • 36: How Many Stars Are There in the Milky Way?
42: How Big Is an Atom? • 101: What Would Happen to You in a Black Hole?

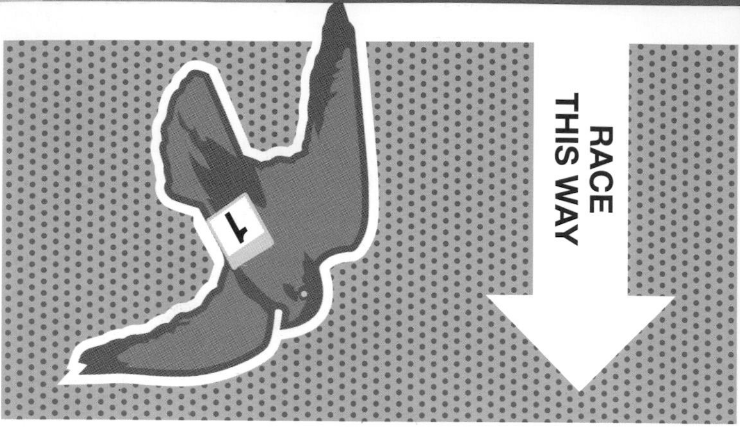

Who Would Win the Animal Olympic 100-Meter Race?

Everyone knows that the fastest animal is the cheetah. Except that it isn't.

Diving Birds and Flying Fish

The creature that would win the Animal Olympic 100 Meters is the peregrine falcon, and it would win it easily. The peregrine falcon has been recorded traveling at speeds of over 200 mph as it dives down to catch prey. Okay, so it would have to be a vertical race for the falcon to win, but if the judges insisted on a horizontal race, a bird would still be the winner: the white-throated spine-tail swift races along at 110 mph. Compared to this, the cheetah ambles by at a top speed of 70 mph—the fastest fish, the sailfish, wouldn't be far behind at 68 mph.

Of course, these speeds are the fastest ones recorded for the different animals over different distances. To make the race completely fair you'd have to decide on the length of the course. But you can be pretty sure that a bird would still win. On the opposite page you'll find the top six contenders for fastest animal in the world.

Fastest in Their Categories

They don't make it into the top six, but they're pretty fast too:

Fastest bird on land:
ostrich (45 mph)

Fastest insect:
dragonfly (35 mph)

Fastest marine mammal:
dall porpoise (35 mph)

Fastest human:
Asafa Powell and Justin Gatlin are currently tied for this title. They each ran 100 m in 9.77 seconds, which is about 22.9 mph. Okay, so we humans are actually pretty slow.

Fastest flying mammal:
big brown bat (16 mph)

The slowest creatures in the world (apart from you, first thing in the morning) would have to include the notorious giant tortoise (0.17 mph) and the three-toed sloth (0.15 mph). But in even less of a rush is the snail, sliding along at 0.03 mph.

Who Would Win the Animal Olympic 100-Meter Race? **Form**

Once you have mastered this **Thing to Know**, stick your Achieved Star here and fill in the form

Achieved

WHO IS THE FASTEST?

The chart below shows the fastest creatures in the animal kingdom. You may think you're pretty fast but compared to the peregrine falcon, the white-throated spine-tail swift, the cheetah, the sailfish, the pronghorn antelope, and the mako shark, you're a snail! You've no hope of ever catching them, even if you were on your bike!

Peregrine falcon (diving vertically)	1 9 9 mph	Sailfish	0 6 8 mph	Your top speed on your bike	0 0 0 mph
White-throated spine-tail swift	1 1 0 mph	Pronghorn antelope	0 6 1 mph	Your top speed running	0 0 0 mph
Cheetah	0 7 0 mph	Mako shark	0 6 0 mph		

Now figure out how much faster you'd need to be to catch the swift

FINISH

To catch the white-throated spine-tail swift I'd have to be 0 0 times faster on my bike / To catch the white-throated spine-tail swift I'd have to be 0 0 times faster running

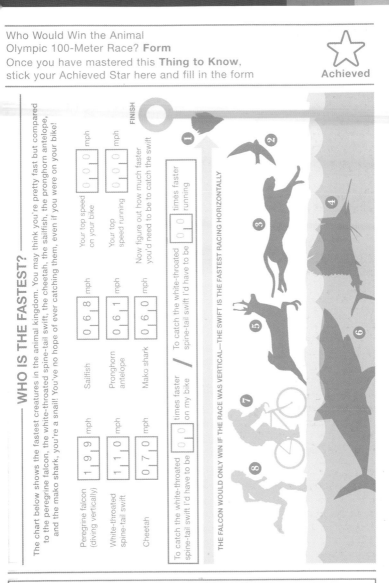

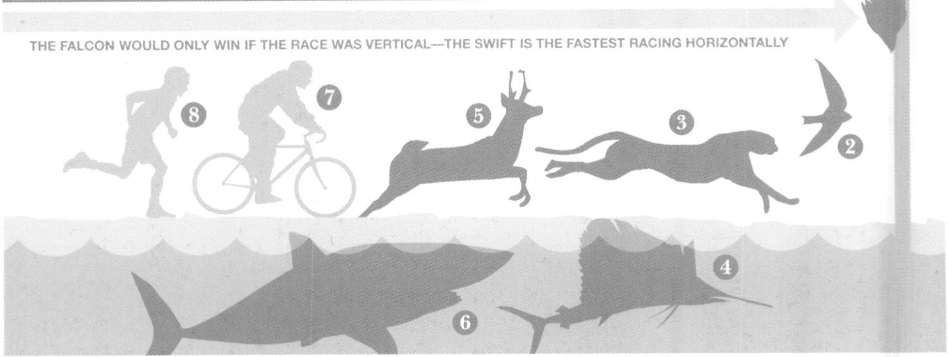
THE FALCON WOULD ONLY WIN IF THE RACE WAS VERTICAL—THE SWIFT IS THE FASTEST RACING HORIZONTALLY
1
2
3
4
5
6
7
8

At the same time you could master these **Things to Know**:
18: What Are the Biggest and Smallest Animals in the World?
41: What Is the World's Most Dangerous Shark?

How Do You Do an Ollie on a Skateboard?

An ollie means smacking the tail of the skateboard on the floor with one foot while pulling up the front of the board into the air with the other, so that the whole board lifts up. It's one of skateboarding's most basic moves, and you can do all kinds of other things once you've mastered it.

Jolly Ollie Days

The hardest part is the timing—it comes with practice. Here's how to do it:

1. Wear plenty of safety gear (better safe than sorry).
2. Put your rear foot on the tail and your front foot a bit more than halfway along the board. The ball of your rear foot should be in the middle of the board and your front foot should be nearly straight across the board.
3. Crouch down. Push your rear foot down on the tail of the board and straighten your legs. (This should make the board bounce up.)
4. As the board comes up, slide your front foot to the nose of the board, then press it down.
5. Lift up your back foot. (This should make the tail rise so that the board is level in midair.)
6. As the board descends, bend your knees and pull them toward your chest.

Learn the trick from a stationary position—when you've got the hang of it you can try it moving along and going up and down hills.

G-ollie! Jack Cruwys-Finnigan did 30 ollies in one minute in London in June 2005, setting the world record. The trick was invented by Alan "Ollie" Gelfand, skateboarding legend.

How Do You Do an Ollie
on a Skateboard? **Form**

Once you have mastered this **Thing to Know**, stick your Achieved Star here and fill in the form

Achieved

SKATEBOARD TRICKS

Once you've mastered the ollie, ask a friend to take photographs of you performing the trick as evidence that you can do it. If you've already mastered the ollie and it's too basic for you, get photographs of you performing more complicated and exciting stunts.

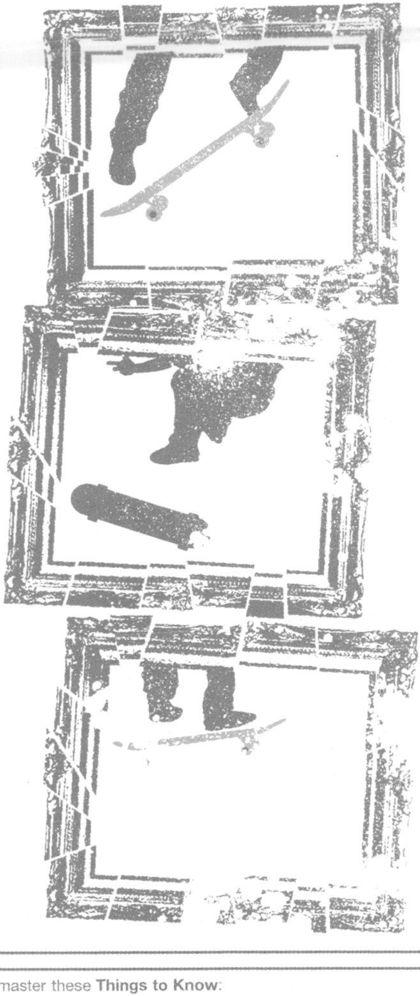

At the same time you could master these **Things to Know**:
9: Who Would Win the Animal Olympic 100-Meter Race?
88: Who Invented the Wheel? • 89: How Do You Do a Wheelie on a Bike?

Who Were the First Chocoholics?

Most people like chocolate—in fact, some of us like it a little too much. But it's hard not to. After all, it contains phenylethylamine, the same chemical that gets released into our brains when we feel happy or in love.

Bitter Sweet

The ancient Maya and the Aztecs of South America were especially fond of the cacao tree, which they called "cacahuatl" (sound like a word you know?). It actually means "bitter water." The Aztecs believed it had been brought to Earth by a god, and it was so precious to them that they used its beans as money. The beans were useful for another reason: they could be crushed into a paste to make a drink—the very first chocolate drink. The Aztecs added spices to the cacao-bean paste, but the drink wasn't like the hot chocolate we drink today: it was much more bitter, seasoned with pepper, and served cold.

In the 16th century, the European conquerors of South America brought the drink back to Europe, but they must have had a sweeter tooth than the Aztecs because they added sugar. The drink became fashionable for those who could afford it. Eventually, in the 1800s, people figured out how to mold it into solid shapes, and the chocolate bar was born.

Today chocolate is popular in most parts of the world. The average American eats 10–12 pounds of chocolate per year.

Theobrama is the botanical name for the cacao bean, and in Greek it means "food of the gods." The Maya burned cacao beans as an offering to their gods—on special occasions they even dripped human blood over them. Tasty—if you're a cannibal.

Who Were the First Chocoholics? **Form**

Once you have mastered this **Thing to Know**, stick your Achieved Star here and fill in the form

Achieved

— NO-BAKE CHOCOLATE GRAHAM CRACKER CAKE —

Chocolate graham cracker cake is magic. It's so yummy you'll want to scarf it down immediately, but moderation is the best policy, or you'll end up with a stomachache. And this is rich stuff! Like with other rich foods, go easy and share it!

8 oz graham crackers
4 oz butter or margerine
1 tbsp sugar
2 tbsps corn syrup (or light molasses)
2 tbsps cocoa powder
2 oz glacé cherries (chopped)
2 oz raisins
4 oz semisweet chocolate

1. The second best thing about this recipe (after eating it, that is) is preparing the graham crackers. You need to put them in a plastic bag and smash them with a rolling pin—if you can't find a rolling pin, use your imagination and find some other weighty object. The graham crackers should end up as crumbs.
2. Next, put the butter, sugar, and syrup or molasses into a saucepan, and stir with a wooden spoon over low heat until all the sugar has dissolved.
3. Remove the saucepan from the heat, add the cocoa, and stir the mixture with your wooden spoon until it's shiny.
4. Add half the crushed graham crackers and mix well until they are all coated.
5. Add the chopped cherries, the raisins, and the other half of the graham crackers and keep stirring until the ingredients are well mixed.
6. Spread the mixture out onto a greased and lined 8-in square baking tin. Now use the wooden spoon to smooth the mixture down so it is level—do not use it to gobble up the mixture! Set the tin aside. You've got more chocolatey work to do!
7. Break up the semisweet chocolate into small pieces and place in a large heatproof bowl. Then set a saucepan with a small amount of water over medium heat and sit the bowl over the saucepan. Two things to remember: the bowl shouldn't be sitting in the water, but just over it, and the water shouldn't ever boil, just gently simmer at most. Keep stirring continuously as the chocolate melts. You want it to be smooth and creamy.
8. Turn off the heat and take the bowl of melted chocolate out of the saucepan (be careful—it'll be hot, so use oven mitts or ask an adult to help!). Pour it over your graham cracker cake mixture and spread evenly with a knife.
9. Chill the chocolate graham cracker cake in the refrigerator until set. Then cut it into pieces. Time to dig in!

— THE LION'S SHARE —

Cut the chocolate cake into 12 pieces. How many pieces did you eat? Pick a color for each person, and fill in how many pieces were eaten by

Sister		Brother	
Friend 1		Friend 2	
Grandma		Grandpa	

You

Dad

Mom

Who ate the most?

At the same time you could master these **Things to Know**:
7: What Is the Difference Between a Fruit and a Vegetable? • 13: Did Cannibals Really Exist? • 14: Will Your Stomach Explode if You Eat Too Much?

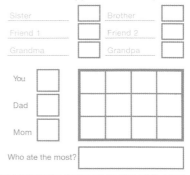

How Big Is the Universe?

No one really knows the size of the universe, or even if it's the only one! It could be that it's infinite—that it has no limits at all—and just thinking about that can boggle your mind. It can also make you feel extremely small.

To Infinity . . . and Beyond!

We are limited in what we can see of the universe. A light-year is a measurement of distance (see **Thing to Know** No. 29), but it also tells us how long light takes to complete the journey. The nearest galaxy to ours is the Andromeda galaxy, more than 2 million light-years away—so what we can see is the Andromeda galaxy 2 million years ago, because it's taken that long for the light to reach us. Scientists think that the universe began about 13.7 billion years ago (see **Thing to Know** No. 1), so the farthest we would ever be able to see would be 13.7 billion light-years away in any direction: we wouldn't be able to see farther than that because it would be impossible for light to reach us from *before* the start of the universe.

This means we've got a limit of what we're able to see of about 28 billion light-years across—which you'd think would be pretty much enough for anyone. But what about an alien who's looking through a telescope at the edge of what we're able to see. What would he or she be able to see on the horizon? And what about the alien sitting on the first alien's horizon? You get the idea. . . .

Getting bigger: Scientists have evidence that our universe is expanding and accelerating outward (see **Thing to Know** No. 1), so while we may not know how big the universe is, we can be certain that it's getting bigger all the time.

How Big Is the Universe? **Form**

Once you have mastered this **Thing to Know,**
stick your Achieved Star here and fill in the form

Achieved

YOUR PLACE IN THE UNIVERSE

The universe is inconceivably big. To give you an idea of how big it is, place pictures of your country, your town, your house, and you below, and try to comprehend your place in the universe.

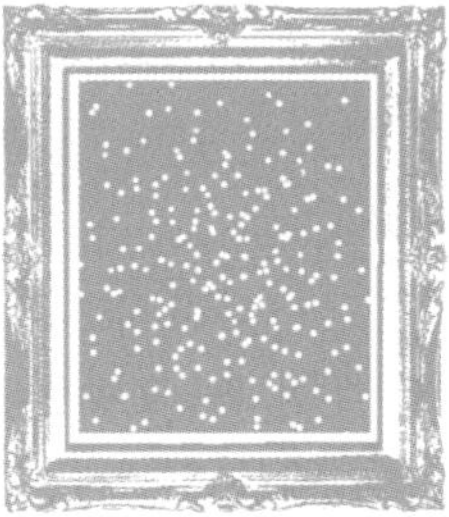

The universe

Galaxies of the universe

The Milky Way

The solar system

Planet Earth

Place an aerial photograph or a map of the country you live in here

Your country

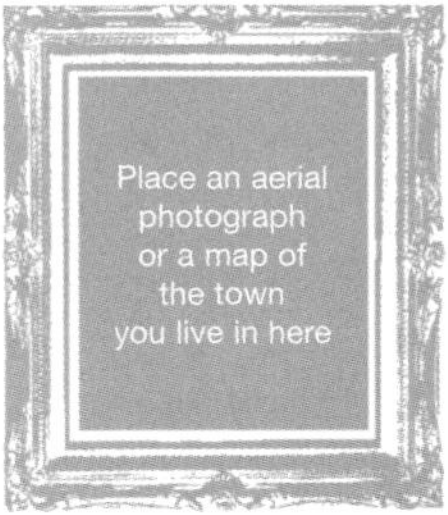
Place an aerial photograph or a map of the town you live in here

Your town

Place a photograph of your house here

Your house

Place a photograph of you here

You

At the same time you could master these **Things to Know**:
1: What Was the Biggest Bang Ever? • 29: How Long Is a Light-Year? • 36: How Many Stars Are There in the Milky Way? • 101: What Would Happen to You in a Black Hole?

Did Cannibals Really Exist?

The Aztecs are famous for making thousands of human sacrifices to their god but they may not have eaten the victims as some reports suggest. Queen Isabella of Spain decreed that conquered people couldn't be enslaved unless they were cannibals, so the Spanish invaders probably used it as an excuse.

Feeling Squeamish? Don't Read On!

But some people really did eat human flesh:

- The Fore tribe of Papua New Guinea used to eat their dead—until 1957, when a brain disease known as "kuru" struck, and it was discovered that the disease was passed on by eating human brains.
- Aboriginal people in Australia used to eat parts of their dead relatives in a ritual ceremony. They were thought to live on through those who ate them
- People have sometimes become cannibals because of famines, like the terrible Irish famine of the mid-1800s or the Russian one in the 1930s.
- There's evidence of Native American cannibals in Colorado about 850 years ago—scientists discovered it by examining remains of human bones, cooking pots, and fossilized human waste.
- Disasters have forced people into cannibalism: in 1972, the survivors of a plane crash in the Andes were forced to eat the frozen bodies of the dead; and in 1846, a band of U.S. pioneers, the Donner party, were strande in the Sierra Nevada mountains and ate their dead companions to avoid starvation.

Still feeling squeamish? The alarming news is that we're probably all descended from cannibals: scientists have discovered that most of us have genes specifically providing immunity to certain diseases that can only have been passed on by eating human brains.

Did Cannibals Really Exist? **Form**

Once you have mastered this **Thing to Know**, stick your Achieved Star here and fill in the form

Achieved

FOOD, GLORIOUS FOOD

Fill out the form below, then make a copy and put in the kitchen for your parents' handy reference.

These are a few of my favorite foods . . .

My favorite breakfast

My favorite main course

My favorite dessert

My favorite drink

My favorite sandwich

My favorite potato chip flavor

My favorite chocolate bar or candy

My favorite vegetable

My favorite fruit

My favorite meat

My favorite cheese

No way! I'm not eating that!

My least favorite breakfast

My least favorite main course

My least favorite dessert

My least favorite drink

My least favorite sandwich

My least favorite potato chip flavor

My least favorite chocolate bar or candy

My least favorite vegetable

My least favorite fruit

My least favorite meat

My least favorite cheese

At the same time you could master these **Things to Know**:
5: Why Is Our Blood Red? • 7: What Is the Difference Between a Fruit and a Vegetable? • 11: Who Were the First Chocoholics? • 91: How Do Bees Make Honey?

Will Your Stomach Explode if You Eat Too Much?

Before you scarf down that extra slice of pizza, or go for an enormous dessert after having demolished that extra slice of pizza, here's some food for thought.

Gut Feeling

Your stomach is like a balloon that can stretch to hold food and shrink when it's empty. It gets to work the minute you've eaten something, producing chemicals to break down food and slimy mucus to protect your stomach lining from the chemicals. At the same time, its powerful muscles squash food to help digest it and to move it out of the stomach into the intestines. These muscles can also expand to fit in all-you-can-eat buffets. An adult's stomach will hold approximately 2 quarts of food but can actually squeeze in the same amount again and more! In fact, it's impossible for your stomach to burst. Stuffing yourself until you feel as though you're going to explode is not recommended though. A part of your brain called the hypothalamus controls your appetite: when it tells you you're full, listen to it.

Some people make a habit of gorging themselves: competitive eaters compete to see who can eat the most in a given time limit. The reigning champion ate 53.5 hot dogs (with buns) in 12 minutes and 18 lb of cow brains in 15 minutes. Come to mention it, cows are pretty good gorgers themselves. Their stomachs (they have four!) can hold more than 163 quarts. Food goes to the first stomach for some mucus, then it's regurgitated and rechewed before being swallowed again.

Bizarre bellies: a starfish can turn one of its stomachs inside out and push it out from the body to capture its prey. Rodents only have one stomach, and many have to eat food twice. This means eating their own waste!

Will Your Stomach Explode if You Eat Too Much? **Form**

Once you have mastered this **Thing to Know**, stick your Achieved Star here and fill in the form

Achieved

INSIDE OUT

Here's a list of some of the sights your food might pass by on its journey through your body. Can you match the right name from the list to the correct internal organ? Answers at the back of the book.

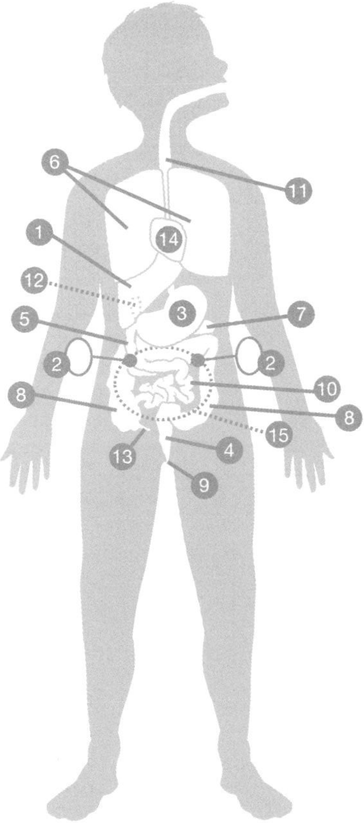

YOUR INTERNAL ORGANS

Small intestine • Lungs • Bladder
Duodenum • Kidneys • Esophagus • Anus
Gallbladder • Large intestine • Heart • Rectum
Stomach • Pancreas • Appendix • Liver

1.
2.
3.
4.
5.
6.
7.
8.
9.
10.
11.
12.
13.
14.
15.

At the same time you could master these **Things to Know**:
5: Why Is Our Blood Red? • 7: What Is the Difference Between a Fruit and a Vegetable? • 11: Who Were the First Chocoholics? • 13: Did Cannibals Really Exist?

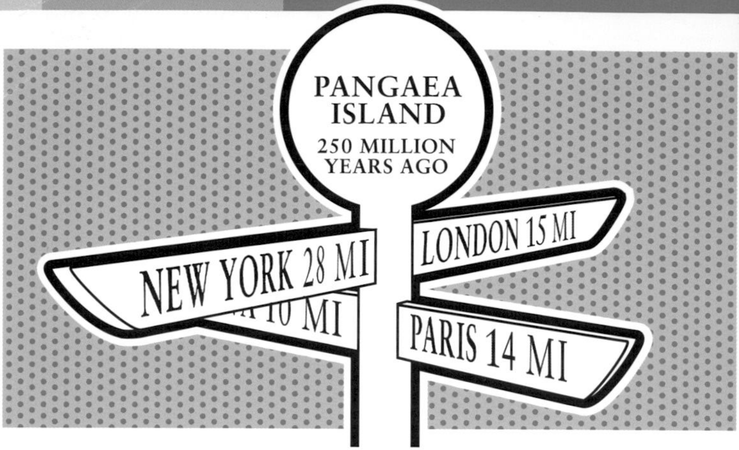

When Was It Possible to Walk from London to New York?

About 225 million years ago the United Kingdom was part of North America—not only could you have walked from New York to London but you wouldn't even have gotten wet! Of course, no one could actually have done this—not only was there no London or New York back then but there weren't even humans!

In-Continents

The continents as we know them today didn't always exist. At one time they were all joined together to form one giant supercontinent called Pangaea. For more than 4.6 billion years, since the beginning of the Earth's history up to the present day, our world has been constantly changing. The power behind these changes is the movement of giant plates in the Earth's outer layers (the "mantle"). This phenomenon is known as "plate tectonics." The plates (sometimes called the "crust") sit on top of a mantle of liquid iron, and over time these plates drift around. Think about it in terms of a hard-boiled egg with a cracked shell: the pieces of shell sit on top of the firm but slippery egg, kind of like the tectonic plates sit on the Earth's mantle.

The process may have been slow but it has transformed our world, splitting up continents and pushing them together. There's evidence of it continuing today. Plates that separate form volcanoes, which in turn form new islands. Plates that collide cause mountains to rise from the ground, and when they slip they cause city-destroying earthquakes.

Feel the Earth move: the plates move approximately 2.4 in per year. Over the course of a million years this is a total of 37 miles. Once upon a time, the Sahara desert used to be at the South Pole and the equator ran across Greenland!

When Was It Possible to Walk from London to New York? **Form**

Once you have mastered this **Thing to Know**, stick your Achieved Star here and fill in the form

Achieved

CHANGING EARTH

Earth was unrecognizable 225 million years ago. All the world's continents were joined together as part of the supercontinent Pangaea. The supercontinent started to break up, slowly forming the Earth as we know it today.

PERMIAN

290–248 MILLION YEARS AGO

TRIASSIC

248–206 MILLION YEARS AGO

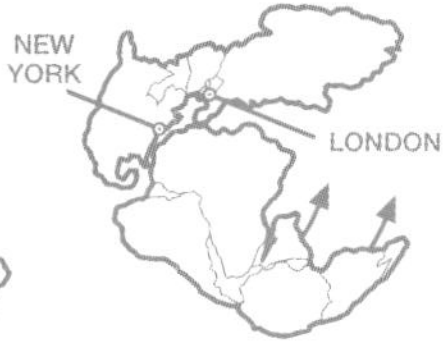

JURASSIC

206–144 MILLION YEARS AGO

CRETACEOUS

144–65 MILLION YEARS AGO

PRESENT DAY

EARTH'S FUTURE

Earth is constantly changing. The Himalayan mountain range continues to grow while glaciers around the world are shrinking. What do you think the Earth will look like in another 65 million years? Draw your ideas below.

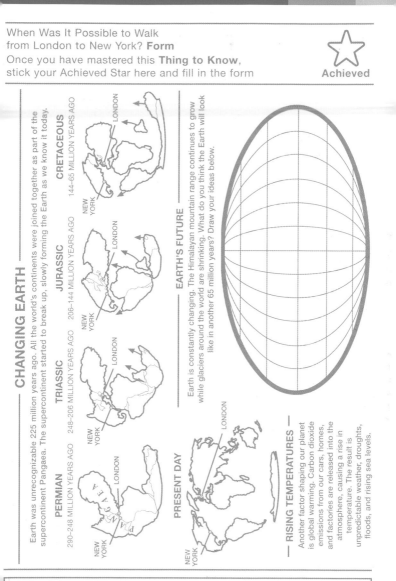

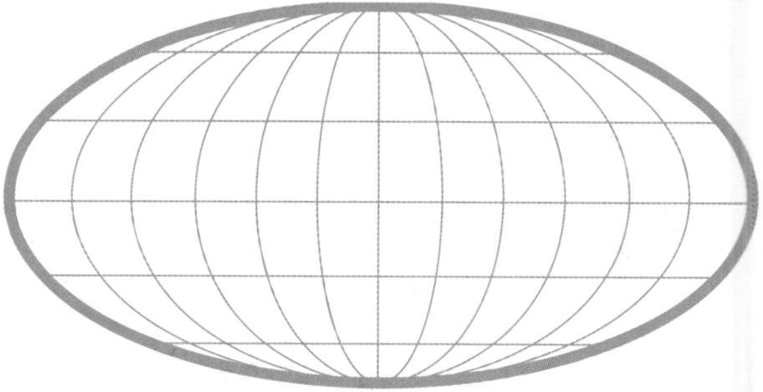

RISING TEMPERATURES

Another factor shaping our planet is global warming. Carbon dioxide emissions from our cars, homes, and factories are released into the atmosphere, causing a rise in temperature. The result is unpredictable weather, droughts, floods, and rising sea levels.

At the same time you could master these **Things to Know**:

16: How Do Mountains Grow? • 19: How Much Does the Earth Weigh?
30: What Is at the Bottom of the Ocean? • 62: How Do You Survive an Earthquake?

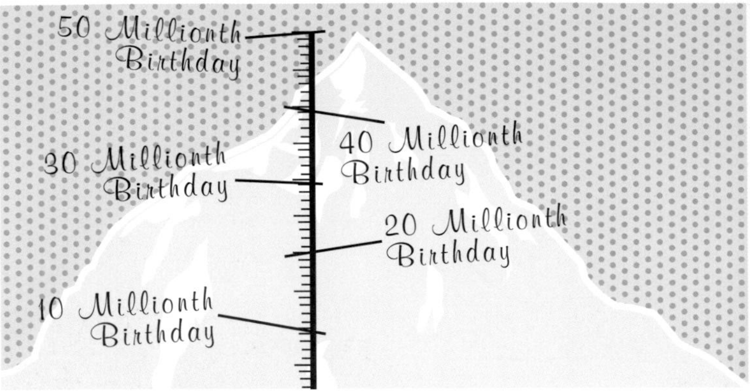

How Do Mountains Grow?

Mountains start out small—they don't suddenly appear out of nowhere. But you're never going to see one get bigger before your eyes, so clearly these processes are very long and very slow.

Making Mountains out of Molehills

There are two main ways for mountains to form:

- The Earth's outer layer (the "mantle") is made up of about 20 plates, which very slowly move against each other. This is what causes earthquakes, but over millions of years it also forms mountains as the plates press together and buckle. Mountain ranges such as the Himalayas were formed when two plates collided like this. In fact, it's still going on. Scientists have figured out that the Himalayas are growing at a rate of about 2.4 in per year.
- Mountains are also formed by volcanoes, when molten magma forces its way to the surface. Examples of this are Mount Fuji in Japan and Mount Erebus in Antarctica. Some volcanic mountains are still active (and so they're still growing), and others died long ago.

Different types of mountains form when plates collide: fold mountains (e.g., the Himalayas) are ones in which layers of rock bend like a roller coaster; fault-block mountains (e.g., Sierra Nevada, California) occur where plates are forced vertically upward at a crack (or "fault") in the crust. Finally, there are dome mountains, which are formed by vast amounts of molten rock pushing up out of the ground.

Fake mountains: some mountains don't grow at all—they're actually pieces of land that have eroded away on all sides to form plateaus. The Grand Canyon in Arizona is a dramatic example of this.

How Do Mountains Grow? **Form**

Once you have mastered this **Thing to Know**,
stick your Achieved Star here and fill in the form

Achieved

MAP OF THE EARTH'S PLATES

The tallest mountains in the world, the Himalayas, are relatively new—having formed 25 to 50 million years ago. The Appalachian Mountains along the eastern coast of North America are much older—they were formed hundreds of millions of years ago when the continental plate of Africa collided with the Americas (as you might have noticed, they drifted apart again).

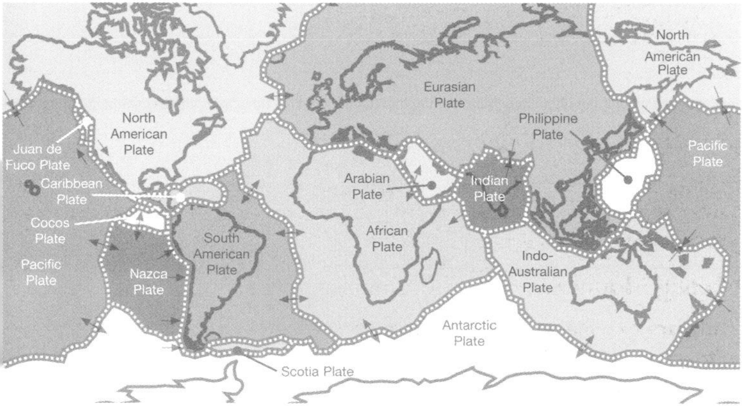

HILLS AND MOUNTAINS

A mountain is a land mass with a peak greater than 2,000 ft. A hill is anything below this size.

What is the name of the highest hill near you?

Have you ever climbed it? y/n

If yes, how many times? 0 0

How high is it? 0 0 0 0 ft

Was it a tough climb? y/n

Did you reach the top? y/n

If no, how far up did you get?

1/4 of the way 1/2 of the way 3/4 of the way

What is the highest mountain you've climbed?

How big is it? 0 0 0 0 ft

How long were you climbing it? 0 0 hours 0 0 mins

Was it a tough climb? y/n

Did you reach the top? y/n

If no, how far up did you get?

1/4 of the way 1/2 of the way 3/4 of the way

At the same time you could master these **Things to Know**:
15: When Was It Possible to Walk from London to New York? • 19: How Much Does the Earth Weigh? • 76: How Do You Survive an Avalanche?

Is Your Teacher an Alien?

Could aliens be among us, planning to take over the Earth and plotting our downfall, or perhaps simply observing our world in the interests of science? Has anyone aroused your suspicions? Could they be aliens in disguise?

The Truth Is Out There

The universe is pretty big, so there's a good chance that there are other races of intelligent beings out there somewhere. However, the fact that the universe is so vast means that it would take a very long time for any aliens to get here (the nearest galaxy is more than 2 million light-years distant—it would take 2 million years to get there if you were traveling at the speed of light). And how would the aliens know we were here in the first place? Nevertheless, scientists have been looking for alien intelligence in our galaxy for about 40 years. But the SETI (Search for ExtraTerrestrial Intelligence) project hasn't detected any signals from aliens yet. If they're out there, they must be farther away than the 40,000 light-years that have been examined by SETI so far.

Of course, this type of evidence (or lack of it) and the enormous distances involved don't necessarily mean anything at all. Perhaps there's a global cover up, hiding the aliens among us, or maybe none of us has yet discovered our alien neighbors. And perhaps alien technology is so advanced that extraterrestrial beings have managed to overcome the limitations of time and space, using wormholes and advanced spaceships. What do you think?

N = R* x fs x fp x nE x fl x fi x fc x L is an equation formulated to calculate how many alien races there are likely to be in the universe. However, what it really does is show how many unknown factors exist that prevent anyone from being able to use the equation.

Is Your Teacher an Alien? **Form**

Once you have mastered this **Thing to Know**, stick your Achieved Star here and fill in the form

Achieved

HOW TO SPOT ALIENS

Are there aliens among us? Is your mom out of this world or is your teacher from another planet? Take this quick test to see if that oddball you know could actually be an alien.

Name of subject

Does your subject have curious eating habits? y/n

If yes, does your subject . . .

- Have no table manners?
- Eat unusually large amounts?
- Eat unusually small amounts?
- Use the wrong silverware?
- Burp loudly after eating?

Does your subject have strange fashion sense? y/n

If yes, does your subject . . .

- Wear inappropriate clothes?
- Always wear the same things?
- Wear ill-fitting clothes?
- Wear mismatching clothes?
- Wear odd socks?

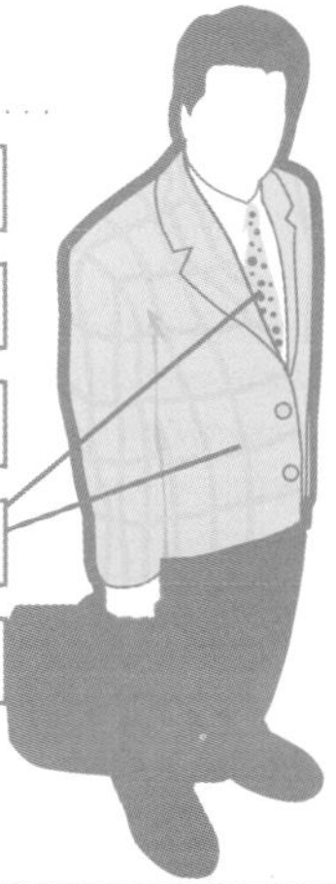

Does your subject think he/she is a comedian, but really is not funny at all? y/n

If yes, does your subject . . .

- Have a strange sense of humor?
- Laugh at his/her own jokes?
- Find bodily functions amusing?
- Not understand other people's jokes?
- Laugh at the wrong time?

Is your subject secretive? y/n

If yes, does your subject . . .

- Keep a diary?
- Keep to him- or herself?
- Keep secrets?
- Make lots of notes?
- Know lots of facts?

Does your subject use words you've never heard before? y/n

Does your subject . . .

- Talk to him- or herself?
- Take a lot of sick days?
- Take lots of pills?
- Dislike certain foods?
- Ask a lot of questions?

CONCLUSION

If you checked the majority of these boxes then your subject is most definitely an alien. Keep a close eye on them and their activities, as you may need to thwart their plans for world domination.

At the same time you could master these **Things to Know**:
2: What Is DNA (and Are We All That Different from Chimps)?
12: How Big Is the Universe? • 44: What Happens in the Bermuda Triangle?

What Are the Biggest and Smallest Animals in the World?

Some animals are so small that if they sat on you, you wouldn't know it. But then there are animals so big that if they sat on you, you wouldn't know it either, because you'd be squashed flat!

Little . . .

The world's smallest animal is hard to judge: it depends what you classify as an animal. Some creatures are just a few microscopic cells. And there are ticks and mites just a few millimeters long. Here are some more tiny beings:

- The smallest animal with a backbone is thought to be the stout infantfish—male fish are just one-quarter inch long.
- The smallest mammal is the Kitti's hog-nosed bat, which is about 1.2 in long and weighs less than 1 oz. A close contender is Savi's pygmy shrew.

. . . and Large

The biggest land animal is an African elephant, which can weigh up to about 6 tons. However, this is tiny compared to the blue whale:

- Blue whales can grow up to 108 ft long (as long as three double-decker buses), though an average-sized adult would be about 80 ft. At birth, a blue whale calf is about 25 ft long and weighs more than an elephant. They weigh up to 190 tons.
- A blue whale's tongue alone weighs as much as a hippo! At this size, they need to eat about 7,000 pounds of food a day.

The heaviest creature that ever lived on Earth *ever*: that would be . . . the blue whale. You might think it'd be a kind of dinosaur, but the biggest dinosaur we know about would only have weighed a little more than half the weight of a blue whale.

What Are the Biggest and Smallest Animals in the World? **Form**

Once you have mastered this **Thing to Know,** stick your Achieved Star here and fill in the form

Achieved

THE WORLD'S BIGGEST CREATURES

Here is a chart to show the size of the world's biggest animals. One of them, you will notice, is no longer around.

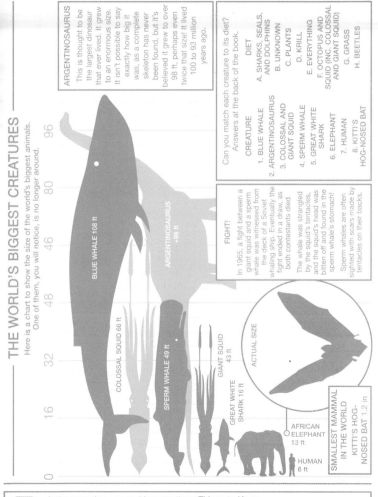

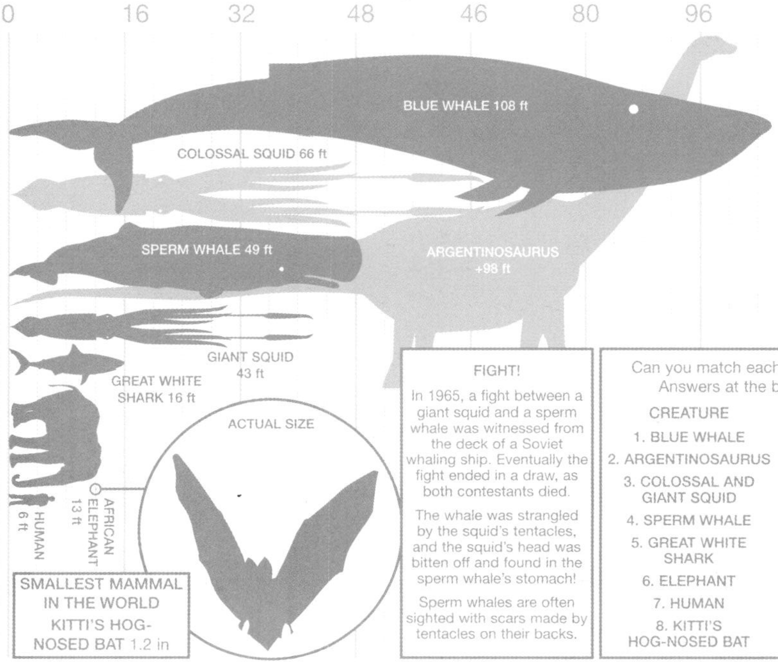

ARGENTINOSAURUS

This is thought to be the largest dinosaur that ever lived. It grew to an enormous size. It isn't possible to say exactly how big it was, as a complete skeleton has never been found, but it's believed it grew to over 98 ft, perhaps even twice that size! It lived 100 to 93 million years ago.

FIGHT!

In 1965, a fight between a giant squid and a sperm whale was witnessed from the deck of a Soviet whaling ship. Eventually the fight ended in a draw, as both contestants died.

The whale was strangled by the squid's tentacles, and the squid's head was bitten off and found in the sperm whale's stomach!

Sperm whales are often sighted with scars made by tentacles on their backs.

Can you match each creature to its diet? Answers at the back of the book.

CREATURE	DIET
1. BLUE WHALE	A. SHARKS, SEALS, AND DOLPHINS
2. ARGENTINOSAURUS	B. UNKNOWN
3. COLOSSAL AND GIANT SQUID	C. PLANTS
4. SPERM WHALE	D. KRILL
5. GREAT WHITE SHARK	E. EVERYTHING
6. ELEPHANT	F. OCTOPUS AND SQUID (INC. COLOSSAL AND GIANT SQUID)
7. HUMAN	G. GRASS
8. KITTI'S HOG-NOSED BAT	H. BEETLES

At the same time you could master these **Things to Know:**
2: What Is DNA (and Are We All That Different from Chimps)? • 9: Who Would Win the Animal Olympic 100-Meter Race? • 30: What Is at the Bottom of the Ocean?

How Much Does the Earth Weigh?

This is probably one of those nagging questions that keeps you awake at night. Okay, maybe not, but you must be asking yourself how it's possible to weigh anything planet-sized. And if not, you're about to find out anyway.

Big Deal

To be accurate we should really talk about mass rather than weight, because weight is a force exerted due to gravity—so if you weighed a hippopotamus on Earth it might weigh 3 tons, but the same hippo would weigh only 110 lb on the Moon (because gravity on the Moon is much less than on Earth). But the mass of the hippo (how much hippo there is) would be the same.

Obviously you can't stick the Earth on a scale and weigh it, but you can measure its mass using an equation worked out by Isaac Newton. All objects have a gravitational attraction for one another (even hippos). From this, you can work out the Earth's mass using an equation that takes into account the distance between Earth and another object in space, and something called the Gravitational Constant. After much head scratching, the answer you'd get would be 13,170,000,000,000,000,000,000,000 lb (just over 13 million billion billion pounds).

Now, this number doesn't mean much to most people. They stop counting after a few zeros. So to give you a better understanding of just how heavy this is, go to the next page where you can do a few calculations of your own.

Big brother: Jupiter, the largest planet in our solar system, has a mass 318 times the Earth's. In fact it's 2.5 times the mass of all the other planets in the solar system put together. That's one giant planet.

How Much Does the Earth Weigh?

How Much Does the Earth Weigh? **Form**

Once you have mastered this **Thing to Know**, stick your Achieved Star here and fill in the form

Achieved

WEIGHTY EQUATIONS

How many of you would it take to equal the weight of the Earth? Try your hand at answering this and other similar questions below.

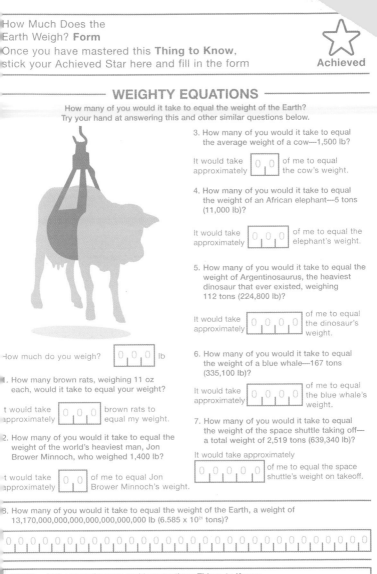

How much do you weigh? 0,0,0 lb

1. How many brown rats, weighing 11 oz each, would it take to equal your weight?

It would take approximately 0,0,0 brown rats to equal my weight.

2. How many of you would it take to equal the weight of the world's heaviest man, Jon Brower Minnoch, who weighed 1,400 lb?

It would take approximately 0,0 of me to equal Jon Brower Minnoch's weight.

3. How many of you would it take to equal the average weight of a cow—1,500 lb?

It would take approximately 0,0 of me to equal the cow's weight.

4. How many of you would it take to equal the weight of an African elephant—5 tons (11,000 lb)?

It would take approximately 0,0,0 of me to equal the elephant's weight.

5. How many of you would it take to equal the weight of Argentinosaurus, the heaviest dinosaur that ever existed, weighing 112 tons (224,800 lb)?

It would take approximately 0,0,0,0 of me to equal the dinosaur's weight.

6. How many of you would it take to equal the weight of a blue whale—167 tons (335,100 lb)?

It would take approximately 0,0,0,0 of me to equal the blue whale's weight.

7. How many of you would it take to equal the weight of the space shuttle taking off—a total weight of 2,519 tons (639,340 lb)?

It would take approximately 0,0,0,0,0 of me to equal the space shuttle's weight on takeoff.

8. How many of you would it take to equal the weight of the Earth, a weight of 13,170,000,000,000,000,000,000,000 lb (6.585×10^{21} tons)?

0,0,0,0,0,0,0,0,0,0,0,0,0,0,0,0,0,0,0,0,0,0,0,0,0

At the same time you could master these **Things to Know**:
18: What Are the Biggest and Smallest Animals in the World?
22: Why Don't We Fall Off the Earth? • 52: Could a Rock Destroy Our Planet?

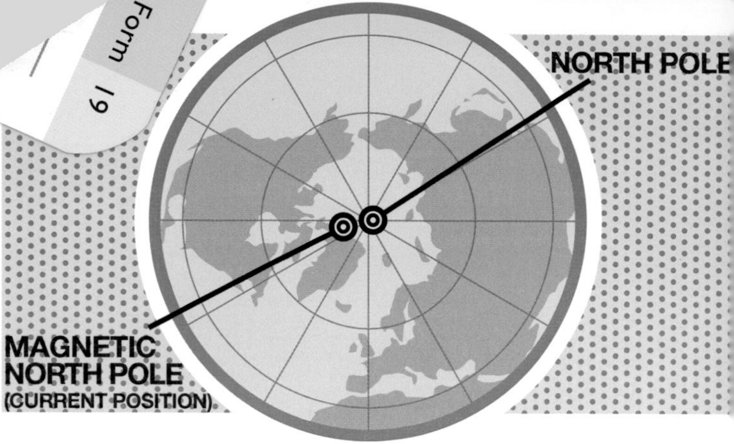

Which Way Is North?

If you've ever been hopelessly lost in the woods with darkness closing in, you might well have asked this question in a desperate kind of way. Or you might have been very glad that you had a compass in your pocket.

Magnetic Attraction

The needle of a compass is a small magnet. The Earth is like a giant magnet because its core is made of liquid iron (at least, scientists are pretty sure it is—no one's been down there to check). Since magnets are attracted to other magnets, the needle on a compass is attracted to the magnetic field produced by the Earth, and it will point to the North Pole.

Even though it's very big, the Earth's magnetic field is weak, so don't use a compass near metal objects or other magnets—it'll lead you completely the wrong way. If you don't have a compass, there are other ways to find north:

- **Use the stars.** In the Northern Hemisphere you need to find the North Star; in the Southern Hemisphere you need to find the Southern Cross.
- **Use the Sun.** Put a stick in the ground and mark the end of its shadow at different times throughout the day. If you are in the Northern Hemisphere, the shortest shadow will point north.
- **Point the hour hand of a watch at the Sun**, then draw an imaginary line between the hour hand and twelve o'clock—the line will point south.
- **Look at the trees.** Trees tend to have fewer branches facing north, but more moss and lichen tend to grow on the north side of trees and rocks.

When north isn't north: a compass will point north, but not to the North Pole. That's because the Earth's magnetic field doesn't quite line up with the North Pole—there's a difference of about 15 mi.

Which Way Is North? **Form**

Once you have mastered this **Thing to Know,**
stick your Achieved Star here and fill in the form

Achieved

FINDING TRUE NORTH

Try your hand at finding north without a compass.

USE THE STARS

Finding north in the Northern Hemisphere is simple thanks to Polaris, the North Star.

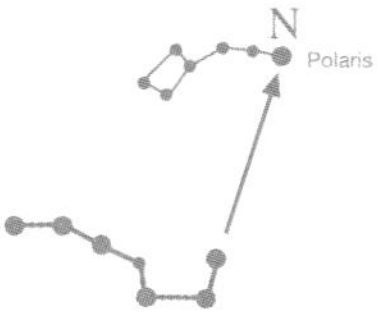

Look for the Plough, also called the Big Dipper. Once you've found it, trace a line straight up from the last two stars until you come to a bright star. This is Polaris.

Finding north in the Southern Hemisphere is harder because there is no star bright enough to guide you. The easiest way is to find south, by looking for the Crux, also called the Southern Cross.

Once you've found it, trace a line from the center of the cross downward for approximately five times its length. This imaginary point marks south.

Did you find north this way? y/n

USE THE SUN

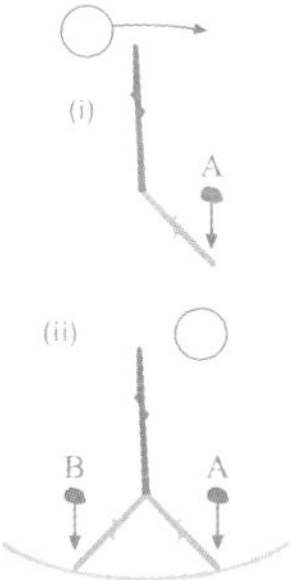

Things you will need:
a couple of sticks, two stones, and a piece of string

(i) Plant one of the sticks vertically into the ground. Sometime in the morning mark the top of the shadow of the stick with a stone.

(ii) Tie one end of your string to the stick in the ground, and the other end to your second stick. With the string tight, use the second stick to draw an arc from the first stone. As the Sun moves during the day, the stick's shadow will get longer and eventually shorter again. Later in the afternoon, when the top of the shadow of the stick comes into contact with the arc you drew, place another stone.

(iii) The line between the two stones is the east–west line and north is the cross section between the stones. North is pointing away from the stick.

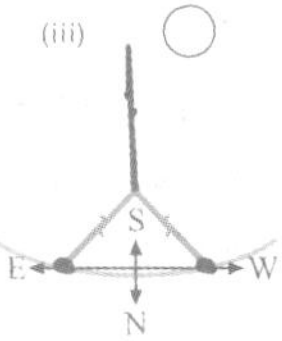

Did you find north this way? y/n

USE YOUR WATCH

NORTHERN HEMISPHERE

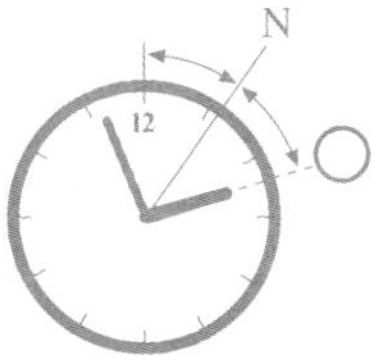

To find north in the Northern Hemisphere, point the hour hand of your watch at the Sun. Trace a line from the center of your watch to the point halfway between 12 and the hour hand. This line points north.

To find north in the Southern Hemisphere point 12 at the Sun. Trace a line from the center of your watch to the point halfway between 12 and the hour hand. Again, this line points north.

Did you find north this way? y/n

SOUTHERN HEMISPHERE

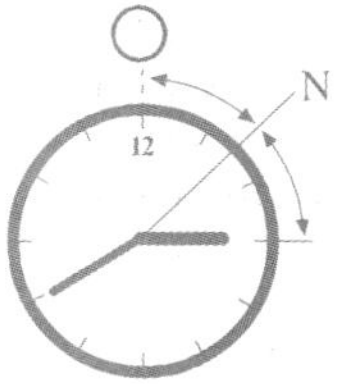

At the same time you could master these **Things to Know**:
36: How Many Stars Are There in the Milky Way? • 53: Where Does the Sun Go at Night? • 66: Why Do Stars Twinkle? • 83: Where Is the Night Sky Multicolored?

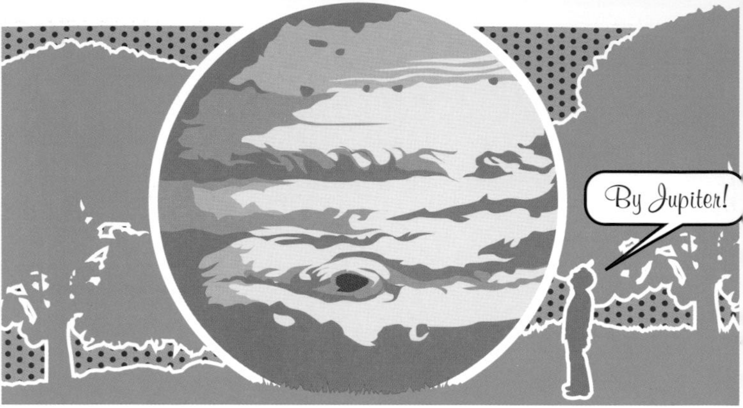

What Is the Solar System (and Could It Fit in Your Yard)?

The solar system is our little piece of the universe—the part that orbits the Sun.

Buck the System

The solar system is made up of the following bits and pieces:

- **The Sun**—our nearest star and the center of the solar system, a giant ball of burning fuel, providing us with light and heat.
- **Eight planets**—in order from nearest the Sun, they are Mercury, Venus, Earth, Mars, Jupiter, Saturn, Uranus, and Neptune.
- **The asteroid belt**—a band of lumps of rock or metal (or a bit of both), orbiting the Sun between Mars and Jupiter. The biggest asteroid is 621 mi across, and the smallest is a tiny speck.
- **Satellites**—natural satellites are often called moons. They're like planets except that they orbit other planets rather than the Sun. Mars and Venus don't have any; others have many, like Jupiter, which also has the biggest moon in the solar system—it's called Ganymede, and it's bigger than Mercury. There are also man-made satellites orbiting the Earth—like space stations.
- **Comets**—chunks of ice and dust whizzing around the Sun in odd orbits.

The solar system is mostly empty space—the distances between planets are enormous. To get an idea of just how enormous, imagine Earth was the size of a pea . . . now look at the form to see how it compares with the size of the rest of the solar system.

Pluto: Pluto is much smaller than many of the moons of other planets, and recently its status was downgraded from an official planet to a dwarf planet. Poor Pluto.

What Is the Solar System (and Could It Fit in Your Yard)? **Form**

Once you have mastered this **Thing to Know,** stick your Achieved Star here and fill in the form

Achieved

The planet sizes here and the distances between them are relative.

1. SUN
This huge circle represents the size of the Sun.
The Sun is huge compared to the planets in our solar system.

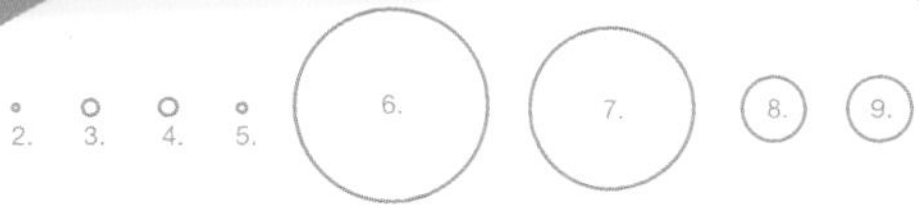

RE-CREATE THE SOLAR SYSTEM IN YOUR YARD

THINGS YOU WILL NEED: a soccer ball, a grain of sand, two peas, a grain of rice, a golf ball, a Ping-Pong ball, two grapes, and a tape measure

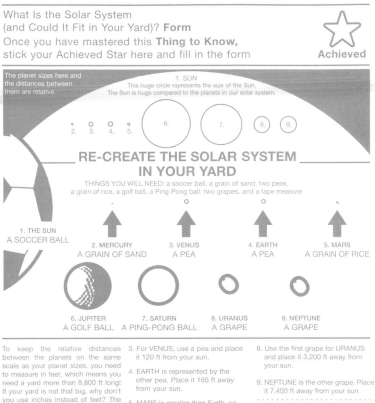

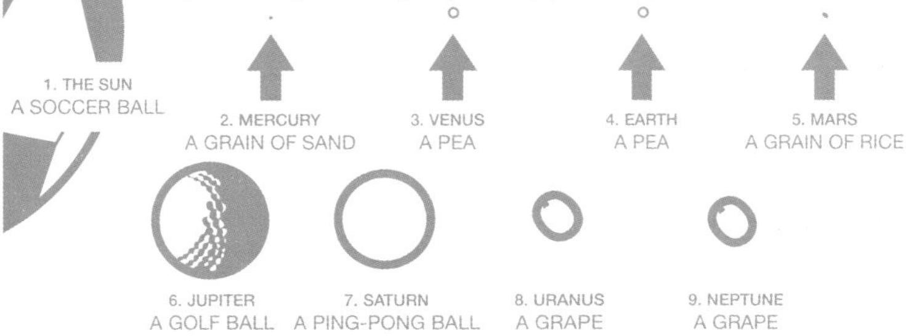

To keep the relative distances between the planets on the same scale as your planet sizes, you need to measure in feet, which means you need a yard more than 8,800 ft long! If your yard is not that big, why don't you use inches instead of feet? The list at the end gives the distances in inches, at a scale of 100 times smaller than those listed below.

1. To represent THE SUN on your model, use a soccer ball.
2. At this scale MERCURY is a grain of sand and barely visible. Place it 60 ft away.
3. For VENUS, use a pea and place it 120 ft from your sun.
4. EARTH is represented by the other pea. Place it 165 ft away from your sun.
5. MARS is smaller than Earth, so a grain of rice will do. Place it 250 ft away from your sun.
6. JUPITER is the largest planet in our solar system, so use a golf ball to represent it. Place it 850 ft away from your sun.
7. Place SATURN, the second largest planet and represented by a Ping-Pong ball, 1,550 ft from your sun.
8. Use the first grape for URANUS and place it 3,200 ft away from your sun.
9. NEPTUNE is the other grape. Place it 7,400 ft away from your sun.

If you use the measurements below, imagine the distances 100 times bigger to get an idea of the scale of the solar system. You may still need to move into a field.

MERCURY 7 in
VENUS 14 in
EARTH 20 in
MARS 30 in
JUPITER 102 in
SATURN 186 in
URANUS 384 in
NEPTUNE 888 in

At the same time you could master these **Things to Know**:
12: How Big Is the Universe? • 29: How Long Is a Light-Year? • 36: How Many Stars Are There in the Milky Way? • 101: What Would Happen to You in a Black Hole?

Why Don't We Fall Off the Earth?

Do you know how fast we're spinning? It's enough to make you feel dizzy. The Earth spins through space at about 1,038 mph, so how come anything stays put on its surface?

A Matter of Gravity

It's not obvious that the Earth is a sphere, which is why it took people so long to figure it out. It looks flat from down here, and the fact that we don't fall off and plummet through space seems to support this idea. The reason planets aren't shaped like cubes, pyramids, or giant tortoises is that a sphere is the shape you get when a large amount of matter is pulled together so that all the different pieces of material are packed as closely as possible. The thing doing the pulling is gravity—this is the force that attracts every object in the universe to every other object. Luckily, this doesn't mean that we're irresistibly drawn to things and end up stuck to lampposts, because the gravity here isn't strong enough. But the Earth's gravity *is* strong enough to keep us on the ground.

Everything on the planet that has mass—tables, elephants, you, socks, microscopic mites—is being pulled toward the center of the Earth by gravity. The more massive something is, the stronger the pull on it. That's why some things feel heavier than others. Even the atmosphere is kept in place because of the gravitational pull of the Earth on particles in the atmosphere—which is just as well, otherwise we wouldn't be able to breathe!

Top spin: the Earth spins around once every 24 hours, but if it suddenly started spinning really fast, we'd all be thrown off into space. Don't panic though—it would need to spin more than 800 times faster than it does now for this to happen.

Why Don't We Fall Off the Earth? **Form**

Once you have mastered this **Thing to Know,** stick your Achieved Star here and fill in the form

Achieved

— WHICH FALLS FASTER, A STONE OR A FEATHER? —

The astronomer Galileo Galilei (1564–1642) was intrigued by the way objects fall to Earth. Legend has it that Galileo climbed to the top of the leaning tower of Pisa armed with two balls—they were the same size but different weights. He dropped them simultaneously from the top of the tower and they landed on the ground at the same time. This amazed people as they had always believed that heavy objects fall to Earth faster than light ones. This experiment proved that theory to be totally wrong.

But if you drop a stone and a feather at the same time from the same height, the stone will always land first. So what is going on? Galileo realized that it wasn't the weight of an object that caused it to fall faster or slower than another, but the effect of air resistance upon it. The feather is an irregular shape and is easily influenced by the resistance of the air.

He proposed that if you dropped a heavy object (a stone) and a light object (a feather) at the same time in a vacuum, then they would both land at the same time.

400 years later an astronaut named David Scott of the Apollo 15 mission to the Moon put Galileo's claim to the test in the vacuum of space. He dropped a hammer and a feather simultaneously from the same height and they both landed on the Moon's surface at the same time, proving Galileo's theory to be right.

EXPERIMENT

For this experiment you need:

two apples of equal size, a grape, a newspaper, and an assistant

1. Place the newspaper on the floor. Ask your eagle-eyed assistant to lie down on his/her stomach in order for their eye level to be as close to the newspaper as possible.
2. Stand on a chair with both your arms outstretched, and an apple in each hand.
3. Drop the apples simultaneously from an equal height.
4. Your assistant should record which hits the newspaper first. Record your results below.

____

5. Subsitute one of the apples with the grape and repeat the experiment. Record your results in the space provided.

____

6. Try using different objects and see if you come to the same conclusions.

Item 1	Item 2

Results

____

What conclusion can you draw from your experiments?

____

When the experiments are over, wash and eat the apples and the grape.

At the same time you could master these **Things to Know**:
18: What Are the Biggest and Smallest Animals in the World? • 19: How Much Does the Earth Weigh? • 59: How Do Planes Get into the Air—and Stay There?

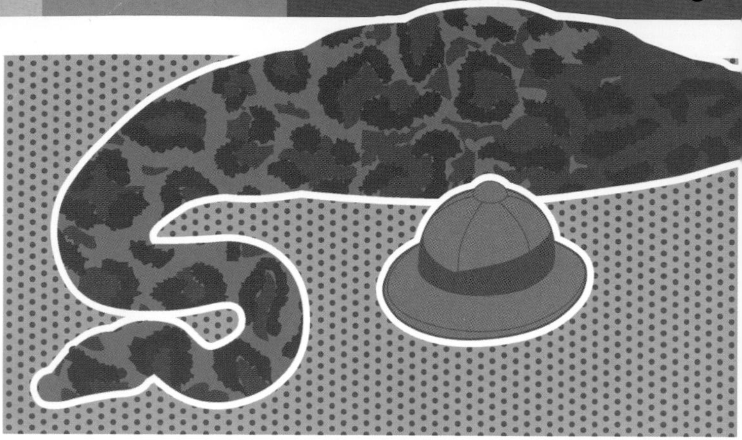

How Does a Snake Swallow Things Bigger Than Its Own Head?

Have you ever wished you were able to swallow something bigger than your own head—whole? Perhaps when you've seen a delicious-looking cake . . .

Snake Snacks

Snakes are long and thin with small heads, no limbs, and teeth that are not able to grind things up, so they have to swallow things whole. Instead of living solely on a diet of spaghetti, snakes have adapted so they can eat things that are bigger than their heads. Some can even eat things that are bigger than they are.

A snake's skull is loosely joined to its jaws by strong ligaments, allowing it to expand, and a bone at the back of the skull acts like a hinge, so that the lower jaw can completely separate from the upper jaw. In this way the snake's head can expand and cope with something huge. The snake can still breathe even when its mouth is completely stuffed with food because the windpipe can move and allows the creature to take in air. The snake pushes the prey down into the gullet, which is almost as big as its stomach—the inside of a snake is very stretchy to accommodate its gargantuan meals.

Snakes don't often fight each other over food, and if they do it can be dangerous: the snakes both start eating the food from either end and the losing snake has been known to be eaten along with the prey!

Snake siesta: all snakes have to increase their temperature by lying in the sun after eating, to make the food easier to digest. If they're not warm enough, they won't have time to digest the food before it rots and might have to regurgitate the prey.

How Does a Snake Swallow Things Bigger Than Its Own Head? **Form**

Once you have mastered this **Thing to Know**, stick your Achieved Star here and fill in the form

Achieved

AMAZING SNAKE FACTS

Test your knowledge of snakes with this quiz. Once you've done the quiz, memorize the correct facts, then impress your friends to earn your star.

1. What color is a black mamba snake?

(a) Brown, gray, or olive
(b) Green, yellow, or orange
(c) Red, black, or brown
(d) Black

2. Which poisonous snake kills more people than any other?

(a) The black mamba of Africa
(b) The saw-scaled (or carpet) viper of West Africa and India
(c) The gaboon viper of Africa
(d) The brown snake of Australia

3. Which snake has the longest fangs and produces the most venom?

(a) The black mamba of Africa
(b) The saw-scaled (or carpet) viper of West Africa and India
(c) The gaboon viper of Africa
(d) The brown snake of Australia

4. What was the age of the oldest snake ever recorded when it died in Philadelphia Zoo in 1977?

(a) 20 years old
(b) 30 years old
(c) 40 years old
(d) 50 years old

5. The longest species of snake is the reticulated python, but how long was the longest python ever recorded?

(a) 33 ft
(b) 66 ft
(c) 98 ft
(d) 131 ft

6. How many species of snake are there and what percentage are poisonous?

(a) Around 1,000 (100% are poisonous)
(b) Around 1,500 (80% are poisonous)
(c) Around 2,000 (50% are poisonous)
(d) Around 2,500 (20% are poisonous)

7. The king cobra is the world's largest poisonous snake. How poisonous is it?

(a) Its poison is strong enough to kill you
(b) Its poison is strong enough to kill an elephant
(c) Both answers
(d) Neither answer

8. What can the paradise tree-snake do that others can't?

(a) Walk
(b) Run
(c) Dance
(d) Fly

9. How does the grass snake escape predators?

(a) By playing dead
(b) By running away
(c) By jumping
(d) By making itself look big

10. How do snakes smell?

(a) With their nose
(b) With their tongue
(c) With their skin
(d) With their tail

Answers at the back of the book.

At the same time you could master these **Things to Know**:
13: Did Cannibals Really Exist? • 14: Will Your Stomach Explode if You Eat Too Much? • 56: What Is the Scariest Thing in the World?

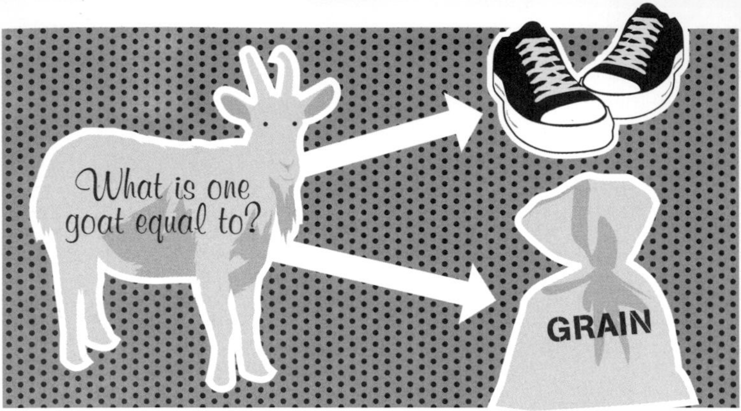

When Did Money Start Making the World Go Around?

Say you had twelve goats and needed a sack of grain and a pair of shoes. Before money was invented, you might have offered one of your goats to a local farmer in exchange for the grain and another goat to a cobbler in return for shoes. Hold on! A whole goat seems a lot for a pair of shoes. Oh, and the cobbler doesn't need any goats. The farmer's up for the deal if you can give him a cow. So do you then have to find someone with a spare cow who wants goats? And how many goats make a camel?

Money Talks

Using money is a lot less complicated than this tricky bartering system. No one knows who exactly came up with the idea, but they are believed to be from China.

- It's thought that cowry shells were used as the first-ever money in China around 1200 BC. The first metal money appeared there 200 years later.
- Native Americans also used shells as money. This is first recorded in the 16th century, but they were probably used long before that.
- The first coins were made out of silver. Unlike today's coins, which are symbols of value, these silver coins were valuable in themselves because they were made from a precious metal.
- To avoid carting around heavy coins, the Chinese introduced paper money and used it from about the 9th to the 15th centuries (when they stopped the practice because of high inflation). Elsewhere in the world paper money wasn't used for centuries.

"To pay through the nose," meaning to pay an excessive price for something, is an expression that is supposed to have come from the Vikings in Ireland in the 9th century. They slit people's noses as a punishment for nonpayment of taxes.

When Did Money Start Making
the World Go Around? **Form**

Once you have mastered this **Thing to Know**,
stick your Achieved Star here and fill in the form

Achieved

WHO NEEDS MONEY?

If your parents don't easily part with their money, try bartering with them. For example, say you want a new computer game and they refuse to give you any money, why not work out a list of chores and each one's monetary value, then offer to trade them for the computer game? Washing dishes might be worth $5.00, mowing the lawn $7.00, and washing the car $10.00. Once you've done these a few times, the total should add up to the total price of the computer game you wanted. Money—who needs it when you can swap your time, energy, and skills for the things you want?

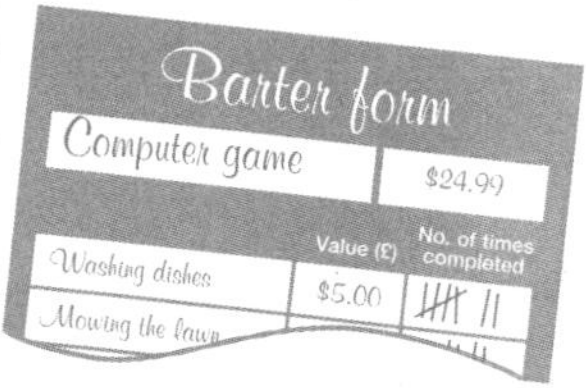

The forms below will help to remind your parents of your agreement. Fill in the chores and prices agreed upon, and make sure one of them signs the form. This way they cannot go back on their word.

BARTER FORM

Put up this form where everyone can monitor your progress.
Photocopy them a few times so you don't ruin your book!

Barter form

Item requested	Cost of item	
	Value ($)	No. of times completed
Name of chore		
Name of chore		
Name of chore		
Name of chore		
Name of chore		
Name of chore		
Name of chore		
Name of chore		

Small print: As your parent/guardian I agree to the value of chores listed above. I also agree to deliver the item requested within seven days of the total chore value achieved matching the item price.

Total

Parent's signature here

Barter form

Item requested	Cost of item	
	Value ($)	No. of times completed
Name of chore		
Name of chore		
Name of chore		
Name of chore		
Name of chore		
Name of chore		
Name of chore		
Name of chore		

Small print: As your parent/guardian I agree to the value of chores listed above. I also agree to deliver the item requested within seven days of the total chore value achieved matching the item price.

Total

Parent's signature here

At the same time you could master these **Things to Know**:
**47: Who Is the Richest Person in the World? • 68: Who Invented Paper?
69: How Can I Win Millions? • 72: Who Was the Most Bloodthirsty Pirate Ever?**

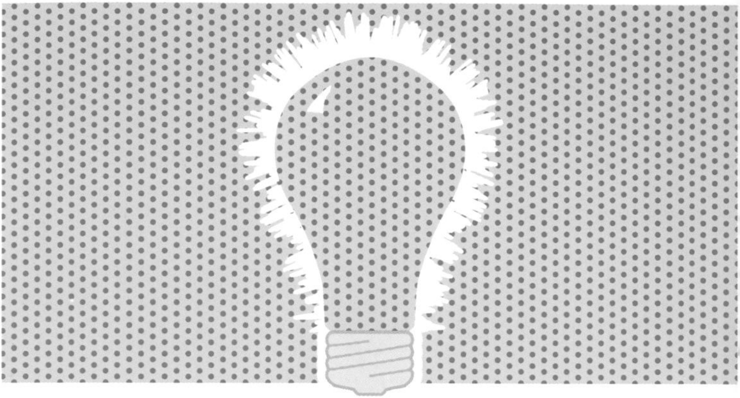

If Light Is Invisible, How Can We See?

We know where light comes from—the Sun, fire, lightbulbs, etc. And we know that without light we wouldn't be able to see and nothing would grow—it would be the end of the world. But what on earth is it?

Lighten Up!

It might be hard to get your head around the fact that we can see because of invisible vibrating fields. Confused? Well, light is actually a form of energy called electromagnetic radiation. It's a part of the electromagnetic spectrum, which is made up of waves of vibrating electric and magnetic fields. Radio waves, microwaves, and X-rays are all part of this spectrum, and the difference between them is in the length of their waves—radio waves, at one end of the spectrum, have the longest wavelength, and gamma rays, at the other, have the shortest. Visible light is just 1,000th of 1% of the whole spectrum.

There are some forms of light that really are invisible, like ultraviolet. The Sun is a source of ultraviolet radiation—we know that because it's those rays that cause our skin to burn! Infrared is another type of invisible light. Although we can't see it, we can feel it as heat.

Light behaves like a stream of particles. It also behaves like a wave. How can it be both at the same time? This "wave-particle duality" is one of the most confusing things in science and one of the key questions of physics.

Get *reddy*: most objects at room temperature or above emit infrared radiation. This means, when there's not enough visible light, infrared images can give us a picture by detecting areas of heat. Infrared is also used in remote controls, burglar alarms, and medical heat lamps.

If Light Is Invisible,
How Can We See? **Form**

Once you have mastered this **Thing to Know,**
stick your Achieved Star here and fill in the form

Achieved

THE ELECTROMAGNETIC SPECTRUM

Visible light is 0.001% of the spectrum. There is so much more to light than we can see. The diagram below breaks down light into its various parts, from gamma rays to radio waves.

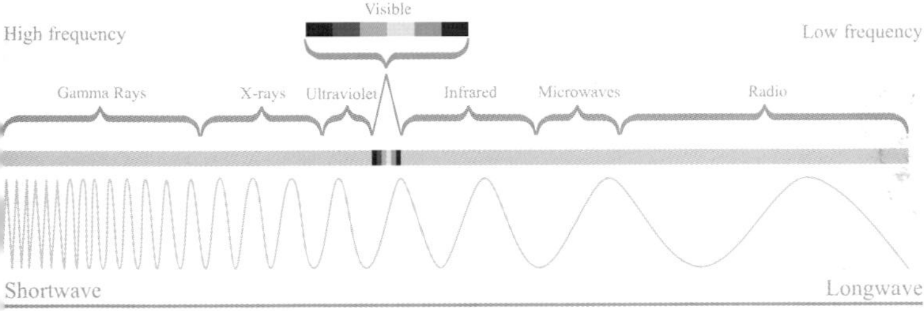

OVER THE RAINBOW

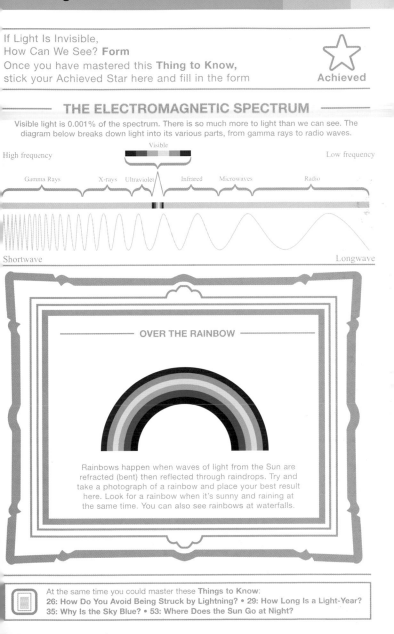

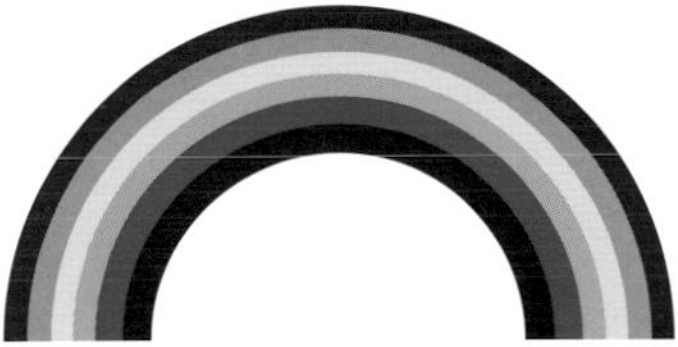

Rainbows happen when waves of light from the Sun are refracted (bent) then reflected through raindrops. Try and take a photograph of a rainbow and place your best result here. Look for a rainbow when it's sunny and raining at the same time. You can also see rainbows at waterfalls.

At the same time you could master these **Things to Know**:
**26: How Do You Avoid Being Struck by Lightning? • 29: How Long Is a Light-Year?
35: Why Is the Sky Blue? • 53: Where Does the Sun Go at Night?**

How Do You Avoid Being Struck by Lightning?

Thunderstorms occur all over the world and lightning is unpredictable, so it's useful to know how to avoid getting toasted.

A Bolt from the Blue

Water and ice droplets in storm clouds bump around and become electrically charged. At the top of the cloud they have a positive charge, and at the bottom, a negative charge. Sometimes the negatively charged bottom is close enough to the positively charged ground (or the top of another cloud) to be attracted to it, and electrical energy is released in a flash of light. Lightning will often strike a tall object, like a church spire or a tall tree, because it's an easier path to the ground than the air. So how can you avoid attracting the attention of a lightning bolt?

- Don't stand near trees or any tall structures.
- If you're in a car, stay there. Lightning will be more attracted to the metal of the car than it will be to you, but don't touch anything metal inside the car.
- Don't hold anything metal, like an umbrella (this would be a handy route for the electricity to get from the air to the earth).
- Keep away from open water, as it's a good conductor of electricity, and don't go sailing (the mast could attract lightning). But if you're in a boat, keep away from anything metal.

Lightning never strikes the same place twice? Untrue! The Empire State Building is struck about 100 times a year. Roy Sullivan, a park ranger from Virginia, was struck a record-breaking seven times. He was injured but survived all seven strikes.

How Do You Avoid Being
Struck by Lightning? **Form**
Once you have mastered this **Thing to Know,**
stick your Achieved Star here and fill in the form

Achieved

TYPES OF LIGHTNING

There are various types of lightning. Check the box if you've seen the type of lightning described.

Forked lightning: many branches of the lightning bolt can be seen

Streak lightning: looks like a single bolt of lightning

Sheet lightning: looks like the cloud is lighting up

Heat lightning: lightning without thunder

Crawler lightning: appears to crawl along the underside of the cloud

Ribbon lightning: parallel streaks of light usually caused by the effect of the wind

Chain or bead lightning: looks like the lightning bolt is broken up

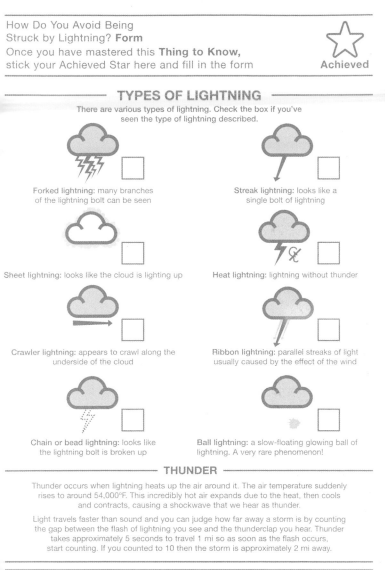

Ball lightning: a slow-floating glowing ball of lightning. A very rare phenomenon!

THUNDER

Thunder occurs when lightning heats up the air around it. The air temperature suddenly rises to around 54,000°F. This incredibly hot air expands due to the heat, then cools and contracts, causing a shockwave that we hear as thunder.

Light travels faster than sound and you can judge how far away a storm is by counting the gap between the flash of lightning you see and the thunderclap you hear. Thunder takes approximately 5 seconds to travel 1 mi so as soon as the flash occurs, start counting. If you counted to 10 then the storm is approximately 2 mi away.

At the same time you could master these **Things to Know**:
43: How Do Clouds Stay Up? • 75: How Can Birds Stand on Electric Wires and Not Be Toasted? • 83: Where Is the Night Sky Multicolored?

What Is the Deadliest Martial Art?

If you ever meet someone who's an expert in a martial art, it's handy to know this in order to decide how scared you should be. Or maybe you want to take up the martial art that's guaranteed to scare other people as much as possible?

Kung Fu Fighting

Any martial arts expert would immediately tell you that being "deadly" isn't really the idea behind martial arts. In fact, they'd probably get a bit annoyed and say you've been watching too many movies, because most forms of martial art focus on self-defense and avoiding conflict. Nor do many martial artists employ weapons. They all follow different philosophies and techniques:

- Karate features sharp, focused punches and kicks.
- Judo focuses on throwing and wrestling.
- Aikido also uses holds and locks rather than blows.
- Choy li fut uses powerful punches.
- Tae kwon do experts perform impressive-looking acrobatic kicks and punches.

So there's no straightforward answer to this question—all martial arts can be deadly, but, of course, it depends on the situation and the expertise of the fighter. The Japanese samurai are probably the most legendary of martial artists whose skills were used for combat, although Japanese ninjas (spies and assassins) have a pretty fearsome reputation too. Both used weapons as well!

The samurai were a class of Japanese warriors, kind of like medieval knights in Europe except they lasted a lot longer—700 years, from the 1100s to the 1800s. It's thought ninjas were around then too, but much less is known about their secret lives.

What Is the Deadliest
Martial Art? **Form**
Once you have mastered this **Thing to Know**,
stick your Achieved Star here and fill in the form

Achieved

DO YOU KUNG FU?

Can you do any martial arts moves? If you can, place photos of you performing them below. If you can't, make some up! Real or invented, write the name of the move below each photo.

At the same time you could master these **Things to Know**:
17: Is Your Teacher an Alien? • 56: What Is the Scariest Thing in the World?
99: Who Was the Greatest Conqueror of All Time?

When Should You Use the Heimlich Maneuver?

The Heimlich Maneuver sounds like the kind of thing you might use in a wrestling match, but in fact it's something you need to know because it can save someone's life if he or she is choking.

Spit It Out

When someone chokes it's because there is a piece of food, or a small object, stuck in the windpipe. He or she can't breathe or speak, so don't expect the person to explain the problem. Instead, leap into action:

- First, ask the victim to lean forward and cough. If this doesn't get rid of the object, continue to the next step. (Don't slap his or her back—this could make matters worse.)
- Stand behind the victim and wrap your arms around his or her waist.
- Make a fist and place the thumb side of it against the victim's body between his or her navel and ribcage.
- Grab your fist with your other hand. Press sharply into the victim's body with a quick thrust, without squeezing the rest of his or her body.
- This movement should eject the choking object from the victim's mouth. If not, keep trying and eventually the object should be removed.

Be alert in cafeterias and restaurants—it's quite common for people to choke on food, and you never know when you might have to step in and save the day.

Invented by Dr. Henry Heimlich in the 1970s, this maneuver has since saved hundreds of thousands of lives—including Cher's and former president Ronald Reagan's. Dr. Heimlich himself has had to use his maneuver only once ever.

When Should You Use the Heimlich Maneuver? **Form**

Once you have mastered this **Thing to Know,** stick your Achieved Star here and fill in the form

Achieved

HEIMLICH MANEUVER

Hopefully in your lifetime you won't ever witness anyone choking, but just in case you do, here is a diagram of how to help someone by using the Heimlich Maneuver.

If you do witness someone choking, administer the Heimlich Maneuver by following the instructions on the opposite page.

WARNING: DO NOT ATTEMPT THE HEIMLICH MANEUVER ON ANYONE WHO ISN'T CHOKING.

Have you ever had to perform the Heimlich Maneuver on someone? y/n

If yes, whom did you help?

What did he or she choke on?

HELP! I NEED SOMEBODY!

Have you ever helped to give someone first aid before? y/n

If yes, how did you help?

Have you ever been in a situation where someone has given you first aid? y/n

If yes, what happened?

At the same time you could master these **Things to Know**:
11: Who Were the First Chocoholics? • 14: Will Your Stomach Explode if You Eat Too Much? • 23: How Does a Snake Swallow Things Bigger Than Its Own Head?

How Long Is a Light-Year?

If you were expecting the answer to be "three Earth years" or "500 times the time it takes to travel from Earth to Mars," you'd be way off track. A light-year is a measurement of distance, not time—a common mistake, and one of those things you can point out every now and then, and feel smug and smart about it.

Light-Years Ahead

A light-year is the distance it takes light to travel through a vacuum in a year. (It's traveling through a vacuum because some substances can slow light down.) Since light cracks along at a speed of about 186,300 mi per second, a light-year is a very long way. Light can travel 7.5 times around the Earth in a single second. In a year, the distance light travels is roughly 5,900,000,000,000 mi. You can see why it's easier to measure these kinds of huge distances in light-years rather than in miles.

Some Light-Year Distances

The nearest star to us (apart from the Sun) is Proxima Centauri, at about 4.2 light-years away.

Our galaxy measures about 100,000 light-years across.

The Andromeda galaxy is about 2.3 *million* light-years away.

Because the light has taken more than 2 million years to travel the distance from the Andromeda galaxy, we're seeing the star as it was more than 2 million years ago. Anything could have happened to it in the meantime. It might not even be there anymore!

Greedy astronomers! Light-years just aren't big enough for some astronomers: they use parsecs to measure distances in space. A parsec = 206,265 times the distance from Earth to the Sun, or 3.26 light-years. Proxima Centauri is about 1.3 parsecs away.

How Long Is a Light-Year? **Form**

Once you have mastered this **Thing to Know,**
stick your Achieved Star here and fill in the form

Achieved

LIGHT-SPEED EQUATIONS

We know that light travels at 186,282 mi per second, so can you figure out the answers to the following questions?

Conversion Table

In 1 second light can travel
186,282 mi

In 1 minute light can travel
11,176,944 mi

In 1 hour light can travel
670,616,629 mi

In 1 day light can travel
16,094,799,105 mi

A year is equal to

12 months • 52 weeks
365 days • 8,760 hours
525,600 minutes
31,536,000 seconds

1. Traveling at the speed of light, how many times could you make the trip from New York to London, a distance of 3,470 mi, in one light second?

   The answer is 0 0 . 0 0 times

2. How many times can light travel around the Earth in a second, given that the circumference of the Earth is 24,902 mi?

   The answer is 0 0 . 0 0 times

3. What is the distance between the Earth and the Moon in light seconds, a distance of 238,897 mi?

   The answer is 0 0 . 0 0 light seconds

4. How many minutes does it take sunlight to reach us, given that the Sun is 93,000,000 mi from the Earth?

   The answer is 0 0 . 0 0 minutes

5. How many years would it take the world's fastest bird, the white-throated spinetail swift, whose top speed is 110 mph, to fly the same distance as above nonstop?

   The answer is 0 0 . 0 0 years

6. Pluto is 3,670,054,382 mi from the Sun. How many hours does it take sunlight to get there?

   The answer is 0 0 . 0 0 hours

7. Voyager 1, launched September 5, 1977, has left our solar system and is just under 92,955,807,000 mi from the Sun. It has taken 30 years to get that far. How long would it have taken at the speed of light?

   The answer is 0 0 . 0 0 days

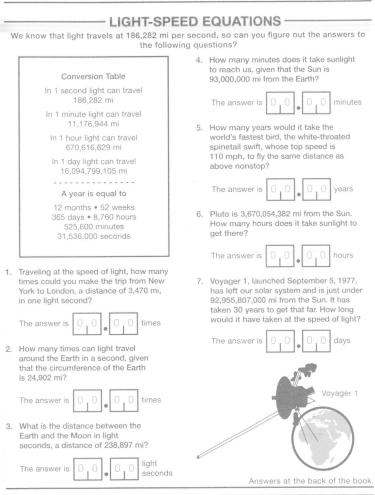

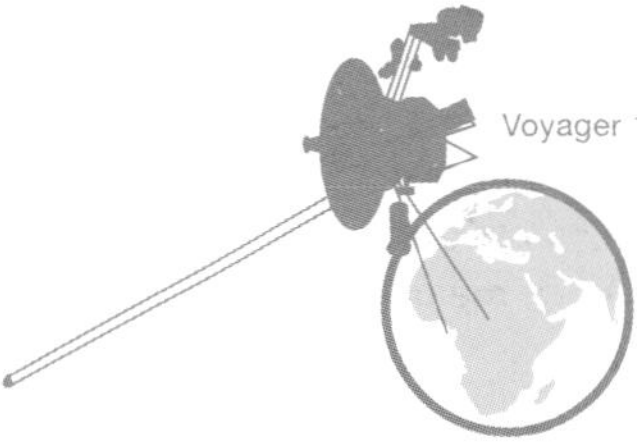

Answers at the back of the book.

At the same time you could master these **Things to Know**:
12: How Big Is the Universe? • 25: If Light Is Invisible, How Can We See?
26: How Do You Avoid Being Struck by Lightning?

This ocean isn't big enough for both of us!

What Is at the Bottom of the Ocean?

Most of the Earth's surface is covered by sea—yet we know more about the surface of the Moon than we do about the ocean bed. That's because it's so huge and so deep. Monterey Bay, off the coast of California, is the area of seabed that's been studied most in the world, but only 1% of it has been explored.

The Deep

On average, the sea is 2.5 mi deep. The ocean floor is even more rugged than the rest of the Earth's surface, and there are thousands of mountains, known as seamounts, that were (and continue to be) formed by volcanic eruptions under the sea. One enormous underwater mountain range stretches for 43,496 mi around the Earth.

The deepest part of the ocean is in the western Pacific. It's called the Mariana Trench and is about 7 mi (or 36,000 ft) deep. If you took Mount Everest and put it inside the trench, there would still be *1 mi* of water above it.

All Creatures Great and Small

Down in the ocean depths live some of the strangest creatures on the planet.

Beautiful deep-sea corals live as far down as 4 mi and can be up to 23 ft high.

Vent tube worms live 1 mi deep or more. They have no mouth or stomach and live by supplying bacteria inside their bodies with oxygen.

The deep-sea angler must be one of the ugliest fish. It lures prey by dangling a flashing light-producing organ in front of its jaws.

Lots of deep-sea creatures glow in the dark: glowing sucker octopuses give out a blue-green light.

Bone-eating worms specialize in feeding on dead whales more than a mile deep. Their bodies bore into the bones and suck out the fat.

Everest shmeverest: the Pacific has the biggest mountains and deepest gorges in the world. If measured from its base underwater, Mauna Kea, a volcano in Hawaii, would be the tallest on our planet—a mile taller than Everest!

What Is at the Bottom of the Ocean? **Form**

Once you have mastered this **Thing to Know**, stick your Achieved Star here and fill in the form

Achieved

THE MARIANA TRENCH

This is the deepest recorded part of any of the oceans. Below is a cross section to show how deep the trench is compared to other oceans and well-known landmarks.

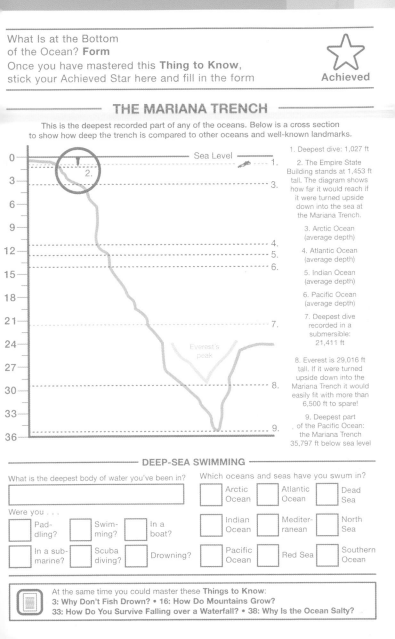

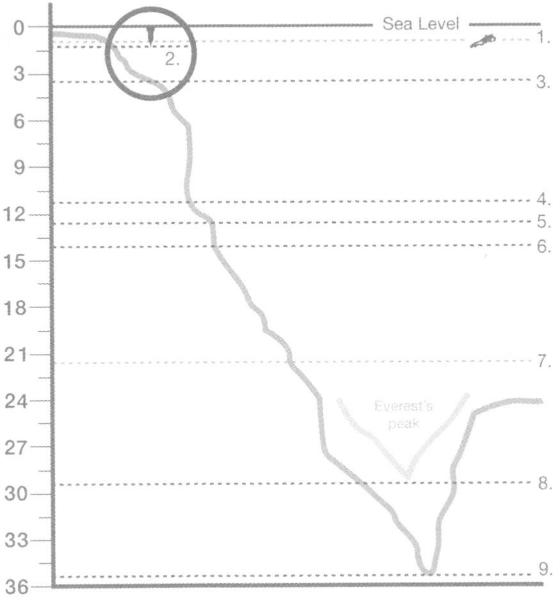

1. Deepest dive: 1,027 ft
2. The Empire State Building stands at 1,453 ft tall. The diagram shows how far it would reach if it were turned upside down into the sea at the Mariana Trench.
3. Arctic Ocean (average depth)
4. Atlantic Ocean (average depth)
5. Indian Ocean (average depth)
6. Pacific Ocean (average depth)
7. Deepest dive recorded in a submersible: 21,411 ft
8. Everest is 29,016 ft tall. If it were turned upside down into the Mariana Trench it would easily fit with more than 6,500 ft to spare!
9. Deepest part of the Pacific Ocean: the Mariana Trench 35,797 ft below sea level

DEEP-SEA SWIMMING

What is the deepest body of water you've been in?

Were you . . .

- ☐ Pad-dling?
- ☐ Swim-ming?
- ☐ In a boat?
- ☐ In a sub-marine?
- ☐ Scuba diving?
- ☐ Drowning?

Which oceans and seas have you swum in?

- ☐ Arctic Ocean
- ☐ Atlantic Ocean
- ☐ Dead Sea
- ☐ Indian Ocean
- ☐ Mediter-ranean
- ☐ North Sea
- ☐ Pacific Ocean
- ☐ Red Sea
- ☐ Southern Ocean

At the same time you could master these **Things to Know**:
**3: Why Don't Fish Drown? • 16: How Do Mountains Grow?
33: How Do You Survive Falling over a Waterfall? • 38: Why Is the Ocean Salty?**

Can a Cockroach Really Live for a Week Without Its Head?

Cockroaches are famous for being almost indestructible, but surviving a week of headlessness is pushing it. What a headache! Can this really be true?

Losing Your Head

Yes, indeed! And here's how they do it:

- Cockroaches don't breathe through their mouths: they have holes in their bodies called spiracles that allow them to breathe.
- What passes for a cockroach's brain isn't concentrated in the head but distributed throughout its body.
- Cutting off a cockroach's head doesn't make it bleed uncontrollably because it doesn't have blood pressure in the same way that we do.

Cockroaches do need food and water though, and without their mouth parts they do eventually die—they can probably go for a week or more without water, and much longer without food.

Ten Things You'd Rather Not Know About Cockroaches

1. They have six legs and at least 18 knees.
2. They have white blood.
3. They can hold their breath for 40 minutes.
4. There are more than 5,000 species of cockroach.
5. They can run at about 3 mph—that's about as fast as you walk.
6. A crushed cockroach is supposed to help heal a wound—though you might not want to try this at home.
7. They eat almost anything—soap, glue, their own cast-off skins, and sometimes each other.
8. They're found everywhere in the world except at the North and South Poles.
9. The world's biggest cockroach is 6 in long. Its wingspan is 12 in. It comes from South America.
10. The Madagascan Giant Hissing Cockroach is often kept as a pet.

Headless chickens: it's common for a chicken to run around for a few moments after its head has been chopped off. But Miracle Mike from Colorado survived for 18 months without his head—enough of his brain stem had been left to let him function almost normally.

Can a Cockroach Really Live for a Week Without Its Head? **Form**
Once you have mastered this **Thing to Know,** stick your Achieved Star here and fill in the form

Achieved

AMAZING INSECT FACTS

Test your knowledge of insects with this quiz. Once you've done the quiz, memorize the correct facts, then impress your friends to earn your star.

1. There are 1.75 million known animal species on Earth. What percentage of these are insects?

(a) 25
(b) 50
(c) 75
(d) 100

2. What is the most common form of insect?

(a) Moths/butterflies
(b) Wasps/bees
(c) Flies/mosquitoes
(d) Beetles

3. How fast can a dragonfly fly?

(a) Up to 9 mph
(b) Up to 19 mph
(c) Up to 22 mph
(d) Up to 37 mph

4. How many times its own length can a grasshopper jump?

(a) 10
(b) 20
(c) 30
(d) 40

5. How many times its own body weight can an ant carry?

(a) 50
(b) 100
(c) 150
(d) 200

6. How many times its own height can a flea jump?

(a) 60
(b) 130
(c) 200
(d) 270

7. Which of these spider facts is false?

(a) Spiders are not insects.
(b) Nearly all spiders are poisonous.
(c) All spiders spin webs.
(d) Spiders have up to eight eyes, but their eyesight is really bad.

8. What is the world's largest beetle called?

(a) Stag
(b) Goliath
(c) Dung
(d) Rhinoceros

(9. What doesn't a luna moth have?

(a) Wings
(b) A mouth
(c) Feelers
(d) Legs

10. What have praying mantis been known to eat?

(a) Small birds
(b) Lizards
(c) Frogs
(d) All of the above

Answers at the back of the book.

At the same time you could master these **Things to Know**:
18: What Are the Biggest and Smallest Animals in the World? • 54: Are Bats Really Blind? • 90: What Is the World's Most Poisonous Creature?

What Is an Ice Age (and When Are We Due for Another One)?

For billions of years there have been warm periods and cold periods in the Earth's climate. An ice age is a cold period, when the North and South Poles are covered in ice, and it can last for tens of millions of years. Now let's think . . . polar bears frolicking in the snow, penguins shivering in the Antarctic wasteland. Yep, you got it. We're in the middle of an ice age at the moment!

Chilling Out

There have been major ice ages lasting hundreds of millions of years—it's thought that the first one lasted from 2.7 to 2.3 billion years ago. One theory suggests that between about 800 and 600 million years ago, during the Cryogenian Period, the Earth was like a giant snowball, with the oceans frozen over completely. Since then, the Earth has warmed up a lot then cooled back down a bit several times. The present ice age started about 40 million years ago and became more severe about 3 million years ago.

During the present ice age, huge ice sheets have advanced and retreated. Right now we're having a warmer period within the ice age, and the glaciers have retreated. The last time they advanced down into Europe and North America was from about 30,000 to 10,000 years ago—this is what many people refer to as the Ice Age, but really it was just a colder section of the much longer ice age that's still going on.

Flood warning: currently 10% of land on Earth is covered by glaciers—it was three times that amount during the most recent colder period that ended about 10,000 years ago. If all the land ice melted today, the sea level would rise by about 230 ft.

What Is an Ice Age (and When Are We Due for Another One)? **Form**

Once you have mastered this **Thing to Know**, stick your Achieved Star here and fill in the form

Achieved

THE LAST ICE AGE

The map below shows the extent to which the ice covered the northern part of our planet 30,000 to 10,000 years ago. It also covered parts of the southern region of the planet.

ICE CYCLES

Have you ever had these n-ice experiences?

Have you ever been ice skating? y/n

What ice-skating skills do you have (if any)?

Last time you ice-skated how many times did you fall? 0 0 times

How many bruises did you count the next day? 0 0 bruises

How do you rate your ice-skating skills?

Poor · Okay · Good · Very good · Excellent

Have you ever walked on a glacier? y/n

If yes, where was the glacier?

Was it tough to climb? y/n

Could you hear the ice cracking and groaning around you? y/n

How long were you climbing for? 0 0 hours 0 0 mins

What equipment did you need (if any)?

At the same time you could master these **Things to Know**:
20: Which Way Is North? • 50: Where on Earth Is the Coldest Place? • 51: How Do You Survive on a Desert Island? • 76: How Do You Survive an Avalanche?

How Do You Survive Falling over a Waterfall?

Obviously, this will depend a lot on which waterfall you're falling over. Try to avoid the top ten highest, or you won't stand much of a chance whatever you do.

Making a Splash

The best thing you can do is to avoid swimming anywhere near a waterfall, because you can easily be swept away by the current of the river. But suppose you've been a bit reckless, here's the best way to survive:

- Take a deep breath as you're about to go over the waterfall.
- As you go over, jump to propel yourself as far away from the edge of the waterfall as possible, otherwise you could be dashed against the rocks as you go down or at the bottom.
- Try to go over the waterfall feetfirst. If you go over headfirst you're in grave danger of bashing your head on those rocks.
- Try to keep your body in a straight line as you drop down by squeezing your feet together and putting your arms around your head to protect it. Flailing limbs are more likely to get broken.
- The force of your fall will make you plunge deep into the water. Start swimming the moment you hit the water to reach the surface as soon as possible. And swim away from the waterfall to avoid getting trapped behind the wall of water or rocks.

Daredevils have been plunging over Niagara Falls for more than 100 years. Annie Taylor was the first person to try it when she went over the falls in a wooden barrel in 1901 and survived unharmed. But several people have died in the attempt.

How Do You Survive Falling over a Waterfall? **Form**

Once you have mastered this **Thing to Know,** stick your Achieved Star here and fill in the form

Achieved

WATERFALLS

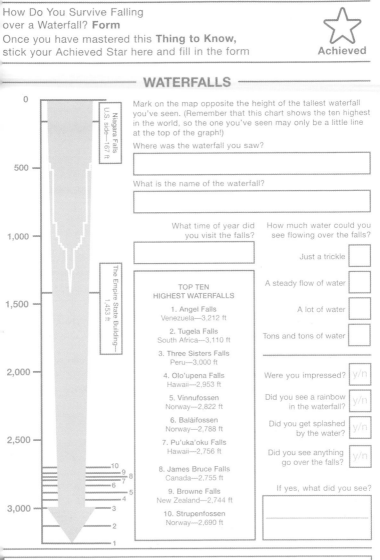

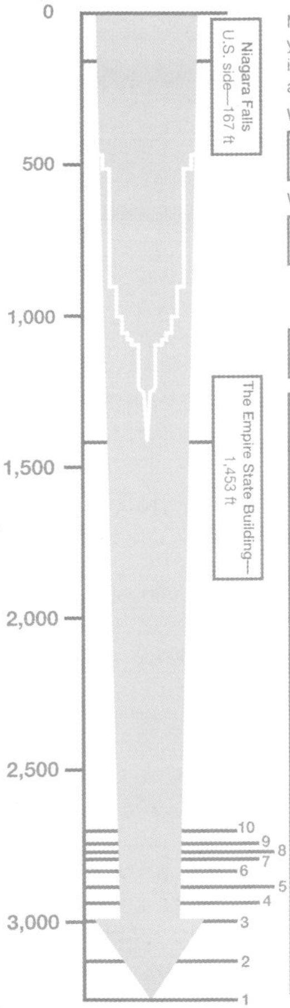

Mark on the map opposite the height of the tallest waterfall you've seen. (Remember that this chart shows the ten highest in the world, so the one you've seen may only be a little line at the top of the graph!)

Where was the waterfall you saw?

What is the name of the waterfall?

What time of year did you visit the falls?

TOP TEN HIGHEST WATERFALLS

1. Angel Falls
Venezuela—3,212 ft
2. Tugela Falls
South Africa—3,110 ft
3. Three Sisters Falls
Peru—3,000 ft
4. Olo'upena Falls
Hawaii—2,953 ft
5. Vinnufossen
Norway—2,822 ft
6. Balåifossen
Norway—2,788 ft
7. Pu'uka'oku Falls
Hawaii—2,756 ft
8. James Bruce Falls
Canada—2,755 ft
9. Browne Falls
New Zealand—2,744 ft
10. Strupenfossen
Norway—2,690 ft

How much water could you see flowing over the falls?

- Just a trickle
- A steady flow of water
- A lot of water
- Tons and tons of water

Were you impressed? y/n

Did you see a rainbow in the waterfall? y/n

Did you get splashed by the water? y/n

Did you see anything go over the falls? y/n

If yes, what did you see?

At the same time you could master these **Things to Know**:
3: Why Don't Fish Drown? • 30: What Is at the Bottom of the Ocean?
38: Why Is the Ocean Salty? • 76: How Do You Survive an Avalanche?

I am!
No, you're not, I am!
Furry fools! I am!

What Is the World's Favorite Pet?

Lots of people are crazy about their pets, especially in the U.S., where more than half of all households share their home with an animal. This is pretty surprising when you consider the hygiene standards of most pets. They can be responsible for all sorts of disgusting diseases. When they lick you, the chances are that they've recently been licking something you wouldn't touch with a ten-foot pole! Despite this, pets are common in Europe, America, and Asia (though not in Africa).

Reigning Cats and Dogs

Cats and dogs are the most popular pets in the world by a long shot. In recent years, cats have taken over from dogs as the favorite pet in the United States and Britain—there's one cat for every five people in the United States, and one cat for every seven people in Britain. Cats seem to be the most popular pets in China too (though cats are also eaten in China!). But it's a very close race between dogs and cats for the world's most popular pet.

The World's Most Popular Pets

Cats

Dogs

Rabbits

Budgies, canaries, and other birds

Goldfish

Hamsters

Guinea pigs

Rats and mice

Gerbils

Tropical fish

Most Popular Pet Names in the U.S.:

Dogs
Max, Baily, Buddy, and Molly

Cats
Max, Tigger, Smokey, and Tiger

Powerful pets: Napoleon's wife, Josephine, kept an orangutan, which sat at the dinner table dressed in a jacket. Charles V of Spain kept seven pet seals, and Julius Caesar owned a pet giraffe.

What Is the World's Favorite Pet? **Form**

Once you have mastered this **Thing to Know**, stick your Achieved Star here and fill in the form

Achieved

YOUR PETS

Keep a record of your pets below. If you have more than three pets, just list your favorite ones. If you don't have a pet, ask a friend or family member about his or hers.

Name of pet 1	Name of pet 2	Name of pet 3
What animal is your pet?	What animal is your pet?	What animal is your pet?
When did you get him/her?	When did you get him/her?	When did you get him/her?
m m d d y y y y	m m d d y y y y	m m d d y y y y
Is he/she still alive? y/n	Is he/she still alive? y/n	Is he/she still alive? y/n
Place a picture here	Place a picture here	Place a picture here
What's the best thing about your pet?	What's the best thing about your pet?	What's the best thing about your pet?

At the same time you could master these **Things to Know**:
49: Does One Dog Year Equal Seven Human Years? • 77: Why Do People Kiss (and Animals Don't)? • 95: Are Cats and Dogs Color-Blind (and How Do We Know)?

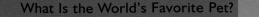

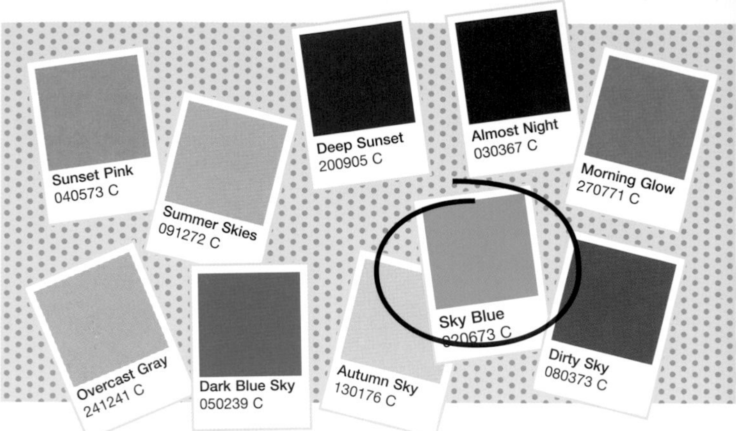

Why Is the Sky Blue?

This is the kind of question that people sometimes ask just to annoy you. So you might as well be ready with an answer.

Give Me Sunshine

Light from the Sun or a lightbulb looks white, but in fact it's made up of all the colors of the rainbow. Color depends on the wavelength and frequency of the light: red colors have the longest wavelengths and lowest frequencies; blues have the shortest wavelengths and highest frequencies. (See **Thing to Know** No. 25 for more on light and the electromagnetic spectrum.)

Particles of dust and droplets of water in clouds are bigger than the wavelength of visible light. When light hits the particles in a cloud, all of the different wavelengths in the light are reflected, so the cloud appears white. But the molecules of gas in the air are smaller than the wavelength of visible light. On a clear day, when there aren't any clouds, the light bumps into the gas molecules and reacts differently: some of it is absorbed and then released in a different direction. The shorter wavelengths—the blue color—are more likely to be absorbed and released in this way than the other colors of light. That's why the sky appears blue on a clear day: because the molecules in the atmosphere are scattering blue light toward you.

Why is the sunset red? Sunlight has to travel farther through the atmosphere when the Sun is setting, so most of the light is reflected and scattered before it reaches us—except for red, because it has the longest wavelength of the spectrum of visible light.

Why Is the Sky Blue? **Form**

Once you have mastered this **Thing to Know,** stick your Achieved Star here and fill in the form

Achieved

BLUE SKIES

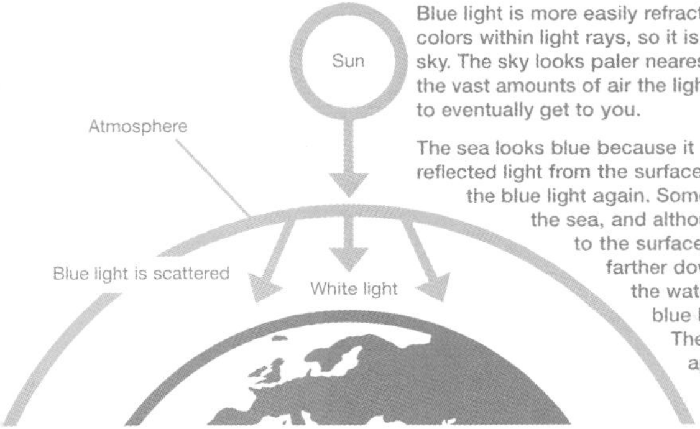
Sun
Atmosphere
Blue light is scattered
White light

Blue light is more easily refracted than the other colors within light rays, so it is scattered across the sky. The sky looks paler nearest to the horizon due to the vast amounts of air the light has to pass through to eventually get to you.

The sea looks blue because it reflects the sky, and reflected light from the surface of the sea scatters the blue light again. Some light also penetrates the sea, and although the water nearest to the surface appears blue, the farther down you go, the darker the water becomes, as the blue light cannot penetrate. The water eventually appears black, as no light can penetrate.

SUNRISE & SUNSET

The Sun and sky appear orange and red because these colors have long wavelengths and travel farther. Blue has a short wavelength and can't reach as far.

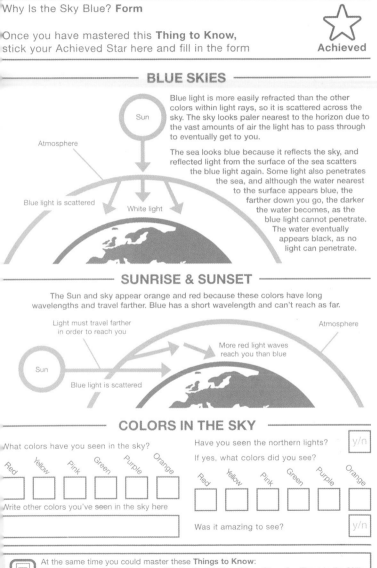

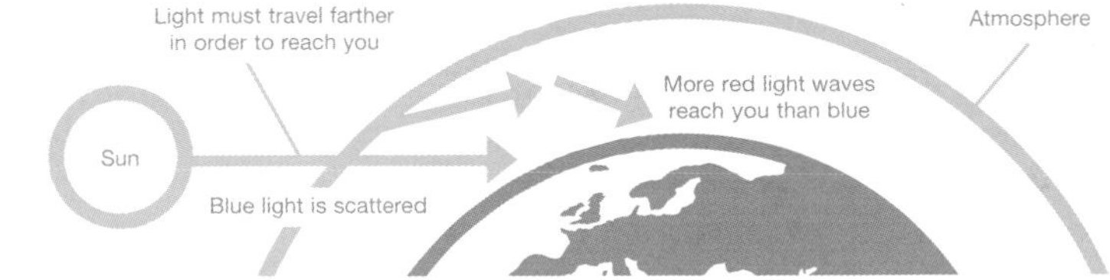
Light must travel farther in order to reach you
Atmosphere
More red light waves reach you than blue
Sun
Blue light is scattered

COLORS IN THE SKY

What colors have you seen in the sky?

Red ☐ Yellow ☐ Pink ☐ Green ☐ Purple ☐ Orange ☐

Write other colors you've seen in the sky here

Have you seen the northern lights? y/n

If yes, what colors did you see?

Red ☐ Yellow ☐ Pink ☐ Green ☐ Purple ☐ Orange ☐

Was it amazing to see? y/n

At the same time you could master these **Things to Know**:
25: If Light Is Invisible, How Can We See? • 36: How Many Stars Are There in the Milky Way? • 43: How Do Clouds Stay Up? • 83: Where Is the Night Sky Multicolored?

How Many Stars Are There in the Milky Way?

Have you ever looked up into the night sky and tried to count all the stars? Did you get an aching neck? You probably ran out of numbers or patience.

Starry-Eyed

A galaxy is a huge group of stars, all held together by gravity. Some galaxies are elliptical (like a stretched circle), some are just irregular blobs, and some—like ours (the Milky Way)—are shaped like spirals. If you have perfec eyesight, it's still likely you'll be able to see only about 2,500 stars in the sky from one place at one time. If you could see all the stars it's possible to see from Earth without a telescope, the number would increase to 8,000. Of course, this is only a tiny fraction of all the stars in the galaxy.

The Milky Way is about 100,000 light-years from one side to the other, and about 10,000 light-years deep. That's big enough to contain a *lot* of stars: the most recent estimates are about 400 billion! We haven't been able to photograph the entire galaxy because we haven't been able to send a spacecraft outside of it to take one. But on a clear night away from artificial light you might be able to see it as a band of white light—like a path in the sky.

Remember, our galaxy is just one of many in the universe (no one knows how many). In our "Local Group" alone there are about 40 galaxies. Two are large spiral ones—the Milky Way and Andromeda. The rest are much smaller.

Why "Milky Way"? No, it's not named after the chocolate bar. It's a translation of the Latin Via Lactea, which in turn is derived from the Greek word for milk. Guess what that is. *Galaktikos*! Now you know where the word *galaxy* came from too!

How Many Stars Are There in the Milky Way? **Form**

Once you have mastered this **Thing to Know,** stick your Achieved Star here and fill in the form

Achieved

CONSTELLATIONS

Can you spot the following constellations in the night sky among the millions of other stars? If you're having trouble finding them, go to www.heavens-above.com for help.

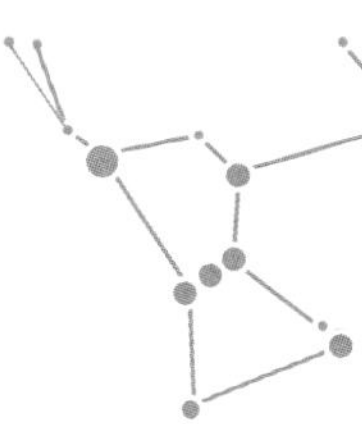

Orion ☐

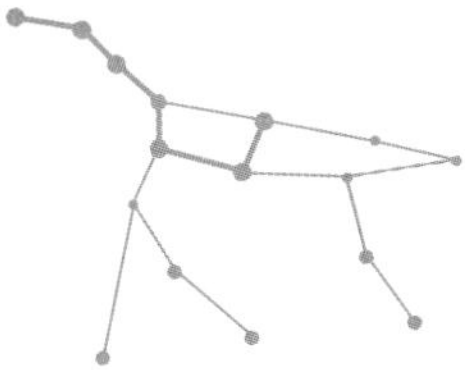

Ursa Major ☐

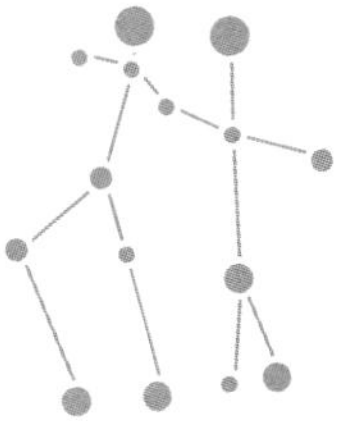

Gemini ☐

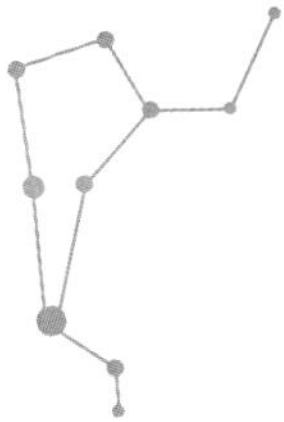

Boötes ☐

Scorpius ☐

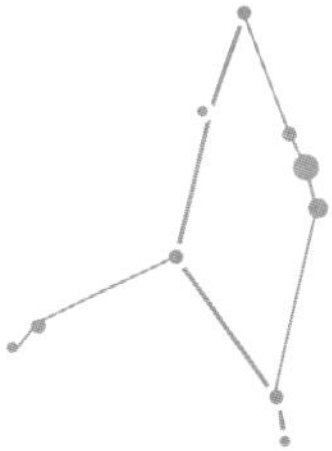

Aquila ☐

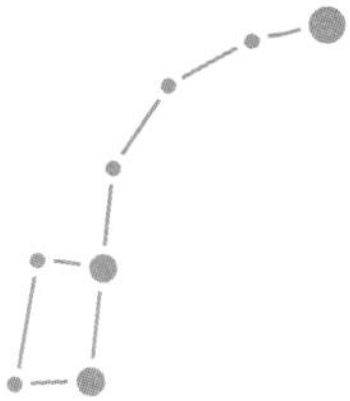

Ursa Minor ☐

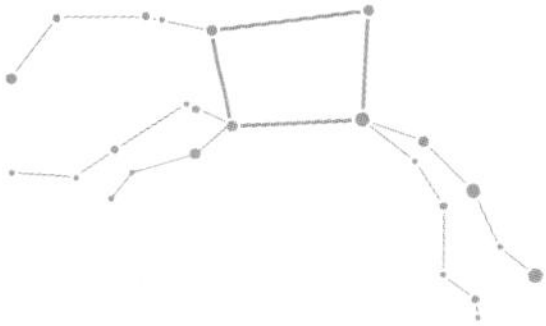

Pegasus ☐

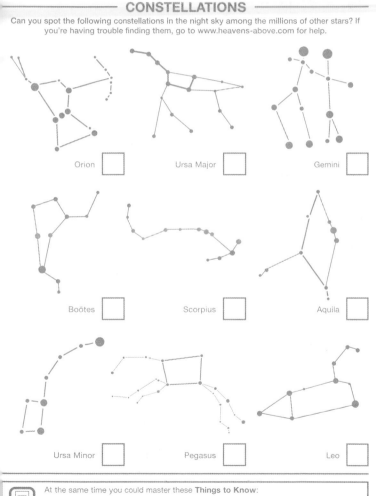

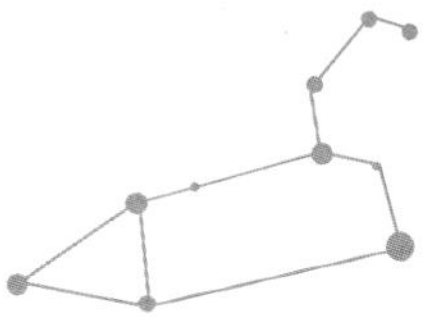

Leo ☐

At the same time you could master these **Things to Know**:
1: What Was the Biggest Bang Ever? • 12: How Big Is the Universe?
66: Why Do Stars Twinkle? • 101: What Would Happen to You in a Black Hole?

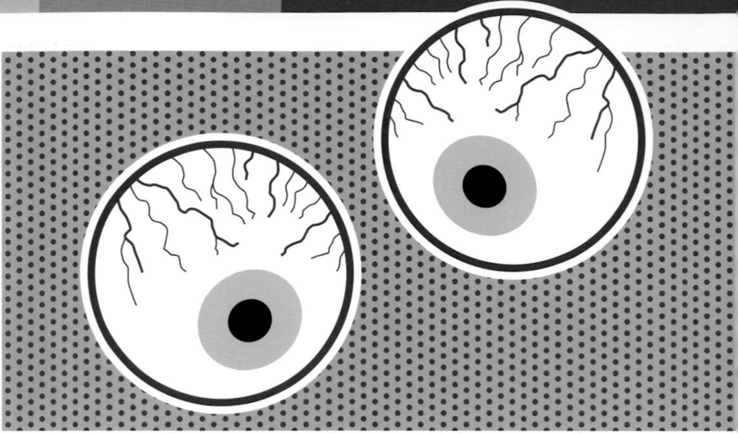

Can You Sneeze with Your Eyes Open?

Ever heard the rumor that if you sneeze with your eyes open, your eyeballs will pop out? Can this really be true? Read on for the eye-opening truth.

Nothing to Sneeze At

Sneezing is your body's way of getting rid of an irritation in your nose. Your nose is a sensitive organ, so all kinds of things might irritate it: allergies (e.g., to pollen or animals), pepper, dust, even bright light makes some people sneeze.

Although it seems simple, sneezing is a pretty complicated process—there's even a special part of your brain that's devoted to making a sneeze. Your diaphragm (the muscle you use to breathe) and muscles in your abdomen, chest, and throat all have to work together, and the muscles that control your eyelids play a part too, making you shut your eyes when you sneeze. Why you should have a reflex to shut your eyes while sneezing is a mystery, but it's definitely not because your eyes would fall out if you didn't. Some people don't have the reflex to close their eyes when they sneeze, and you'll be pleased to know that they keep their eyeballs in place anyway.

When you sneeze, millions of tiny snot particles are propelled out of your nose at about 40 mph. And just one sneeze can contain millions of viruses. So always use a tissue.

Bless you, times a million: in 1981, Donna Griffiths, a 12-year-old schoolgirl from Worcestershire, England, started sneezing. She stopped a world-record-breaking 978 days later. It's estimated she sneezed more than a million times in the first year alone.

Can You Sneeze with Your Eyes Open? **Form**

Once you have mastered this **Thing to Know,** stick your Achieved Star here and fill in the form

Achieved

SNEEZING REMEDIES

How many times do you usually sneeze in a row?

1 | 2 | 3 | 4 | more than 4

How do you usually stop yourself from sneezing?

TRY THESE REMEDIES

REMEDY 1: Apply pressure between your top lip and your nose.

Did this remedy work? y/n

If no, how many times did you sneeze? ___ times

Do you think this remedy is just an old wives' tale? y/n

REMEDY 2: Try to hold your breath for as long as possible.

Did this remedy work? y/n

If no, how many times did you sneeze? ___ times

Do you think this remedy is just an old wives' tale? y/n

REMEDY 3: Think of anything distracting, like your pet or a math problem.

Did this remedy work? y/n

If no, how many times did you sneeze? ___ times

Do you think this remedy is just an old wives' tale? y/n

REMEDY 4: Press the top of your mouth with your tongue.

Did this remedy work? y/n

If no, how many times did you sneeze? ___ times

Do you think this remedy is just an old wives' tale? y/n

REMEDY 5: Without moving your head, look up with your eyes.

Did this remedy work? y/n

If no, how many times did you sneeze? ___ times

Do you think this remedy is just an old wives' tale? y/n

REMEDY 6: If you dare, hold your eyes open.

Did this remedy work? y/n

If no, how many times did you sneeze? ___ times

Do you think this remedy is just an old wives' tale? y/n

IF YOU WANT TO SNEEZE

Sometimes you feel like you're about to sneeze, but then you don't. Next time, try looking at something bright to make the sneeze come. It doesn't work with everyone.

Did this tip work for you? y/n

If yes, how many times did you sneeze? ___ times

At the same time you could master these **Things to Know**:
64: Do Animals Cry? • 65: Why Do We Get Hiccups?
97: What Is the World's Deadliest Disease?

Why Is the Ocean Salty?

If you've ever been at the ocean and tried to impress your friends with an underwater handstand then accidentally swallowed a mouthful of seawater, you probably noticed that it's pretty salty. But have you ever wondered why?

A Pinch of Salt

River water contains salt too, but not nearly as much as seawater, and usually not enough for us to notice it. It comes from minerals in the soil and rocks that the water passes through before it gets into the rivers. The salt that the rivers and streams carry with them every year into the ocean is only a tiny proportion of all the salt in the sea, but it gets left behind when water evaporates and falls as rain. Over hundreds of millions of years, the salt content has built up to make the oceans as salty as they are today. The sea is about 3.5% salt, most of it sodium chloride—the kind you might put on your fries.

The sea gets salt from other places too: hydrothermal vents are places in the seabed where water has seeped into the Earth's crust, heated up, dissolved minerals from the crust, and flowed back into the sea. More salt is added when underwater volcanoes erupt.

You might expect the ocean to be getting saltier, but it isn't. As new salt is added, dissolved salts form new minerals on the ocean floor. In fact, the ocean has had the same salt content for millions of years.

Fiery water: the superhot water spewing out of hydrothermal vents looks like black smoke, and the minerals it contains build the rims of the vents into tall towers. They're nicknamed "black smokers." The temperature of the water can reach 750°F.

Why Is the Ocean Salty? **Form**

Once you have mastered this **Thing to Know,**
stick your Achieved Star here and fill in the form

Achieved

THE DEAD SEA

The Dead Sea is the saltiest body of water on Earth. It's ten times saltier than the oceans and it isn't even a real sea! The Dead Sea is actually a lake in Israel. It's called the Dead Sea because nothing can live in it. The reason the lake is so salty is because all the rivers in the area run into it, but there isn't a river that runs out to the sea. The only way for the water to escape is through evaporation, and as it is in a hot part of the world the water evaporates quickly, leaving the salty minerals behind. And the lake will become saltier still, because it's getting smaller. The salt in the water is so abundant that people can't even swim in the water. We float on top of it!

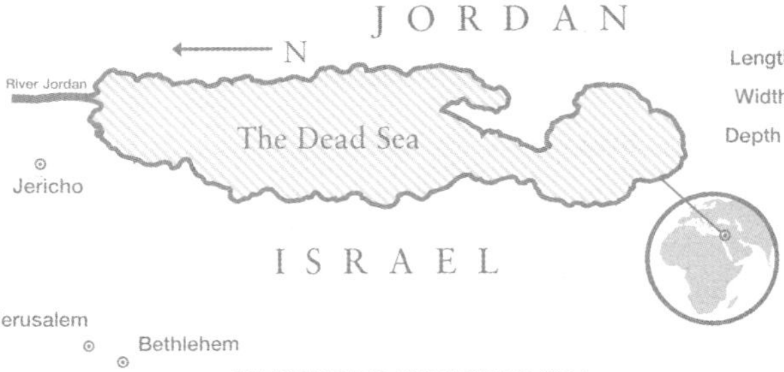

Length 48 mi

Width 11 mi

Depth 1,373 ft

MAKE YOUR OWN DEAD SEA

The Ocean:
3.5% salinity

1. Fill a large container with 1 qt of water, then put an egg in it. Does it float?
2. Take the egg out of the water and add 1.2 oz of salt, mixing well. This is the salinity of seawater. Now try the egg. What happened?
3. Now add another 11 oz of salt to the water and mix again. This is the salinity of the Dead Sea. Try the egg one more time. What happened?

The Dead Sea:
35% salinity

MAKE SALT CRYSTALS

Salt crystals are beautiful and fun to watch forming. All you need to make your own is

a glass • water • salt • food coloring
cotton thread • a paper clip • a pencil

Take the glass and fill it with hot water (the hotter the better).

Take the salt and stir it in. Keep stirring until you see that no more salt is dissolving.

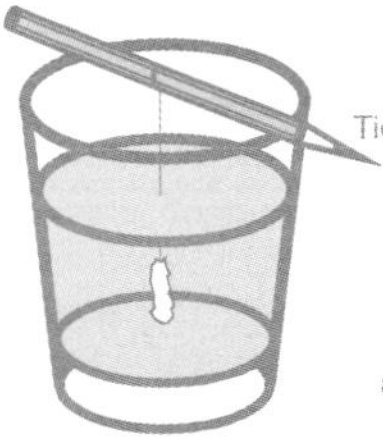

If you want your crystals to be more interesting, add a few drops of food coloring.

Tie one end of the thread to the paper clip and the other to the pencil. Dangle the paper clip into the mixture. Make sure the paper clip isn't touching the bottom.

Finally, wait until crystals start to appear all over the paper clip. This may take a couple of days.

At the same time you could master these **Things to Know**:
3: Why Don't Fish Drown? • 30: What Is at the Bottom of the Ocean?
33: How Do You Survive Falling over a Waterfall?

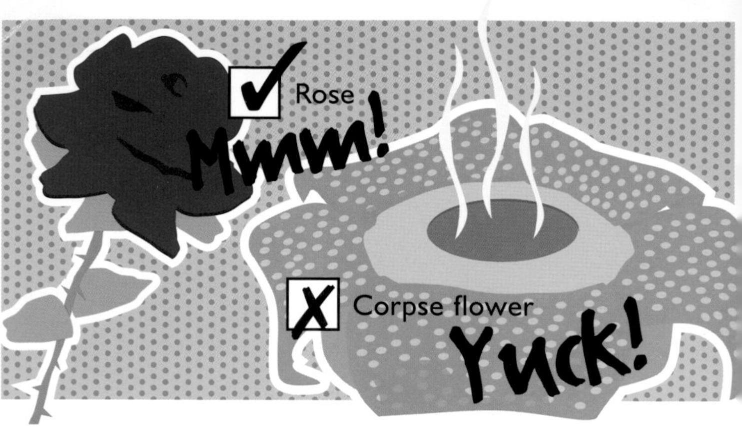

What Is the Worst Smell Ever?

It's a matter of taste, really. Perhaps you're grossed out by babies' diapers, dogs' breath, rotting vegetables, or fresh fish. Most people are, but what is it about these things that make them so bad, and some worse than others?

The Worst Whiff

Our sense of smell is basically an early-warning system. It's not as sensitive as most animals', but then we face fewer threats. At least we can smell smoke from a fire or leaking gas. And we know when food has passed its sell-by date and gone bad, because it smells awful—as would a dead animal, rotting in a tropical heat. The one thing many of the worst stenches have in common is that they contain sulfur compounds. Consider these natural stink bombs . . .

- **Skunk:** this furry little creature can spray its ferocious fumes out of its backside with incredible accuracy, up to a distance of 10 ft, and the human nose can detect it up to a mile away downwind!
- **Titam aram, or corpse flower:** it grows in the jungles of Sumatra and is the world's biggest flower . . . and the foulest smelling. Using sulfur-based chemicals, it creates its revolting reek in order to attract beetles and flies, which pollinate the plant.
- **Durian fruit:** this fruit, which comes from Southeast Asia, is famous for its terrible raw sewage smell. It's so bad that durians have been banned on public transport in Singapore.

Scientists are probably responsible for concocting the worst smells ever: stink bombs for use in warfare and smells used to test cleaning products. One technique is simply to mix two awful smells, especially ones that have associations of danger.

What Is the Worst Smell Ever? **Form**

Once you have mastered this **Thing to Know,**
stick your Achieved Star here and fill in the form

Achieved

YOU SMELL!

What do you consider to be your favorite smells and what are the smells you can't stand? Make a record of them below.

Coffee	out of 10	Bacon cooking	out of 10	Roses	out of 10	Bread baking	out of 10
Fireworks	out of 10	Rain	out of 10	Fresh-cut grass	out of 10	A wet dog	out of 10
Dad's aftershave	out of 10	Your school	out of 10	Your underarms	out of 10	Matches	out of 10
Blue cheese	out of 10	Your bedroom	out of 10	Hospitals	out of 10	Swimming pools	out of 10
The dentist's office	out of 10	Babies	out of 10	A bonfire	out of 10	Mom's perfume	out of 10
Dog poop	out of 10	Soil	out of 10	Tuna from a can	out of 10	Your family car	out of 10
The trash can	out of 10	Cigarette smoke	out of 10	Your sneakers	out of 10	Gas stations	out of 10

Do you think you have a sensitive nose? y/n

Rate how good you think you smell

Not good at all—yuck! | Not too bad | Okay | Pretty sweet | Heavenly

What do you do to smell good?

Is it enough? y/n

Who is the best-smelling person you know?

Describe their smell

Who is the worst-smelling person you know?

Rate how badly you think they smell

A bit stinky | I have to hold my nose | Worse than the dog | The trash can smells better | Not as bad as me!

At the same time you could master these **Things to Know**:
48: What Makes Farts So Smelly?
84: What Is the Sixth Sense?

How Did the Ancient Egyptians Make the Pyramids?

In ancient Egypt they didn't have bulldozers, cranes, forklifts, etc.—and yet the pyramids are huge! Clearly, a lot of people went to a lot of trouble to build them

People Power

The ancient Egyptians were fond of pyramids—there are 67 of them. The Grea Pyramid, the tomb of Khufu, is about 440 ft high and made up of 2,300,000 blocks of stone, each about 2.75 tons in weight. We don't know for certain how these huge tombs were built. One theory goes that aliens built them using advanced technology from another world. A more likely theory follows:

- Architects chose the pyramid shape because it's so stable.
- The Egyptian ruler, the pharaoh, employed a huge number of workers (maybe as many as 100,000), probably just for the part of the year when th River Nile flooded and there wasn't much farming to be done. Some expert think the workers were all slaves, but others think they were probably ordinary farmers who were expected to do public works when they weren working the land.
- Limestone blocks were quarried nearby using stone and copper tools, then moved to the building site on rafts across the Nile and then on sleds.
- It's likely the workers then used ramps, which were built up as the pyramic grew, made from earth and used for hauling up the stone blocks. The ramp were removed from the top down as the pyramids were finished.
- Levers were used for getting each stone into its final position.

Topped: the Great Pyramid in Giza was the tallest building in the world for more than 4,000 years. Its height was unsurpassed until the completion of some of Europe's great medieval cathedrals in the 1300s.

How Did the Ancient Egyptians
Make the Pyramids? **Form**
Once you have mastered this **Thing to Know**,
stick your Achieved Star here and fill in the form

Achieved

HIEROGLYPHICS

Figure out what your name would look like in hieroglyphics.
Some letters like E and I, F and V, and U and W have the same symbol.

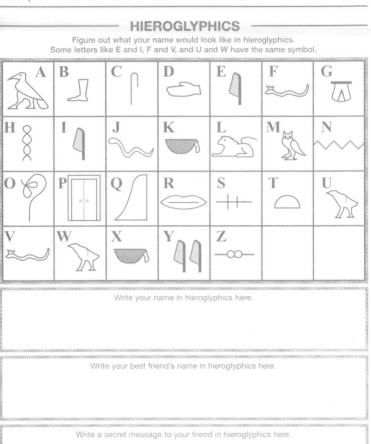

Write your name in hieroglyphics here.

Write your best friend's name in hieroglyphics here.

Write a secret message to your friend in hieroglyphics here.

At the same time you could master these **Things to Know**:
4: What Were the Seven Wonders of the World? • 74: How Dangerous Is Quicksand? • 93: Did People Make Everything from Stone in the Stone Age?

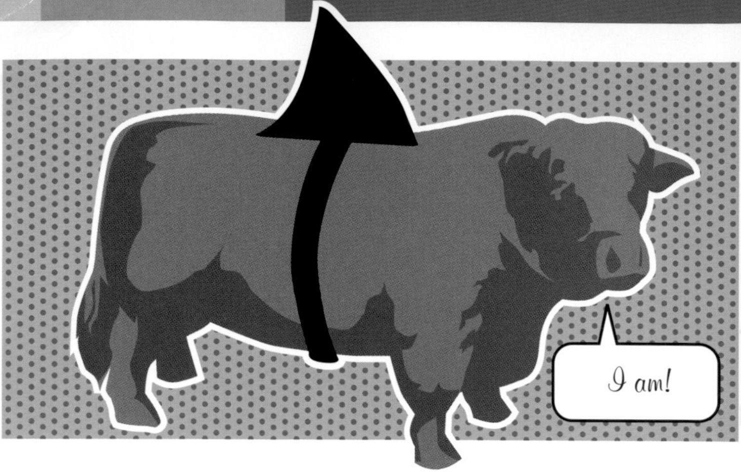

What Is the World's Most Dangerous Shark?

Yes, yes, most sharks aren't dangerous and many are endangered species that need our protection. But they DO have big teeth and they're REALLY scary. We need to know which ones to avoid.

Armed to the Teeth

There are about 350 different kinds of shark, but the good news is that only about 30 of them have been known to attack humans, and only 3 kinds regularly attack humans. Phew! There's some debate over which type of shark is the most dangerous to people. The problem is that when you're being attacked by a shark, it can be pretty difficult to tell what kind it is (with all that thrashing around, blood, etc.). Here are three main contenders:

- **The great white:** these sharks are big—generally about 9–13 ft but great whites have been known to measure 23 ft in length. They usually attack people when they mistake them for seals.
- **The bull shark:** bull sharks aren't as big as great whites—generally less than 8 ft long—but they often attack prey as big as or bigger than themselves. And they tend to stay close to the shore—just where you might be swimming. Bull sharks can live in freshwater as well as saltwater.
- **The tiger shark:** these sharks have been known to grow up to almost 20 ft, but on average they're about 10 ft long. They eat almost anything: a suit of medieval armor, deer antlers, and a chicken coop are some of the stranger items that have been found inside tiger sharks' stomachs.

The stats: in a year there are likely to be about 100 reported shark attacks, with less than 10% being fatal. Statistically you're most likely to be a victim of a shark attack if you're surfing or windsurfing in the United States (where about 80% of shark attacks happen).

What Is the World's Most Dangerous Shark? **Form**

Once you have mastered this **Thing to Know**, stick your Achieved Star here and fill in the form

Achieved

SHARKS

Here are some of the most notorious sharks. The diver alongside shows the relative size of a human. Some types of shark are smaller than us, while others, like these, are whoppers!

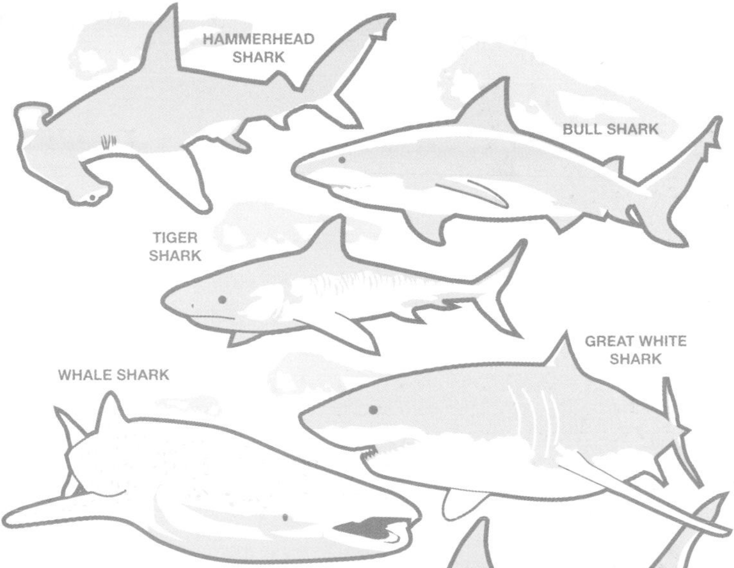

MEGALODON

Megalodon, a prehistoric shark, died out more than 1.6 million years ago. Its teeth were more than 8 in long, its jaws were 6 ft wide, and its favorite food was whales.

Megalodon comes from the ancient Greek words *megalos* and *don*, which translates as "big tooth."

HOW CLOSE HAVE YOU BEEN TO A SHARK?

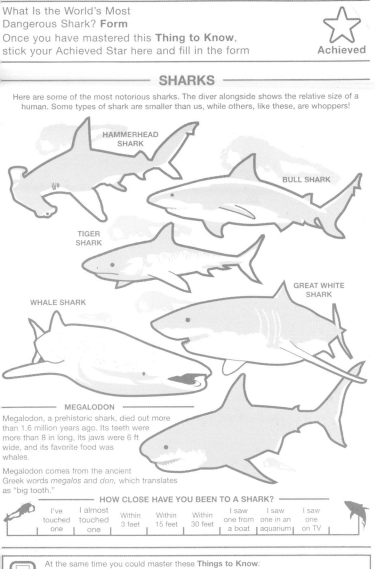

At the same time you could master these **Things to Know**:
3: Why Don't Fish Drown? • 30: What Is at the Bottom of the Ocean?
38: Why Is the Ocean Salty? • 56: What Is the Scariest Thing in the World?

How Big Is an Atom?

Or rather, how small is it? Atoms—the basic units of matter—make up everything in the world, including you. As you've probably guessed, they're pretty tiny.

The Mighty Atom

Different types of atoms vary in size a bit, but all measure roughly a tenth of a millionth of a millimeter across (0.0000001 mm)—that's about a million times smaller than the width of a human hair. (Although atoms don't vary much in size, they vary a lot in weight—a plutonium atom weighs 200 times as much as a hydrogen atom, but it's only three times the size.)

You might think that atoms must be the smallest things in existence, but they're made up of even smaller ("subatomic") particles:

- Inside an atom, electrons are whizzing around a nucleus, which is at the center of the atom.
- The nucleus is tiny—100,000 times smaller than the atom itself. If an atom were the size of an Olympic-sized stadium, the nucleus would be the size of a coin. And yet the nucleus is the densest part of the atom—most of an atom is empty space with electrons in it.
- Inside the nucleus are even tinier particles: protons and neutrons.
- Protons and neutrons are made up of minute particles called quarks.
- As far as we know, there's nothing smaller than a quark. But one day scientists might discover that quarks are made up of even smaller particles.

The word *atom* comes from the ancient Greek word meaning "uncuttable"—Democritus, an ancient Greek philosopher, came up with the word to describe the smallest particles of which everything else is made.

How Big Is an Atom? **Form**

Once you have mastered this **Thing to Know,** stick your Achieved Star here and fill in the form

Achieved

ALL THE SMALL THINGS

Test your knowledge of the world's smallest things with this quiz. Once you've done the quiz, memorize the correct facts, then impress your friends to earn your star.

1. **What is the smallest country in the world, at 0.2 square mi?**

(a) Monaco
(b) Liechtenstein
(c) San Marino
(d) Vatican City

2. **What is only 0.3 in long?**

(a) The world's smallest insect
(b) The world's smallest mammal
(c) The world's smallest fish
(d) The world's smallest bird

3. **Who or what was 54 in tall?**

(a) The world's smallest man
(b) The world's smallest elephant
(c) The world's smallest rhino
(d) The world's smallest whale

4. **The plant wolffia (or watermeal) is the world's smallest flowering plant. How small is it?**

(a) 0.02 in long and 0.01 in wide
(b) 0.06 in long and 0.05 in wide
(c) 0.10 in long and 0.09 in wide
(d) 0.14 in long and 0.13 in wide

5. **Mill Ends Park in Portland, Oregon, is the smallest park in the world. How small is it?**

(a) 3-in-wide circle
(b) 6-in-wide circle
(c) 12-in-wide circle
(d) 24-in-wide circle

6. **Thumbelina, a dwarf miniature horse, is the smallest horse in the world. How small is she?**

(a) 6 in tall
(b) 12 in tall
(c) 17 in tall
(d) 24 in tall

7. **The world's smallest book is a copy of the New Testament. It contains 180,568 words. How small is it?**

(a) 0.02 in x 0.02 in
(b) 0.04 in x 0.04 in
(c) 0.20 in x 0.20 in
(d) 0.40 in x 0.40 in

8. **The world's smallest dog is a Chihuahua called Heaven Sent Brandy. How small is she?**

(a) 3.6 in long
(b) 4.9 in long
(c) 6.0 in long
(d) 8.5 in long

9. **Where is the world's smallest house, measuring 74 x 122 x 100 in?**

(a) Japan
(b) Wales
(c) China
(d) Peru

10. **What do the lions in a safari park in Liverpool think small cars are?**

(a) Prey
(b) Other lions
(c) Bushes
(d) Tin cans

Answers at the back of the book.

At the same time you could master these **Things to Know**:
1: What Was the Biggest Bang Ever? • 12: How Big Is the Universe?
18: What Are the Biggest and Smallest Animals in the World?

How Do Clouds Stay Up?

If clouds are made up of water droplets and ice, which are heavier than air, how do they stay up? Even a feather will fall through the air!

Wandering Lonely . . .

If you added them up together, the droplets of ice and water in a cloud woul weigh many tons. Imagine a cloud 1,640 ft long, 1,640 ft high, and 1,640 ft wide: it'd weigh 275 tons—that's as much as 35 male African elephants. The droplets are absolutely tiny though—you'd need 2 billion of them to make a teaspoon of water—and they're so light that they fall incredibly slowly. Yes, clouds are falling, but their descent is countered by warm air currents rising from the ground, which continually push the cloud particles back up.

So what happens when the air cools—at night, for instance? Why don't the clouds fall from the sky? Well, you may have noticed how those large puffy clouds (cumulus clouds) often descend in the evening. Fortunately, as they get lower, the warm air near the ground starts to heat them up again and evaporate the water droplets. The clouds disappear well before they reach the ground!

Clouds don't always stay up, of course—that's why it rains. When the warm air rising from the ground cools down, it condenses and adds to the droplets of water already in the cloud. When the droplets in the cloud are too heavy for any rising warm air to keep them up, they fall to the ground as rain.

If you like clouds, look out for noctilucent clouds. These beautiful clouds seem to glow in the sky at high altitudes. They're believed to be formed of ice crystals but no one knows for sure—they're so high up that they're difficult to study.

How Do Clouds Stay Up? **Form**

Once you have mastered this **Thing to Know**, stick your Achieved Star here and fill in the form

Achieved

CLOUD FORMATIONS

Here are the different types of cloud formations that can be seen in the sky. Once you've seen a formation, check it on the list.

☐ Cirrus

Thin, wispy, detached, white, high cloud

☐ Cirrostratus

Thin, wispy, veillike, high cloud

☐ Cirrocumulus

Delicate, high cloud, appearing in a series of ripples that cover the sky

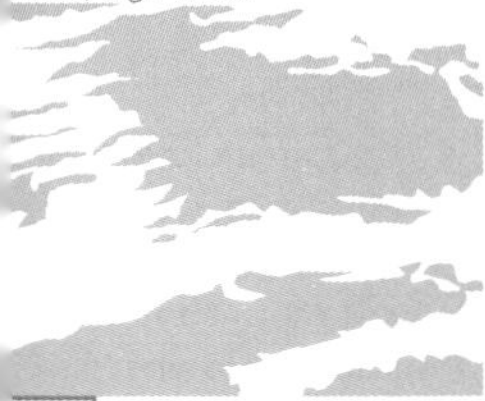

☐ Altostratus

Fairly thin, uniform layers of grayish, mid-height cloud

☐ Altocumulus

Puffy, medium-sized, white or gray, mid-height cloud

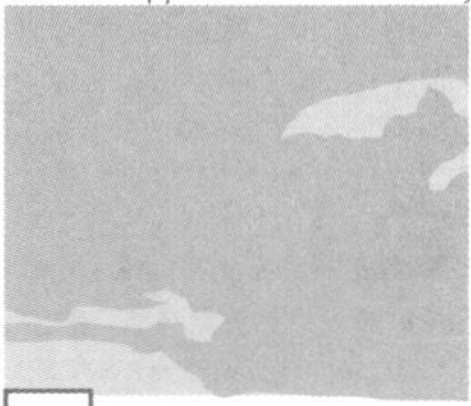

☐ Nimbostratus

Dark, puffy, low layers of rain-bearing cloud

☐ Cumulus

Low cloud with a flat base and puffy, rounded top

☐ Stratus

Thick and thin, low layers of gray cloud; overcast skies

☐ Cumulonimbus

Tall, dense, low. rain-bearing cloud

At the same time you could master these **Things to Know**:
30: What Is at the Bottom of the Ocean? • 35: Why Is the Sky Blue? • 38: Why Is the Ocean Salty? • 59: How Do Planes Get into the Air—and Stay There?

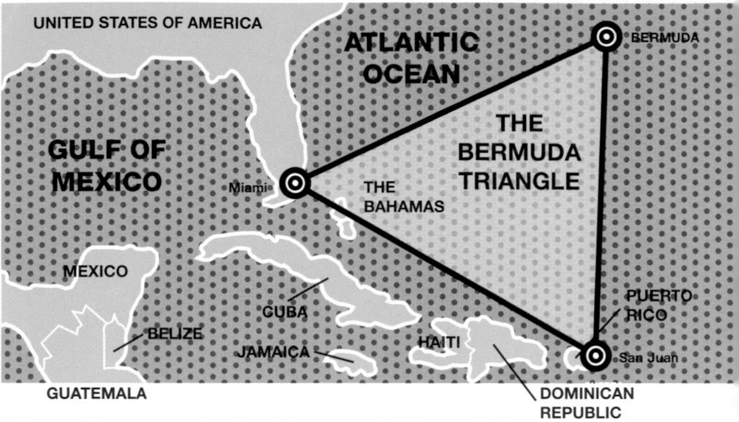

What Happens in the Bermuda Triangle?

The Bermuda Triangle isn't a type of percussion instrument but an area of the Atlantic Ocean between Bermuda, Miami, and Puerto Rico, where ships and planes seem to have a weird habit of disappearing.

The Tale of Flight 19

The area got its nickname in the 1960s, but reports of strange happenings predate that by centuries—even Columbus's ships are supposed to have had problems in the Bermuda Triangle. But the event that really gave the area its spooky reputation is the tale of Flight 19, a 1945 wartime training exercise involving five planes. The leader of the five aircraft became confused about directions, claiming that his compass wasn't working. All the planes began heading out to sea instead of back to land, and eventually they ran out of fue and crashed into the ocean. The planes were never found. It's a tragic tale, but there's probably no mystery about it—it's not surprising that wreckage is seldom found from crashes near the Bermuda Triangle, because the deepest part of the Atlantic is close by (and Flight 19 crashed in stormy weather).

People have become fascinated with the Bermuda Triangle and the various ships and planes that have gone missing there, but there's little evidence that the area is any more dangerous than other parts of the ocean. Local coast guards blame the unpredictable weather for any accidents, discounting theories that a race of submarine aliens periodically lures pilots to their doom

More sea mystery: an area in the Philippine Sea is Asia's Bermuda Triangle, known as the Devil's Sea or Dragon's Triangle. Legend has it that sea dragons in that part are prone to conjuring whirlpools, storms, and thick fog.

What Happens in the Bermuda Triangle? **Form**

Once you have mastered this **Thing to Know**, stick your Achieved Star here and fill in the form

Achieved

THE UNEXPLAINED

Here are some other unanswered or debatable questions. What's your opinion?

Does the abominable snowman really exist? y/n Why do you think that?

Does the Loch Ness monster really exist? y/n Why do you think that?

Have aliens visited Earth? y/n Why do you think that?

Is there such a thing as telepathy or a sixth sense? y/n Why do you think that?

Are crop circles the work of aliens? y/n Why do you think that?

Does God exist? y/n Why do you think that?

IT'S A MYSTERY

Unusual things happen all the time. The majority of the time they can be explained away, but occasionally the causes are more mysterious. If you've had a strange experience, record the incident here.

Have you ever had a paranormal experience? y/n

If yes, write your story below

Do you think there's a logical explanation? y/n

If yes, what could it be?

At the same time you could master these **Things to Know**:
17: Is Your Teacher an Alien? • 30: What Is at the Bottom of the Ocean? • 59: How Do Planes Get into the Air—and Stay There?

Why Do Some Animals Shed Their Skin?

Imagine you shed your skin like a lizard or a snake—it'd be like having a ghostly twin. Conversation might be kind of dull and shallow though.

Skin Deep

Different animals shed their skins in different ways:

- All animals shed their skin as they grow. Humans, like many other animals, shed skin cells every day, but they're so small we don't notice them.
- Lizards shed skin in chunks, and you can sometimes see lizards with pieces of skin hanging off—it might look horrible, but they're not in pain—they've already grown a new skin underneath the old one.
- When snakes have grown a new skin, their old one peels off in one shot. The creatures rub against something rough until the old skin splits, then the snake peels it off slowly, starting with its nose. You can sometimes find complete snake skins—like a papery mold of the snake.
- Insects and crustaceans (e.g., crabs) have the hard, armorlike part of their bodies on the outside—it's called an exoskeleton. When their bodies grow too big for the outer casing, they have to get rid of it and make a new one.
- Hermit crabs aren't true crabs and don't have their own hard shells: they find shells to live in that used to belong to other animals. When they grow too big for the shell they're in, they hunt around for a new one that's the right size and quickly slip into it naked (while no one's looking, of course).

Skinned alive! Household dust is mostly made up of dead human skin cells shed by you and your family. Microscopic creatures called dust mites like to chew on these discarded bits. Unfortunately, lots of people are allergic to the dust mites' droppings.

Why Do Some Animals
Shed Their Skin? **Form**

Once you have mastered this **Thing to Know**, stick your Achieved Star here and fill in the form

Achieved

KNOWLEDGE THAT'S ONLY SKIN DEEP

Which of the following statements are true and which are false?

QUIZ 1: SKIN FACTS

1. The largest organ your body has is your skin. T/F
2. Your skin regulates your body temperature. T/F
3. Skin makes up 5% of your body weight. T/F
4. There are roughly 3 million skin cells per square in of skin on your body. T/F
5. A square in of skin also has about 1,000 sweat glands. T/F
6. Skin has two layers, called the outer and inner layers. T/F
7. Skin grows faster than any other part of your body. T/F
8. If you covered your entire body with paint, you could suffocate and die. T/F
9. The top layer of your skin is all dead cells. T/F
10. You lose 40 dead skin cells every minute. T/F
11. You lose 9 lb of dead skin cells every year. T/F

Answers at the back of the book.

QUIZ 2: SPENDING TIME OUTSIDE

If you're going to spend a lot of time outdoors (e.g., when you're on vacation), should you . . .

1. . . . apply suncreen on a bright, sunny day? y/n
2. . . . apply sunscreen on a cloudy day? y/n
3. . . . apply sunscreen while sitting under a beach umbrella? y/n
4. . . . apply suncreen on the ski slopes? y/n
5. . . . apply sunscreen every day? y/n

The answer to all the QUIZ 2 questions is YES!

If you're going to spend a lot of time outdoors, you need to look after your skin.

1. Even though your skin provides some protection from the sun, it can still be damaged by ultraviolet (UV) rays, which cause various types of skin disease.

2. More than 80% of the Sun's rays can pass through clouds.

3. You should still apply sunscreen even if you're under an umbrella, as the Sun's rays reflect off the surface of the sand onto you.

4. Ski slopes are particularly bad for UV rays, as the bright-white snow reflects sunlight more than a sandy beach.

At the same time you could master these **Things to Know**:
23: How Does a Snake Swallow Things Bigger Than Its Own Head?
86: How Does a Chameleon Change Its Color?

Who Built Stonehenge, How and Why?

Ask most people who built Stonehenge and they'll mutter something about the Druids. But Stonehenge is *much* older than that.

Staggering Stones

Stonehenge was built in three stages:

1. The first Stonehenge was a circular earth bank about 360 ft across with a ditch around it, made by Stone Age people about 5,000 years ago.
2. Later, a wooden structure was made.
3. Stonehenge was completed about 3,600 years ago, during the Bronze Age (the site was abandoned 1,000 years before the Druids were around).

The stone monument we can see today is only a part of what was there originally—over the years, people have broken pieces off some of the stones and carted away others completely.

Two types of stone are used at Stonehenge: the smaller ones come from Wales and weigh about 4 tons each. They must have been brought to Salisbury Plain on rafts over sea and land—the most likely route measures about 235 mi. The bigger stones come from about 19 mi north of Stonehenge, but they weigh up to 55 tons each! It probably took years to transport them. The stones were bashed into shape using stone hammers, including the special joints that were made to hold the upright stones and the beams together.

Why all the effort? No one knows exactly—it's an ancient mystery. Could Stonehenge have been some kind of temple? The stones line up with the sunrise at midsummer and the sunset at midwinter, so perhaps people worshiped a sun god.

Who Built Stonehenge, How and Why? **Form**

Once you have mastered this **Thing to Know**, stick your Achieved Star here and fill in the form

Achieved

SUNDIAL

On midsummer's and midwinter's days the Sun lines up exactly with the northeast entrance of Stonehenge, making it a kind of giant sundial.

The illustration below is the base of a sundial. Make a slit down the page along the dotted line (a) or, if you don't want to ruin your book, photocopy this page first.

From a separate piece of paper, cut a triangle 2.8 in x 2.1 in, as shown in diagram (b). This will be your gnomon (the part that casts the shadow). Make sure you have a tab to turn under the base to keep the gnomon upright. Now point the sundial north and tell the time with the shadow made by the gnomon.

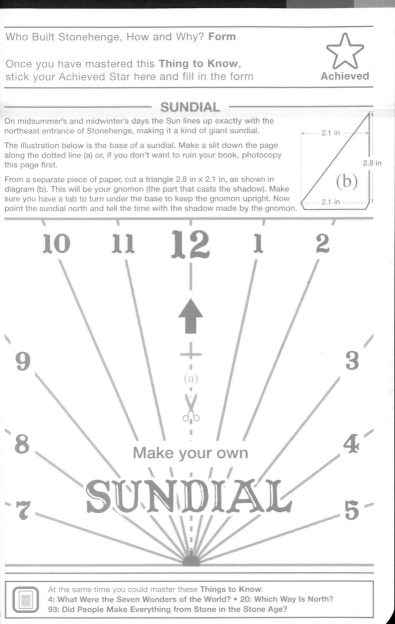

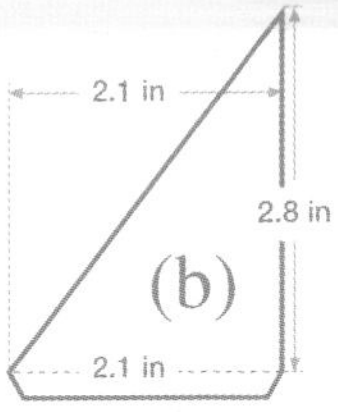

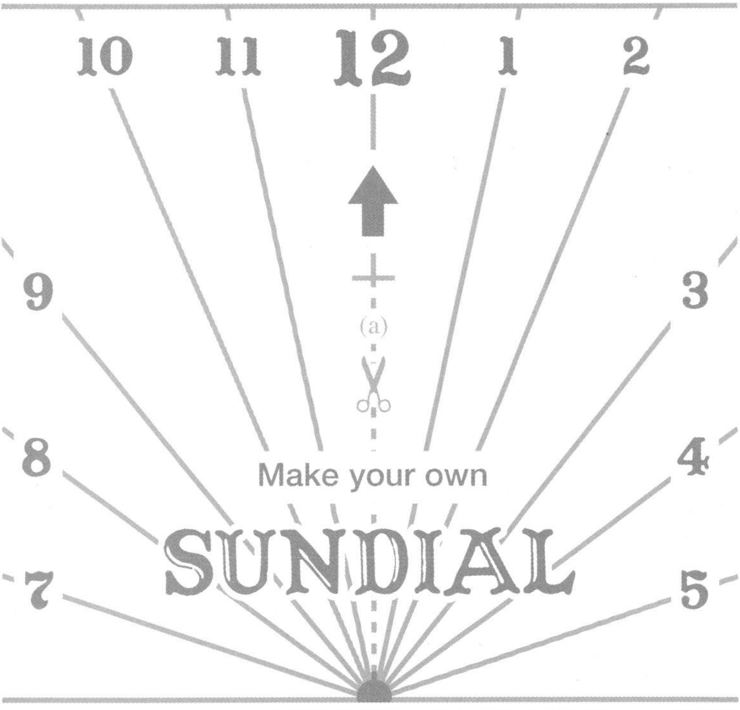

At the same time you could master these **Things to Know**:
4: What Were the Seven Wonders of the World? • 20: Which Way Is North?
93: Did People Make Everything from Stone in the Stone Age?

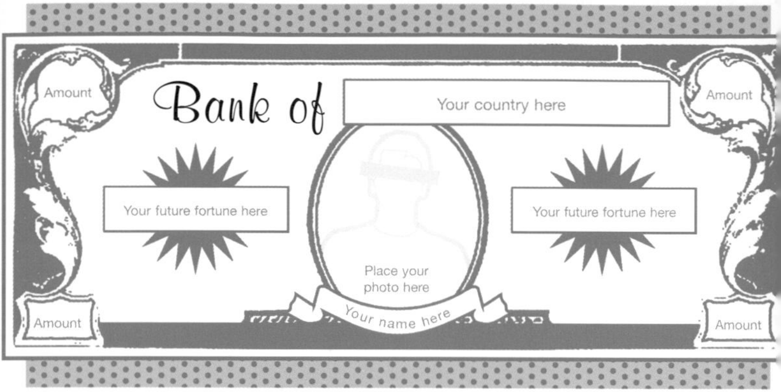

Who Is the Richest Person in the World?

What would you do with 56 billion dollars? According to *Forbes* business magazine, that's the fortune of the richest person in the world.

The Top Five Richest People

Name	Billions	Country
1. William Gates III	56	United States
2. Carlos Slim Helu	53.1	Mexico
3. Warren Buffet	52.4	United States
4. Ingvar Kamprad	28	Sweden
5. Lakshmi Mittal	27.7	India (UK based)

William Gates III, or Bill to his friends, started amassing cash early: when he was 17 he sold his first computer program (a timetable) to his own school for $4,200. But Bill earned most of his enormous wealth from the huge international company Microsoft, which he founded. Most people with that sort of cash would probably spend it on private jets, yachts, expensive cars, sports teams, multi-million-dollar houses all over the world—perhaps a small tropical island. But other than the money he spends on art (he bought a collection of notes by Leonardo da Vinci for over $30 million), Bill doesn't seem to delight in bling. His charitable organization is the second largest in the world and donates billions to aid world health and education—he's one of the few people who have that kind of money lying around.

Bill Gates is so rich that the IRS has a computer devoted solely to his finances. However, his fortune isn't what it used to be: at one time he was worth over $100 billion.

Who Is the Richest Person in the World? **Form**

Once you have mastered this **Thing to Know**, stick your Achieved Star here and fill in the form

Achieved

PREDICTED WEALTH CHART

Use the flowchart below to determine how rich you're going to be in the future. Answer the questions truthfully, as you'll only be lying to yourself if you cheat.

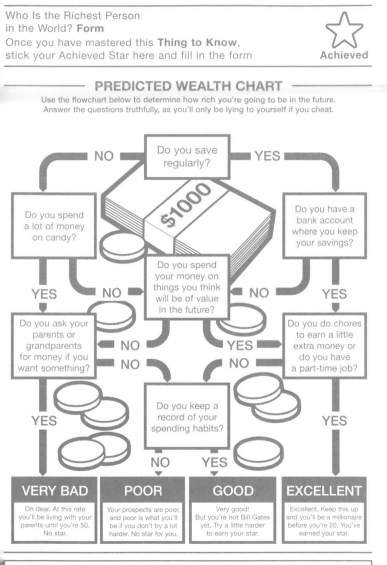

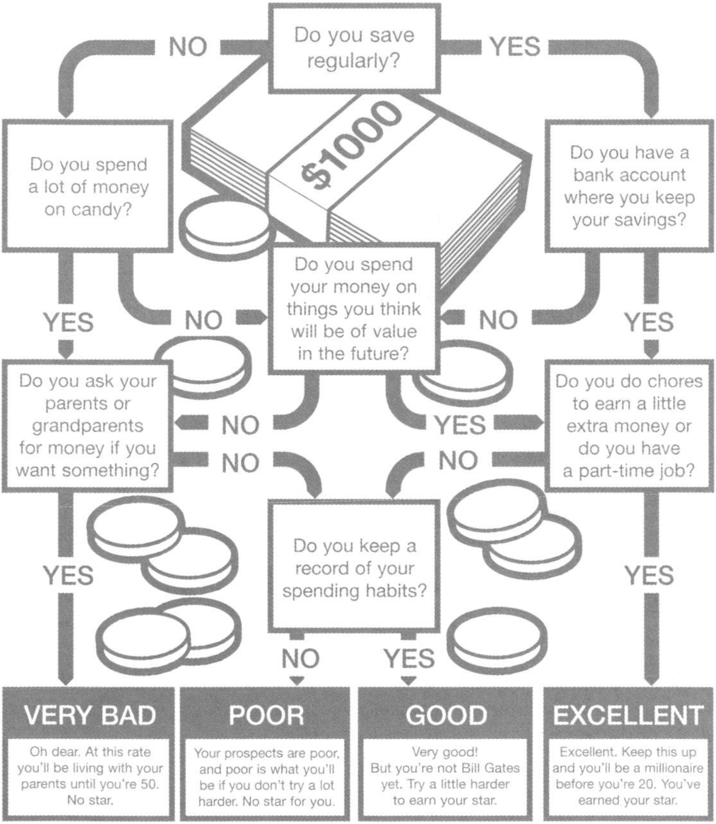
Do you save regularly?
NO
YES
$1000
Do you spend a lot of money on candy?
Do you have a bank account where you keep your savings?
Do you spend your money on things you think will be of value in the future?
YES
NO
NO
YES
Do you ask your parents or grandparents for money if you want something?
NO
YES
NO
NO
Do you do chores to earn a little extra money or do you have a part-time job?
Do you keep a record of your spending habits?
YES
YES
NO
YES
VERY BAD
Oh dear. At this rate you'll be living with your parents until you're 50. No star.
POOR
Your prospects are poor, and poor is what you'll be if you don't try a lot harder. No star for you.
GOOD
Very good! But you're not Bill Gates yet. Try a little harder to earn your star.
EXCELLENT
Excellent. Keep this up and you'll be a millionaire before you're 20. You've earned your star.

At the same time you could master these **Things to Know**:
24: When Did Money Start Making the World Go Around? • 68: Who Invented Paper?
69: How Can I Win Millions? • 78: Who Invented the Internet?

What Makes Farts So Smelly?

Everyone farts—kings, queens, movie stars, judges, presidents, and teachers. But farts vary from person to person and from fart to fart. The differences in the flatus (a fancy word for gas) are due to what people have eaten, how much air they've swallowed, and which bacteria they have living inside them.

It's a Gas!

Farts are made up of several different gases. Here's a breakdown:

- **Carbon dioxide.** Farts contain more of this than any other gas. It's completely odorless—the gas you breathe out is also carbon dioxide.
- **Hydrogen.** Together with carbon dioxide, this forms the majority of your fart. It's odorless on its own but reacts with sulfur to make hydrogen sulfide, which smells like rotten eggs! The more food you eat containing sulfur, the more hydrogen sulfide (and other sulfide-containing gases) you're likely to produce in your farts. It's hard to believe, but the smelly components of a fart are actually less than 0.01% of the whole fart!
- **Methane.** Produced by bacteria, this is highly flammable. Not everyone has methane in their farts—it's thought only about a third of us produce it.
- **Nitrogen.** In fart gas, nitrogen comes from the air we swallow. The gas doesn't smell on its own, but it reacts with other chemicals to make indole and skatole—two especially stinky compounds.
- **Oxygen.** This gas also comes from swallowed air, but most gets absorbed by the body, so there's likely to be less oxygen in farts than any other gas.

Want to cover up your farts? You can buy a fart filter that fits inside your undies. The filter contains charcoal, which works as a kind of fart deodorant. Of course, you could always blame the dog, but beware the old saying, "He who smelt it, dealt it."

What Makes Farts So Smelly? **Form**

Once you have mastered this **Thing to Know,**
stick your Achieved Star here and fill in the form

Achieved

THE FART HALL OF SHAME

Below is your very own fart hall of shame. Read the questions below and write the fart culprit's name on each jar—you may find it's always the same person.

Who farts the most?	Whose farts smell the worst?	Who farts the loudest?	Who farts the longest?

Who says they don't fart but you know they do?	Who seems to be most embarrassed when they fart?	Who farts at totally inappropriate times?	Who seems to enjoy farting the most?

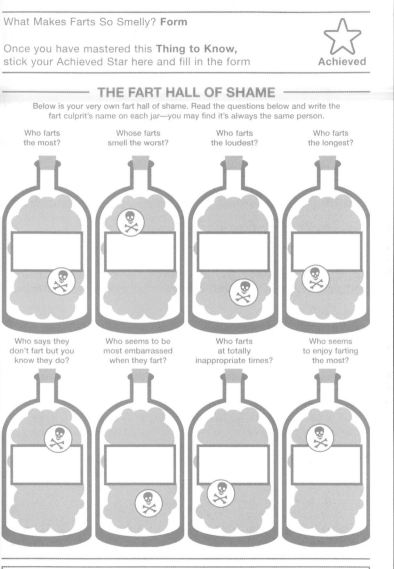

At the same time you could master these **Things to Know**:
39: What Is the Worst Smell Ever? • 73: Pus—What Is It Good For?
84: What Is the Sixth Sense?

Does One Dog Year Equal Seven Human Years?

People like to be as in tune with their pets as possible, so someone came up with this idea as a way of translating a dog's age into human terms. But it doesn't actually work very well: if Rover is one, that would make him seven human years old—but really Rover is almost fully grown.

Paws for Thought

It's better to use a slightly more complicated rule when you're thinking about the age of your dog, using a formula that ties in with the landmarks of doggy life, such as the "15, 10, 5" formula:

- Dogs have done most of their growing up by the age of one. So we could say that a one-year-old dog is the same as a 15-year-old human.
- By the age of two a dog is fully grown—an adult in the prime of life—so we add another ten years and make Rover 25 in human years.
- Then add another five years for each year of Rover's life after that. That means if your dog is five years old, he's 40 in human years.

This works because the average life span of a dog is about 12 years. Check out www.dogbreedinfo.com to find out about different breeds of dogs, as the average life span will vary between breeds.

Animal Life Spans

Animal	Life span
Giant tortoise	193 years
Parrot	80 years
Elephant	70 years
Crocodile	45 years
Horse	25 years
Sheep	15 years
Rabbit	9 years
Hamster	3 years
Worker ant	6 months
Mayfly	24 hours

The oldest pet on record is a goldfish called Tish, from Yorkshire, England, which was 43 years old when it died in 1999. The longest living dog that we know about was an Australian cattle dog named Bluey, which lived to be 29.

Does One Dog Year Equal
Seven Human Years? **Form**

Once you have mastered this **Thing to Know**,
stick your Achieved Star here and fill in the form

Achieved

IT'S A DOG'S LIFE

The charts below will help you figure out how old your dog really is compared to you. The charts compare human years to dog and cat years (i.e., a big dog at five would be 40 human years old). If you don't know the exact date your pet was born, take an educated guess or ask a vet to take one for you!

BIG DOG YEARS

1	2	3	4	5	6	7	8	9	10	11
12	19	26	33	40	47	54	61	68	75	82

When was your dog born? y y y y

Your age now 0 0 years old

Your dog's age now 0 0 . 0 years old

SMALL DOG YEARS

1	2	3	4	5	6	7	8	9	10	11
15	24	28	32	36	40	44	48	52	56	60

When was your dog born? y y y y

Your age now 0 0 years old

Your dog's age now 0 0 . 0 years old

CAT YEARS

1	2	3	4	5	6	7	8	9	10	11	12	13	14	15	16	17	18	19	20
16	24	28	32	36	40	44	48	52	56	60	64	67	70	72	74	76	78	80	82

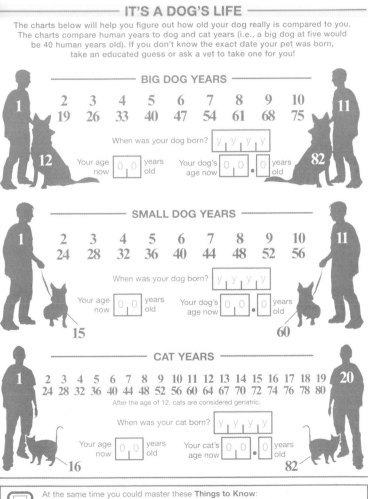

After the age of 12, cats are considered geriatric.

When was your cat born? y y y y

Your age now 0 0 years old

Your cat's age now 0 0 . 0 years old

At the same time you could master these **Things to Know**:
34: What Is the World's Favorite Pet? • 64: Do Animals Cry?
95: Are Cats and Dogs Color-Blind (and How Do We Know)?

I'm fed up with this weather, Neville. Next winter we're going to Fiji!

Where on Earth Is the Coldest Place?

If you think where you live can be chilly, you've probably never been to Antarctica.

Getting Cold Feet

The lowest temperature ever recorded on Earth was –129 degrees F at the Russian base Vostok in Antarctica—the South Pole. All but 2% of the continent is covered by layers of solid ice up to 3 mi thick. Here are some more things you should know about Antarctica:

- It has six months of daylight (September to February) followed by six months of darkness (March to August).
- 90% of the world's ice is found there.
- It holds the world records for the Earth's driest and windiest place (Antarctic winds get up to 199 mph), as well as the world's coldest.
- It does have an area without ice—the Dry Valleys, where it hasn't rained for 2 million years!

There's more debate about the hottest place on Earth. The highest temperature ever recorded was 136 degrees F at Al' Aziziyah, Libya, in 1922. But the place with the hottest average temperature is Dakol in the Danakil Depression, northeastern Ethiopia—with around 95 degrees F. The reason it's so hot is because it's very low down—328 ft below sea level in some places. This is the same reason for the extreme heat in Death Valley, California, which is another contender for the hottest place in the world.

Cold comfort: only a couple inches of rain fall in a year anywhere in the Antarctic, just slightly more than the Sahara, so technically it's a desert—despite the lack of sun and sand.

Where on Earth Is the Coldest Place? **Form**

Once you have mastered this **Thing to Know**, stick your Achieved Star here and fill in the form

Achieved

HOT & COLD FLASHES

The coldest temperature ever recorded on Earth was –129°F. But what are the coldest and the hottest temperatures you've experienced?

Coldest Place

Where were you? And why were you there?

How cold did you feel?

A little chilly | Pretty cold | Chilled to the bone | F-f-freezing! | So cold it hurt!

What did you do to warm up?

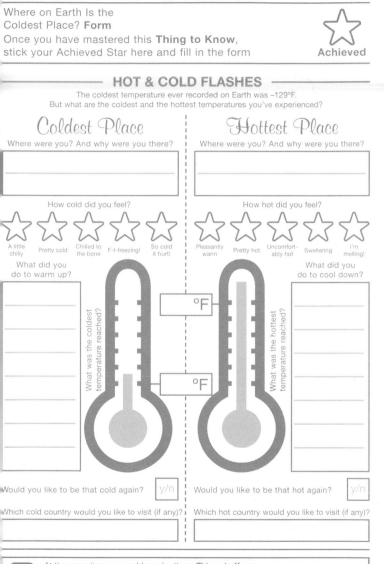

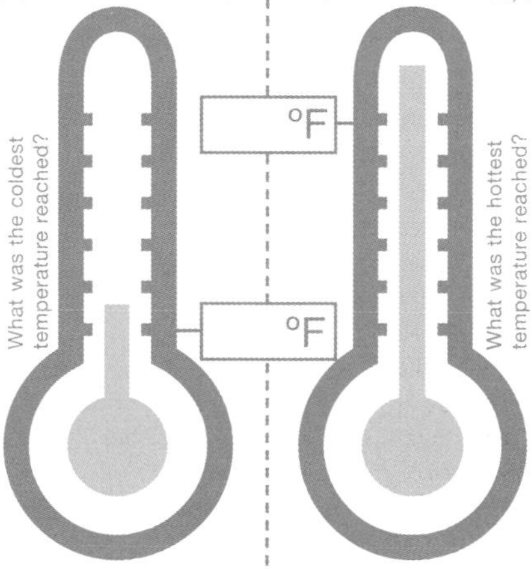

What was the coldest temperature reached?
°F
°F
What was the hottest temperature reached?

Would you like to be that cold again? y/n

Which cold country would you like to visit (if any)?

Hottest Place

Where were you? And why were you there?

How hot did you feel?

Pleasantly warm | Pretty hot | Uncomfortably hot | Sweltering | I'm melting!

What did you do to cool down?

Would you like to be that hot again? y/n

Which hot country would you like to visit (if any)?

At the same time you could master these **Things to Know**:
32: What Is an Ice Age (and When Are We Due for Another One)? • 51: How Do You Survive on a Desert Island? • 76: How Do You Survive an Avalanche?

How Do You Survive on a Desert Island?

If you somehow end up marooned, you'll need to know a few survival tips.

Water, Water Everywhere

You won't survive long without drinking water. Look for a spring or stream. Check that the water isn't polluted, and always filter it (through a cloth if you don't have anything better). If you can, boil it before you drink it, even if you think it's clean. Also:

- Make or use a container to collect rainwater.
- If there are sand dunes on your desert island, fresh water can often be found behind them. Dig down and try the water—fresh water should float to the top of any salty water that's seeped through from the ocean.
- Some plants, like the prickly pear, store water in their fleshy leaves. But make sure you know the plant isn't poisonous!

You'll need something to keep you warm and dry. Look for a dry rocky outcrop, or even a fallen tree—this could form the basis of your shelter.

- Use whatever is on hand to make your shelter—reeds, palm leaves, twigs. Tr weaving branches to make a more permanent shelter.
- To keep warm, line your shelter with dry ferns, leaves, pine needles, or grass. And wear a hat (or make something to cover your head)! 20% of your body's heat is lost from your head.

You'll probably want to be rescued. You could try lighting a bonfire to attract ship or plane—but make sure it doesn't get out of control. Of course, if you'r marooned on a desert island, it's essential to send a message in a bottle.

Daniel Defoe's novel *Robinson Crusoe* is based on a real-life desert islander named Alexander Selkirk, who was marooned alone on a remote island 400 mi off the coast of Chile for more than four years before being rescued.

How Do You Survive on a Desert Island? **Form**

Once you have mastered this **Thing to Know**, stick your Achieved Star here and fill in the form

Achieved

DESERT ISLAND LISTS

If you were stuck on a desert island for a year, what would be the things you'd like to have with you and why?

ITEM 1

Why would you want to have item 1?

ITEM 2

Why would you want to have item 2?

ITEM 3

Why would you want to have item 3?

ITEM 4

Why would you want to have item 4?

Some ideas for food:

- Try making a fishing rod or a spear.
- You can eat most types of seaweed. If you can, boil it for a few hours first, though.
- Insects, worms, and snails are a good source of protein. Mmmm, yummy!
- If you notice any bees on your island, honey is a great energy source (but you'll have to get past the bees first).

What food would you miss the most?

Do you think you'd struggle living on the island? y/n

How well do you think you would cope?

Very badly | Badly | Okay | Very well | Amazingly well

How would you attempt to escape the island?

At the same time you could master these **Things to Know**:
7: What Is the Difference Between a Fruit and a Vegetable? • 13: Did Cannibals Really Exist? • 41: What Is the World's Most Dangerous Shark?

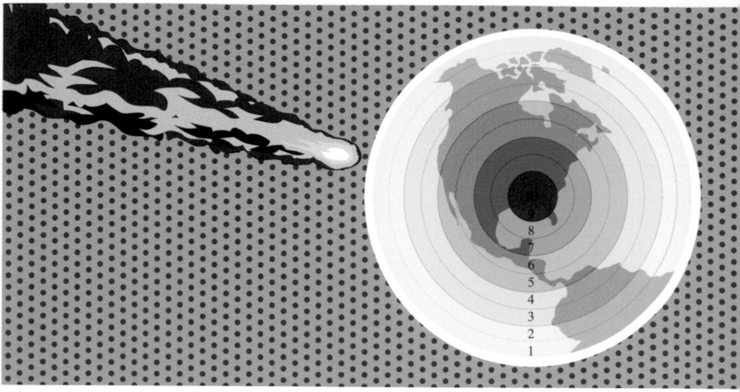

Could a Rock Destroy Our Planet?

Having a bad day? Well, it could be worse. A meteorite could come hurtling down and smash the TV. Or worse, wipe out everything. Feeling better?

Star Struck

- A meteorite is a lump of rock that's big and hard enough to get through the atmosphere and hit Earth. Most are fragments from the asteroid belt between Jupiter and Mars, and a few come from the Moon or Mars.
- Most meteorites are very small. No one's ever been known to be killed by a meteorite, though a few people have been injured (one woman was sitting on her sofa in Alabama when a meteorite smashed through the roof and hit her on the leg). There are exceptions, of course, like the huge meteorite that's thought to have killed off the dinosaurs about 65 million years ago. Its crater, in Central America, is about 112 mi across.
- About 120 impact craters from meteorites have been found on Earth, but most meteorites aren't big or heavy enough to make craters.

To cause serious damage, a meteorite would need to be about 1 mi across or bigger. The chances of one hitting Earth have been calculated at about one in a million years—so we're due for one soon. Apart from the unfortunate people and animals in the way, the main danger would be that the dust created would block out the Sun and stop plants from growing. But the effects wouldn't last; the world wouldn't end—it would take a really big meteorite for that to happen.

More flying rocks: meteorites are often confused with meteors, which are also known as shooting stars. These are bits of rock flying through space too—we see them as streaks of light in the night sky as they burn up in Earth's atmosphere.

Could a Rock Destroy
Our Planet? **Form**

Once you have mastered this **Thing to Know,**
stick your Achieved Star here and fill in the form

Achieved

IMPACT CRATERS

The map below highlights some of the impact craters that have been found on Earth caused by meteorites. Approximately five new craters are found every year. Unlike the Moon, many of Earth's craters have disappeared because Earth is slowly but constantly changing, due to climatic, tectonic, and volcanic activity. Highlighted are the five biggest impact crater sites that have been discovered in the world to date.

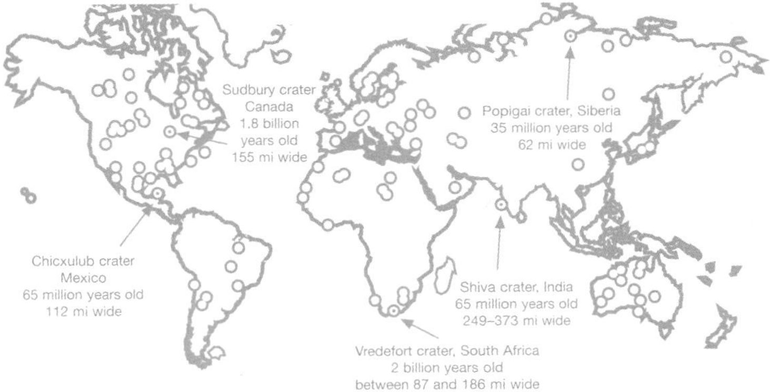

EARTH'S CRATERS

Have you ever seen a crater on Earth? y/n

If yes, where did you see it?

How old was it?

Were you impressed? y/n

MOON'S CRATERS

Do you like looking up at the Moon? y/n

How many Moon craters can you count with the naked eye?

0 0 0 0 0 0 0 0

How many Moon craters can you count with a telescope?

0 0 0 0 0 0 0 0

Name the Moon's most famous landmarks and craters. (Search the Internet for the answers.)

At the same time you could master these **Things to Know**:
6: What Is the Oldest Living Thing in the World? • 19: How Much Does the Earth Weigh? • 21: What Is the Solar System (and Could It Fit in Your Yard)?

Yawn! It's way past my bedtime.

Where Does the Sun Go at Night?

The answer to this question sounds obvious, but you may find that there's a little more to it than at first appears.

Night and Day

Very simply, during the day it's light because the Earth is facing the Sun (at least, the part of the Earth where you happen to be). At night it gets dark because the Earth (or the part of it you're on) is facing away from the Sun. The Earth is spinning on its axis, which runs from the North Pole to the South Pole through the center of the Earth, and it takes 24 hours for it to make one complete spin. For roughly half this time it'll be facing the Sun—this is the daytime—and for the other half (again, roughly) it'll be facing away from the Sun—this is the nighttime.

But some people aren't content with that explanation and insist on making things a lot more complicated. The stars in the sky are just like our sun. Of course, they're much farther away but, since there are so many of them, why don't they make it as bright at night as it is during the day? Believe it or not, there's no obvious answer to this question, and scientists have puzzled over it for years. They've come up with two theories: first, that the light doesn't reach us because of the expanding universe; and second, that the age of the universe (see **Thing to Know** No. 1) puts a limit on the amount of light we receive from stars, because it takes a long time for it to reach us over such vast distances.

Dark looks: lots of different animals hunt at night and have adapted so that they can see in the dark. Some have bigger eyes to allow in more light. Cats have a reflective layer in their eyes so that they can make the most of whatever light is available.

Where Does the Sun
Go at Night? **Form**

Once you have mastered this **Thing to Know**, stick your Achieved Star here and fill in the form

Achieved

NOCTURNAL CREATURES

There are many creatures around the world that only come out at night. Here are some you might have seen in your town, your yard, the countryside, or perhaps when you've been on vacation. Check the box if you've spotted these animals at night.

Firefly ☐

Bat ☐

Mouse ☐

Rat ☐

Owl ☐

Toad ☐

Hedgehog ☐

Fox ☐

Turtle ☐

Crocodile ☐

Beaver ☐

Kangaroo ☐

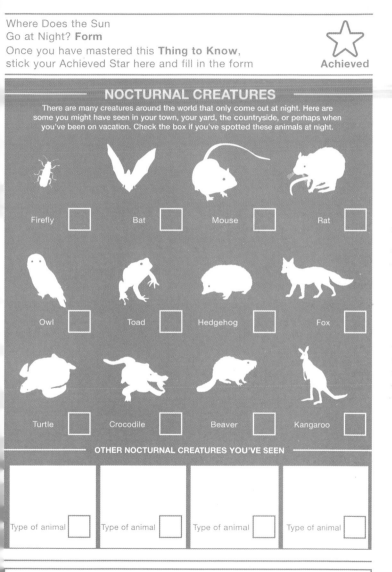

OTHER NOCTURNAL CREATURES YOU'VE SEEN

Type of animal ☐

Type of animal ☐

Type of animal ☐

Type of animal ☐

At the same time you could master these **Things to Know**:
25: If Light Is Invisible, How Can We See? • 54: Are Bats Really Blind? • 60: Why Does the Moon Change Shape? • 94: What Makes Things Glow in the Dark?

Are Bats Really Blind?

No, bats aren't blind. Sure, most of them probably wouldn't get very far dow the rows on an optician's wall chart, but then bats aren't really into books.

Bat Sense

Bats' eyes are sensitive to light and give them some information about the world around them, but for getting around they rely on echolocation. Bats make high-frequency sounds that reflect back to them. This lets them know where objects are so that they're able to navigate and to target the night-flying insects they live on. Here are some more bat facts:

- Bats are the only flying mammals in the world.
- There are about 1,000 species of bat in the world.
- Vampire bats live on blood—usually from big animals such as cows—and they seldom kill their prey. They make cuts in the animal's skin and lap up the blood. They're found in Central and South America—not Transylvania.
- Most bats live on insects and fruit, and some live on frogs and small animals.
- The bones in a bat's wing are like the ones in your arm and hand.
- Bats often live in large colonies, hanging upside down to sleep in their roosts. The biggest roost ever found is in Texas and is home to more than 20 million bats.
- We should be grateful to bats: they can each eat thousands of mosquitoes in a single night.

Batty stories: another myth about these strange creatures is that they can become entangled in long hair. This isn't true either: their echolocation is too sophisticated for them to fly into someone's head. They may be small, but they're not stupid.

Are Bats Really Blind? **Form**

Once you have mastered this **Thing to Know**,
stick your Achieved Star here and fill in the form

TEST YOUR BAT SENSE

Blindfolded and using only your hearing (and a pen!), ask a friend to give you directions to guide the bat to its prey. Answer at the back of the book.

At the same time you could master these **Things to Know**:
18: What Are the Biggest and Smallest Animals in the World? • 53: Where Does the Sun Go at Night? • 56: What Is the Scariest Thing in the World?

What Wiped Out Nearly Half the Population of Europe?

The Black Death was a terrible outbreak of the plague that ravaged Europe in the Middle Ages, from 1347 to 1350. Europe was never quite the same again.

A Spot of Plague

The Black Death was named this because the victims' skin would turn black due to bleeding underneath it. (The "Death" part is fairly obvious.) In fact, it was an outbreak of two types of plague: the bubonic plague, in which victims developed swellings called "buboes" that were spread by fleabites, and the pneumonic plague, which infected the lungs and was spread by contact with other sufferers. But both were caused by the same type of bacterium.

It's very difficult to tell exactly how many people died because accounts vary. Also, people were too busy dying to worry very much about keeping records. But it's thought that up to half the population of Europe was wiped out by the Black Death. The highest death tolls were in big cities, where people were crowded closely together. Not only Europe was affected: parts of Asia and the Middle East had plague outbreaks during the same period.

The disease returned every so often until the 1700s, including in 1665–66 in London. The Great Fire of London in 1666 helped to wipe out the disease.

Cure evil: cures for the Black Death included drinking your own urine, putting a live hen next to the buboes or covering them with dried dead toads, and cutting veins to let out "bad blood."

What Wiped Out Nearly Half the Population of Europe? **Form**

Once you have mastered this **Thing to Know**, stick your Achieved Star here and fill in the form

Achieved

PLAGUED WITH FACTS

Test your knowledge of the plague with this quiz. Once you've done the quiz, memorize the correct facts, then impress your friends to earn your star.

1. **The nursery rhyme "ring-around the rosy" is about the plague, but what is the "ring-around-the-rosy"?**

(a) Dying flowers
(b) A round red rash that appears on the victims' skin
(c) Nosebleeds
(d) Red rings around the victims' eyes

2. **. . . and what does the line "a pocket full of posies" refer to?**

(a) Foul-tasting medicine
(b) Sores
(c) Fragrances to hide the smell of the dying
(d) Gloves for protection from the infected

3. **What is the most common form of the plague?**

(a) Bubonic
(b) Pneumonic
(c) Septicemic
(d) Smallpox

4. **If you contracted bubonic plague where would buboes, which ooze pus and blood, first appear?**

(a) In the groin and under the arms
(b) On your legs
(c) On your hands
(d) Everywhere

Answers at the back of the book.

5. **How many people did the Great Plague of 1665–66 kill?**

(a) 25,000–50,000
(b) 50,000–75,000
(c) 75,000–100,000
(d) 100,000–125,000

6. **What percentage of London's entire population did the Great Plague of 1665–66 kill?**

(a) 25 (b) 50 (c) 75 (d) 100

7. **Which of these were symptoms of the Black Death?**

(a) Headache, fever, and vomiting
(b) Swollen glands, stomachache, and blistering
(c) Exhaustion, fatigue, and delirium
(d) All of the above

8. **What happened to the victims' eyes?**

(a) They'd go red
(b) They'd ooze pus
(c) They'd become difficult to open
(d) All of the above

9. **What was the expected life span of someone who'd contracted the Black Death?**

(a) 2–3 hours (b) 2–3 days
(c) 2–3 weeks (d) 2–3 months

10. **Complete the sentence: Recovery from the Black Death was . . .**

(a) . . . guaranteed (b) . . . likely
(c) . . . possible (d) . . . unusual

At the same time you could master these **Things to Know**:
71: Are You Only Ever a Few Feet from a Rat in a Big City? • 73: Pus—What Is It Good For? • 97: What Is the World's Deadliest Disease?

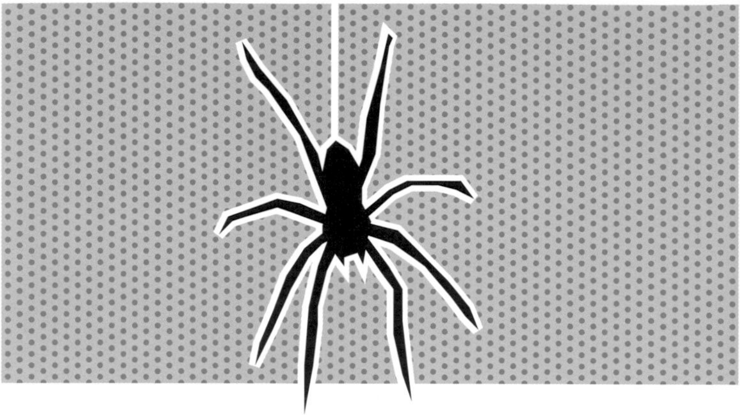

What Is the Scariest Thing in the World?

Your idea of the scariest thing ever might be a headless ghost chasing you through a maze full of rats, spiders, and snakes before forcing you to swim through a shark-and-piranha-infested tank, then driving you over a cliff. But what's terrifying for you may not be in the least bit alarming to someone else

Blind Courage

Fear is a good thing—if we were completely fearless, it wouldn't be long before we were eaten by a crocodile or fell off a tall building. It's very difficult to figure out what people are most afraid of, but among the most common phobias is a fear of spiders. Why we should be afraid of nonaggressive creatures hundreds of times smaller than we are is a mystery. Unless the spider is poisonous, in which case it's totally understandable.

Probably the most common fear, if you grouped several together, is the fear of other people. Most people get sweaty palmed and dry mouthed at the thought of public speaking, for example. And agoraphobia, which affects one person in twenty, can stop sufferers from leaving their homes for years in extreme cases. Perhaps it's pretty reasonable: after all, which other animal is as scheming, unpredictable, and dangerous as people are?

Strange Phobias

Coulrophobia
(clowns)

Trichopathophobia
(hair)

Peladophobia
(bald people)

Genuphobia
(knees)

Amathophobia
(dust)

Hippopotomonstroses
-quippedaliophobia
(long words)

Bromidrosiphobia
(BO)

Pogonophobia
(beards)

Scientists have discovered a fear gene in mice: mice bred without that particular gene (called GRP) are reckless rodents, lacking the normal instinctive fear of open spaces or dangerous environments. One day the research might be used to treat people with phobias.

What Is the Scariest Thing in the World? **Form**

Once you have mastered this **Thing to Know**, stick your Achieved Star here and fill in the form

Achieved

FEAR FACTOR

Here are some of the things people find really scary. How do you feel about them? Rate their fear factor.

FEAR FACTOR

Do spiders scare you? y/n out of 10

FEAR FACTOR

Do snakes scare you? y/n out of 10

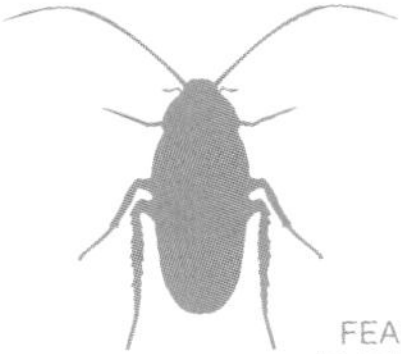

FEAR FACTOR

Do insects scare you? y/n out of 10

FEAR FACTOR

Do mice and/or rats scare you? y/n out of 10

FEAR FACTOR

Do vampires scare you? y/n out of 10

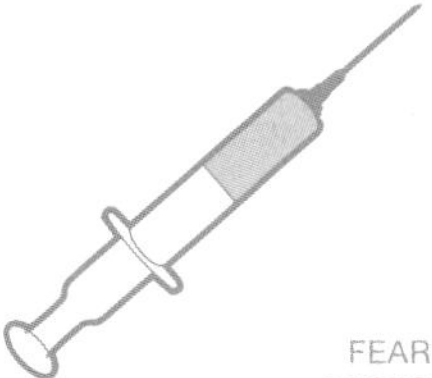

FEAR FACTOR

Do shots scare you? y/n out of 10

FEAR FACTOR

Do ghosts scare you? y/n out of 10

FEAR FACTOR

Do horror movies scare you? y/n out of 10

What scares you the most? Draw your fear below.

FEAR FACTOR

out of 10

At the same time you could master these **Things to Know**:
41: What Is the World's Most Dangerous Shark? • 90: What Is the World's Most Poisonous Creature? • 96: Where Are the Most Haunted Houses in the World?

How Do Oysters Make Pearls?

Oysters are mollusks, the same type of creature as a slug or snail. Now, snail lovers, look away—you won't like the next part. Most mollusks are, on the whole, fairly unattractive creatures. Oysters, however, have two things going for them. They're good to eat (the animal part, that is), and they occasionally produce some very pretty and rather valuable gemstones.

Irritated Oysters

As oysters grow, their shells grow too. Oysters use minerals from the food they eat to make a special substance called nacre, which they use to make their shells. Sometimes small bits of rock get inside the oyster's shell, especially if the animal lives in rough waters, and this irritates the creature. The oyster's reaction is to cover up the piece of grit with the same material it uses to build its shell—nacre. It builds up the nacre in layers to make a ball around the grit, and the end result is a pearl.

Pearls can be "cultured" as well as natural, which means that a pearl harvester has deliberately put an irritant inside the oyster's shell. The result is the same, but natural pearls are more expensive because they're much rarer. Natural pearls can come in a variety of different colors—blue, green, yellow, and even black (black ones are only found in the South Pacific Ocean). The most expensive pearls are perfectly round.

Gender benders: an oyster can change from male to female and vice versa quite naturally during the course of its life. The older it gets, the more likely it is to become female—probably because the bigger the oyster, the more eggs it can produce.

How Do Oysters Make Pearls? **Form**

Once you have mastered this **Thing to Know**, stick your Achieved Star here and fill in the form

Achieved

BIRTHSTONES

Each month of the year is symbolized by a different gemstone. They are believed to represent certain qualities in the people born during that month. Which is your birthstone, and what does that say about you? Color in the gems, and check to see if you got the colors right by turning to the back of the book.

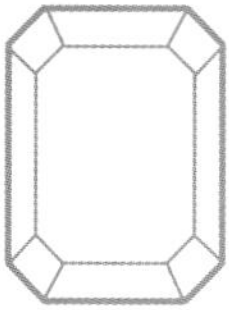

JANUARY
Garnet

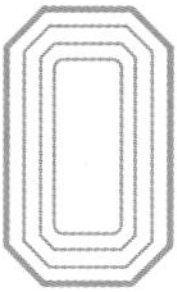

FEBRUARY
Amethyst

MARCH
Aquamarine or bloodstone

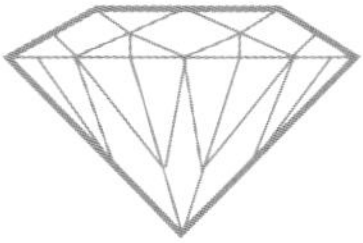

APRIL
Diamond

MAY
Emerald

JUNE
Pearl, moonstone, or alexandrite

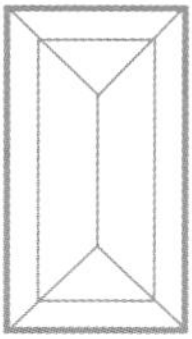

JULY
Ruby

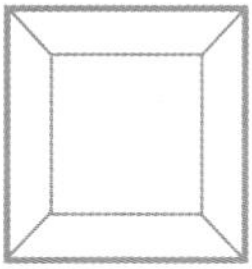

AUGUST
Peridot or sardonyx

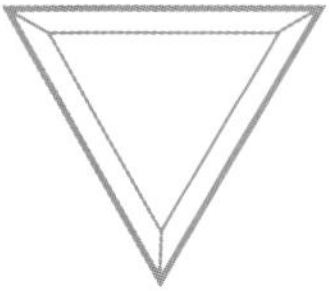

SEPTEMBER
Sapphire

OCTOBER
Opal or tourmaline

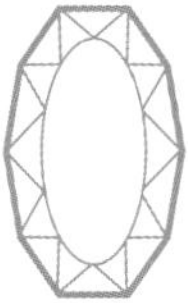

NOVEMBER
Topaz or citrine

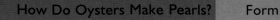

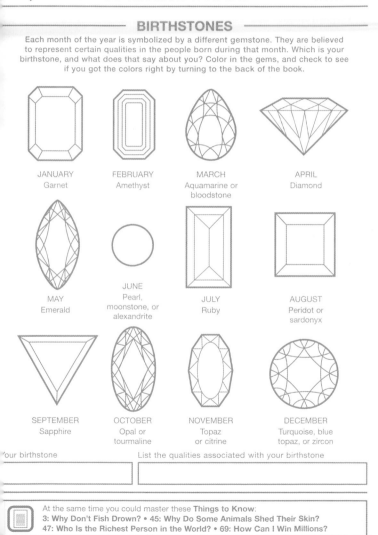

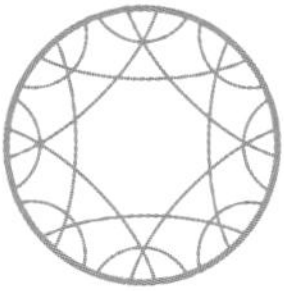

DECEMBER
Turquoise, blue topaz, or zircon

'our birthstone

List the qualities associated with your birthstone

At the same time you could master these **Things to Know**:
3: Why Don't Fish Drown? • 45: Why Do Some Animals Shed Their Skin?
47: Who Is the Richest Person in the World? • 69: How Can I Win Millions?

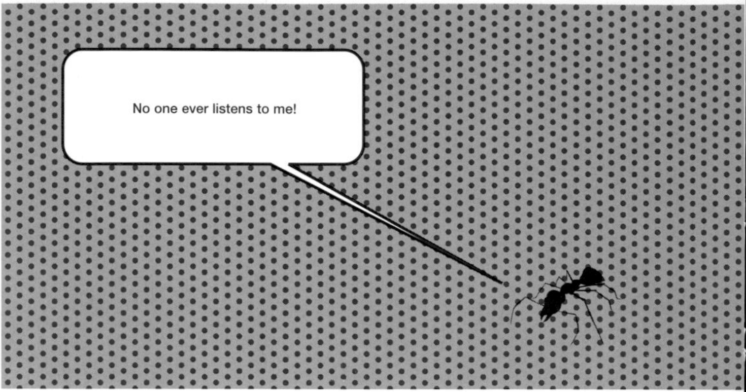

What Is the Quietest Sound We Can Hear?

Even though it's the dead of night and everything seems to be completely silent, listen carefully and you'll probably be able to hear the gentle rustling of the wind in the trees, a clock ticking in another room, the cat padding about quietly . . . or your neighbors' stereo suddenly being played at full blast.

Good Vibrations

Sound is made by vibrations, and the ear very cleverly detects these vibrations and converts them into electrical signals that are sent to the brain. The brain translates these signals and tries to identify them.

If you have normal hearing, sounds can reach your ears from the tiniest of vibrations. You might find this difficult to believe, but the quietest noises we can hear are caused by our eardrums moving about one-tenth the diameter of a hydrogen atom: that's about one-hundredth of a *millionth* of a millimeter.

Sound levels are measured in decibels (dB)—although "loudness" isn't measured by decibels because different individuals experience loudness in different ways. A sound that is too quiet to be heard by someone with normal hearing is set at 0 dB. People who cannot hear sounds below 95 dB are profoundly deaf and usually communciate through sign language or lipreading.

Excuse me? If you have to raise your voice to be heard by someone else, the sound level is probably above 85 dB—prolonged exposure to this kind of volume can cause hearing loss, and any exposure to 140 dB can cause immediate damage.

What Is the Quietest Sound
We Can Hear? **Form**

Once you have mastered this **Thing to Know,**
stick your Achieved Star here and fill in the form

Achieved

HEAR, HEAR!

The chart below is a sound scale that is measured in decibels (dBs). The limit of human hearing is 0 dBs. Try and match the noise or event to the number of decibels it reaches. The first one has been done for you.

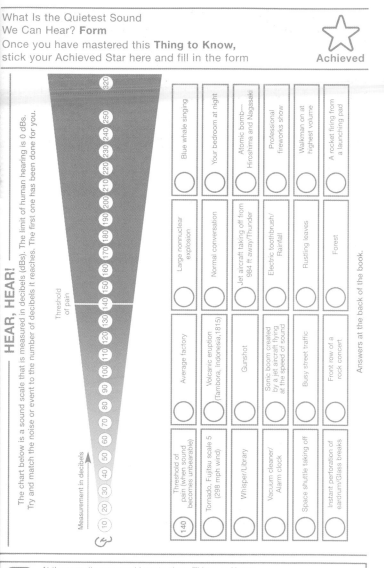

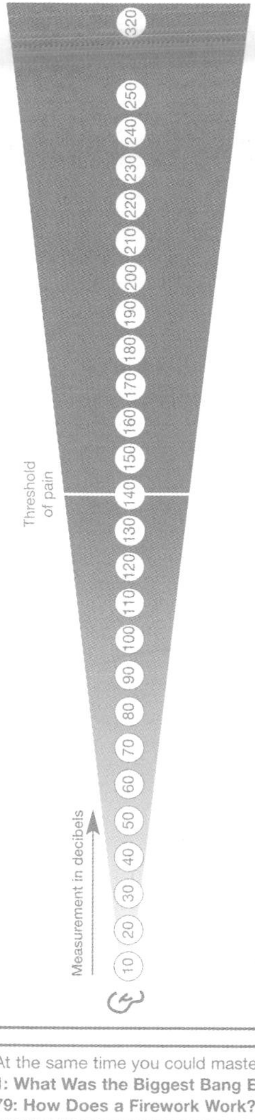

- (140) Threshold of pain (when sound becomes unbearable)
- ( ) Average factory
- ( ) Large nonnuclear explosion
- ( ) Blue whale singing
- ( ) Tornado, Fujitsu scale 5 (298 mph wind)
- ( ) Volcanic eruption (Tambora, Indonesia, 1815)
- ( ) Normal conversation
- ( ) Your bedroom at night
- ( ) Whisper/Library
- ( ) Gunshot
- ( ) Jet aircraft taking off from 984 ft away/Thunder
- ( ) Atomic bomb—Hiroshima and Nagasaki
- ( ) Vacuum cleaner/ Alarm clock
- ( ) Sonic boom created by a jet aircraft flying at the speed of sound
- ( ) Electric toothbrush/ Rainfall
- ( ) Professional fireworks show
- ( ) Space shuttle taking off
- ( ) Busy street traffic
- ( ) Rustling leaves
- ( ) Walkman on at highest volume
- ( ) Instant perforation of eardrum/Glass breaks
- ( ) Front row of a rock concert
- ( ) Forest
- ( ) A rocket firing from a launching pad

Answers at the back of the book.

At the same time you could master these **Things to Know**:
1: What Was the Biggest Bang Ever? • 67: Do Storms Have Eyes?
79: How Does a Firework Work? • 84: What Is the Sixth Sense?

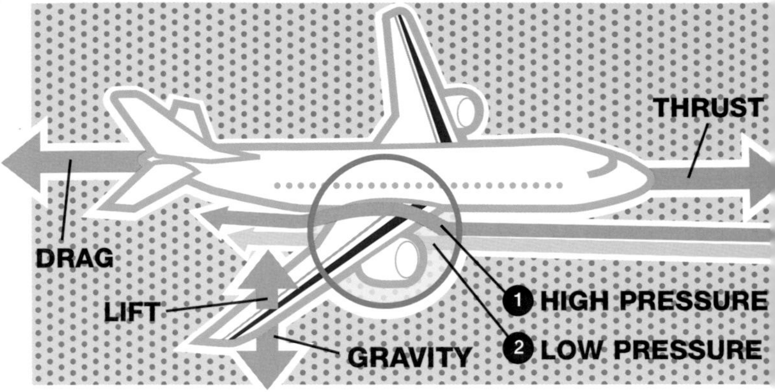

How Do Planes Get into the Air—and Stay There?

Planes are big and heavy, birds are small and light, and yet they have one major thing in common—they can both fly. How does that work?

Winging It

Get a strip of paper and blow along the top of it (not at it or underneath it), and you'll see that the paper lifts up. That's because the air moving along the top of it (your breath) is moving faster than the air underneath it, which means there isn't as much air pressing down on the top as there is air pressing up from the bottom. That makes it lift.

The wings on a plane use the same principle, but, instead of using a giant blowing machine, they use the design of their wings to make air move faster on the top than the bottom. Because the top of a plane's wing is curved, the air has to move faster over it, so there's less pressure from the air on the top than there is from the air pressing up from underneath. Just like the strip of paper, the air below the wing is pushing up more than the air above it is pushing down. As the plane moves forward quickly, the air pressure underneath its wings lifts it up.

A plane has to have enough lift from its wings to lift up its weight, which sounds pretty obvious. If you made a really heavy plane, its wings would have to be ridiculously enormous to get it off the ground. This is why ostriches and emus can't fly—they're too heavy for the size of their wings.

The *Spruce Goose* is the biggest plane ever built. Its wingspan is nearly 330 ft and the plane is more than 213 ft long. But it flew only once ever—in 1947—over a distance of less than a mile.

How Do Planes Get into
the Air—and Stay There? **Form**
Once you have mastered this **Thing to Know,**
stick your Achieved Star here and fill in the form

Achieved

MAKE A PAPER AIRPLANE

To make this great paper airplane, take an 8.5" x 11" piece of paper and fold it in half lengthways then fold it back out again. Then follow these steps.

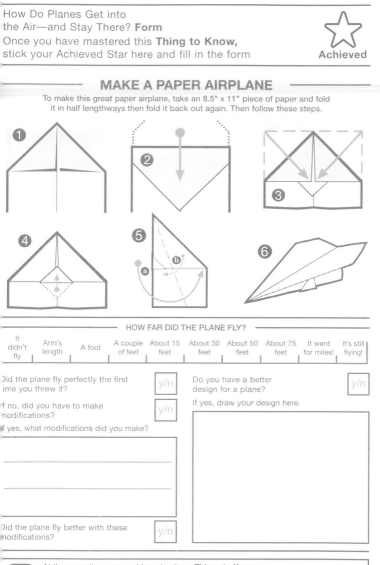

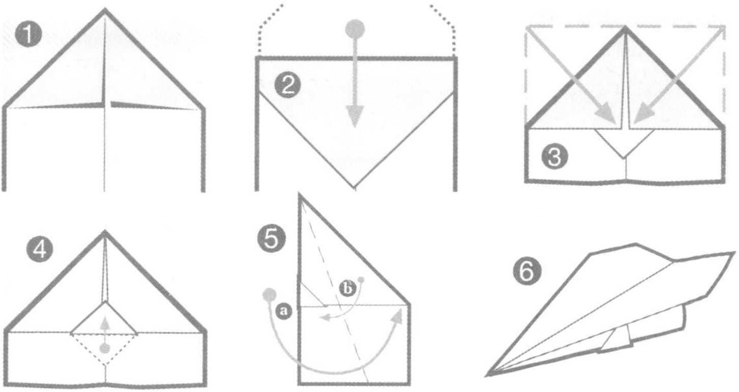

HOW FAR DID THE PLANE FLY?

It didn't fly	Arm's length	A foot	A couple of feet	About 15 feet	About 30 feet	About 50 feet	About 75 feet	It went for miles!	It's still flying!

Did the plane fly perfectly the first time you threw it? y/n

If no, did you have to make modifications? y/n

If yes, what modifications did you make?

Did the plane fly better with these modifications? y/n

Do you have a better design for a plane? y/n

If yes, draw your design here.

At the same time you could master these **Things to Know**:
43: How Do Clouds Stay Up? • 44: What Happens in the Bermuda Triangle?
63: How Many People Are Flying Through the Air at Any One Time?

Why Does the Moon Change Shape?

Are you a lunatic? Does your behavior depend on the phases of the Moon? Do full moons drive you loopy? Okay, so there's no proof of lunacy (in the original sense of the word), but there must be a reason why the Moon changes shape.

Come Over to the Dark Side

We see the Moon at night because it reflects light from the Sun, not because it shines. The shape it appears to us depends on how much of it is in shadow:

- The Moon orbits Earth once every 27.3 days.
- As it moves around Earth, more or less of it is lit up by the Sun.
- We can see only the part of the Moon that is both turned toward Earth and lit by the Sun. So we might see the whole of the Moon or just a crescent, depending on where the Moon is in its 27.3-day orbit.

So, as you probably guessed, the Moon doesn't actually change shape at all: it just looks different at different times. You can try this effect out for yourself in a dark room using a flashlight and an orange!

Some of the planets in our solar system have far more than their fair share of moons.

Jupiter has the most moons of any planet: four big ones and at least 60 smaller ones. Ganymede is the biggest moon in the solar system.

Mars has two moons, but they're both very small.

Saturn has at least 19 moons. The biggest, Titan, even has its own atmosphere.

Several moons in the solar system are bigger than Pluto, which is actually a dwarf planet.

Only Mercury and Venus don't have any moons at all.

The magic of perspective: the Sun and the Moon seem to be about the same size because the Sun is (very roughly) 400 times bigger than the Moon, but it's also (very roughly) 400 times farther away.

Why Does the Moon Change Shape? **Form**

Once you have mastered this **Thing to Know**,
stick your Achieved Star here and fill in the form

PHASES OF THE MOON

A LUNAR MONTH

Keep a record of the moon's phases over a month and see how it changes shape.

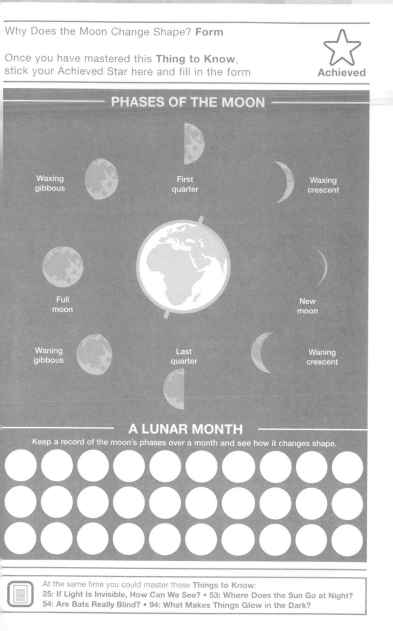

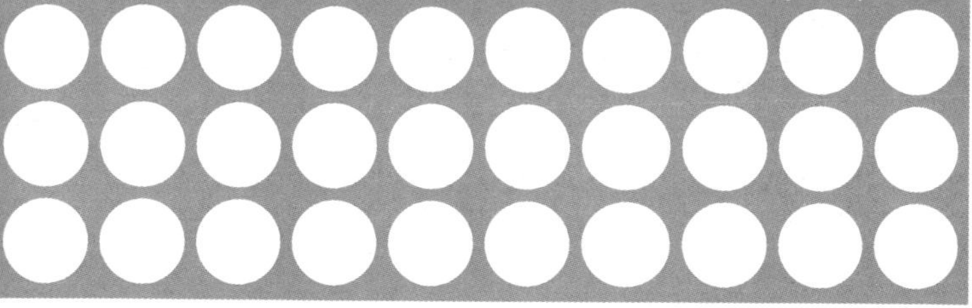

At the same time you could master these **Things to Know**:
25: If Light Is Invisible, How Can We See? • 53: Where Does the Sun Go at Night?
54: Are Bats Really Blind? • 94: What Makes Things Glow in the Dark?

TOURIST MAP
Can you direct me to tourist information, please?

Were All Romans from Rome?

The Roman Empire is famous for having been very big and powerful. At its height it extended from northern Britain to Egypt, including the Mediterranean area. But did the citizens of one city really manage to control all those people?

There's No Place Like Rome

The short answer is *no*. At first you could only be a Roman citizen if you came from Rome, but as the Romans conquered more and more territory, other people became Roman even if they'd never been anywhere near the city of Rome in their lives. The Romans were very good at getting the people they conquered to think and act as they did—and that's one of the reasons they were so successful. Cleverly, they did this not by bullying people into taking on their religion and ways, but by incorporating other religions and traditions into the Roman way of life—and making people Roman citizens.

Rome made people citizens first in the rest of Italy and then throughout the conquered lands. There were different classes of citizenship, but, generally speaking, being a Roman citizen gave you the right to vote, the right to a legal marriage, and the right to be exempt from especially awful punishments like being flogged or crucified without trial. You also got some financial benefits because you didn't have to pay so many taxes. In AD 212, Roman emperor Caracalla gave Roman citizenship to all free people in the whole of the empire (i.e., anyone who wasn't a slave).

Being a slave in the Roman Empire was no picnic. There were plenty of them, but they weren't Roman citizens, of course, and had very few rights. And if they gave evidence in a court of law, the evidence was only valid if they'd been tortured first!

Were All Romans from Rome? **Form**

Once you have mastered this **Thing to Know**, stick your Achieved Star here and fill in the form

Achieved

THE ROMAN EMPIRE

At its peak the Roman Empire engulfed most of modern-day Europe and parts of the Middle East and Africa. The map below shows the expansion of the empire over time. Which countries of the conquest have you visited? Check the boxes below.

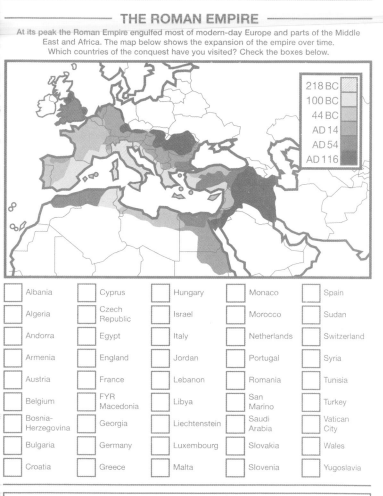

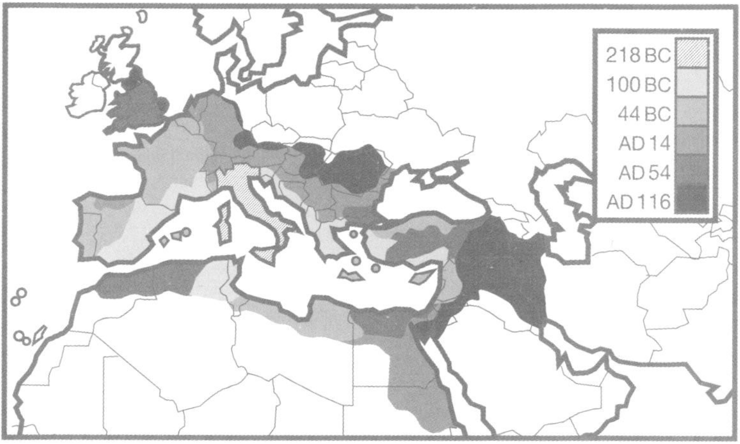

☐ Albania	☐ Cyprus	☐ Hungary	☐ Monaco	☐ Spain
☐ Algeria	☐ Czech Republic	☐ Israel	☐ Morocco	☐ Sudan
☐ Andorra	☐ Egypt	☐ Italy	☐ Netherlands	☐ Switzerland
☐ Armenia	☐ England	☐ Jordan	☐ Portugal	☐ Syria
☐ Austria	☐ France	☐ Lebanon	☐ Romania	☐ Tunisia
☐ Belgium	☐ FYR Macedonia	☐ Libya	☐ San Marino	☐ Turkey
☐ Bosnia-Herzegovina	☐ Georgia	☐ Liechtenstein	☐ Saudi Arabia	☐ Vatican City
☐ Bulgaria	☐ Germany	☐ Luxembourg	☐ Slovakia	☐ Wales
☐ Croatia	☐ Greece	☐ Malta	☐ Slovenia	☐ Yugoslavia

At the same time you could master these **Things to Know**:
4: What Were the Seven Wonders of the World? • 55: What Wiped Out Nearly Half the Population of Europe? • 99: Who Was the Greatest Conqueror of All Time?

How Do You Survive an Earthquake?

Whether or not you live in an earthquake zone, it's best to be prepared.

Shaky Ground

Earthquakes happen because of the movement of plates in the Earth's outer layer (the mantle), which can break and split into new positions. These movements cause vibrations (seismic waves) that travel along the Earth's surface. You're more likely to experience an earthquake if you live near a fault line (a crack or weakness) in one of the plates.

If you're inside a building when an earthquake happens . . .

- Stay inside. Get under a piece of heavy furniture (e.g., a table), or crouch in a corner formed by two inside walls with your arms over your head.
- Keep away from windows and any objects that might fall and injure you.

If you're outside . . .

- Move as far away as possible from buildings, trees, streetlights, etc. Lie on the ground and cover your head.
- If you're in a car, stay in it, but pull over away from buildings, bridges, etc.

After the earthquake it might be helpful to use a piece of cloth to breathe through, to filter the dust. If you're in a building, wait until it's safe before you run outside—there may well be aftershocks.

Over a million earthquakes happen every year. Thankfully, most are too small for anyone to notice. But one of them, somewhere in the world, is likely to be big. In 1989 an earthquake in San Francisco moved the entire area about three feet northward.

How Do You Survive
an Earthquake? **Form**
Once you have mastered this **Thing to Know**,
stick your Achieved Star here and fill in the form

Achieved

EARTHQUAKES

There are approximately 2,600 earthquakes across the world every day, although most of them are hardly noticeable. Below is a chart to show where the majority of earthquakes happen (shaded areas). Quakes usually occur on the Earth's tectonic plate lines (dotted lines).

Have you ever experienced an earthquake? y/n

If yes, where did it happen?

What was the measurement on the Richter scale? 0 0 . 0

Were you scared? y/n

How long did the earthquake continue for? 0 0 mins 0 0 secs

Were there aftershocks? y/n

If yes, how many? 0 0 0

Were you hurt? y/n If yes, how were you hurt?

Was there much damage? y/n If yes, what kind of damage?

At the same time you could master these **Things to Know**:
15: When Was It Possible to Walk from London to New York?
16: How Do Mountains Grow? • 52: Could a Rock Destroy Our Planet?

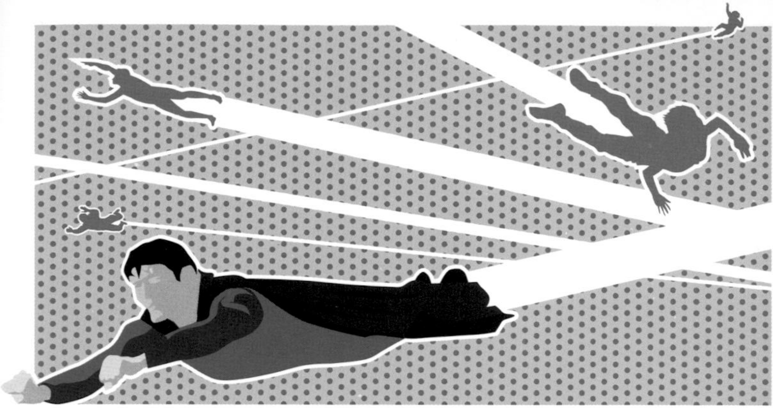

How Many People Are Flying Through the Air at Any One Time

It's a surprising and bizarre thought that there may be more people than birds flying over our heads right now.

Winging It

Air travel has only been around for 100 years or so, and it has only been available to ordinary travelers in the last 50 years. In that time it's become extremely popular—and it's still increasing, even though traveling by plane is extremely bad for the environment.

Every year, there are an estimated 1.5 billion air passengers. That's roughly 4 million per day, or 220,000 every hour (if we do not count a few hours because there aren't many flights at nighttime). It's a staggering thought. How many of them are flying directly over your head depends, of course, on where you happen to be. The busiest airport in the world is Hartsfield-Jackson in Atlanta, Georgia, which handles 83.5 million passengers every year. So if you were hanging around the flight path in Atlanta, you might have thousands of people whizzing over your head every hour.

The World's Busiest Airports

Hartsfield-Jackson Atlanta International
Georgia

O'Hare International Airport
Chicago, Illinois

London Heathrow
England

Tokyo International
Kanto, Japan

Los Angeles International
California

Dallas-Fort Worth International
Texas

Frankfurt International
Hesse, Germany

Charles de Gaulle International
Paris, France

Schiphol
Amsterdam, The Netherlands

If you travel in a car for an hour, you're about 100 times more likely to be injured than if you travel in a plane for an hour. So why are so many people afraid of flying? Is it crashing they fear, or something else? Small spaces, heights, terrorism, turbulence?

How Many People Are Flying Through the Air at Any One Time? **Form**
Once you have mastered this **Thing to Know**, stick your Achieved Star here and fill in the form

Achieved

PLANE SAILING

What is the longest plane journey you've been on?

0,0 hours 0,0 mins

Where was it from?

And to?

How did you pass the time?

Playing games ☐ Looking out the window ☐ Annoying people ☐ Reading ☐ Sleeping ☐ Watching films ☐

What was the time difference in the country you flew to? Plus/minus 0,0 hours

Was it worth the long trip? y/n

Which countries have you flown to?

Which was your favorite country?

Why?

Have you ever been lost in an airport? y/n

Have you ever missed a flight? y/n

Have you ever been delayed for hours and hours? y/n

Which of the following are part of your flying experience?

Terror ☐ Excitement ☐ Sickness ☐ Boredom ☐ Popping ears ☐

Have you ever been through severe turbulence in a plane? y/n

If yes, how scared were you?

1 2 3 4 5

Have you ever met the pilot on a plane? y/n

Have you ever visited the cockpit? y/n

Have you ever been sucked into the toilet on a plane? y/n

At the same time you could master these **Things to Know**:
8: Is Time Travel Possible? • 43: How Do Clouds Stay Up? • 56: What Is the Scariest Thing in the World? • 59: How Do Planes Get into the Air—and Stay There?

I'm cold and lost
and nobody loves me.

Do Animals Cry?

Most land mammals produce tears to wash away dirt and irritants. So, in that way, lots of animals cry. But there's one animal that cries tears when it's in trouble or pain: a large sea creature called a dugong that lives in the Indian Ocean. There are also stories of elephants shedding tears when they're in distress.

Crying Chimps and Laughing Rats

Although most animals don't cry in the way that we do, it doesn't necessarily mean that they don't feel emotions. Chimps are our closest relatives, and it's difficult to hear a baby chimp crying out when it's separated from its mother without assuming that it's crying in just the same way that a baby human would. Dogs sometimes refuse to eat and show other signs of distress when their owners die. However, we can't know what the animals are really feeling when they behave like this, and we can't just assume they're feeling sadness, anguish, or regret in the same way that humans do.

Some animals make noises that sound a bit like laughter (e.g., kookaburras and hyenas), but that's just coincidence—it doesn't mean they've found something funny. On the other hand, lots of different animals play. Rats chirp and chimps pant when they're playing and seem to be enjoying themselves. So maybe a chirp is the rat equivalent of a hearty laugh, although we've no idea what a rat's sense of humor is like. They probably like dirty jokes.

Mourning mutts: the most famous sad dog of all time must be Greyfriars Bobby. When his owner died in 1858, the terrier stood watch over his master's grave, leaving only for food, until his own death 14 years later.

Do Animals Cry? **Form**

Once you have mastered this **Thing to Know**, stick your Achieved Star here and fill in the form

Achieved

HOW SENSITIVE ARE YOU?

Take this quick quiz to find out how much of a softy or a tough nut you are. Answer truthfully, as you'll only be lying to yourself if you cheat.

1. When was the last time you cried?
(a) Sometime in the last week
(b) Sometime in the last month
(c) Not for a long, long time

2. How did you react the last time you fell off your bike or injured yourself?
(a) You cried and headed home.
(b) You took a look at the injury, felt queasy, and had to sit down to recover.
(c) You took a look at the injury and continued as normal, claiming, "It's only a flesh wound."

3. How did you react when the joke was on you or when a friend embarassed you in front of a group of people?
(a) You went bright red and got angry or ran away.
(b) You felt silly but managed to laugh it off.
(c) You turned the joke back onto the joker.

4. How did you feel when you watched the film *Bambi*?
(a) You sobbed like a baby.
(b) You were very moved by it.
(c) You didn't find it sad at all.

5. How did you react the last time you saw a spider in your house?
(a) You screamed or jumped on to a chair and got someone else to get rid of it.
(b) You squashed it or trapped it under a glass.
(c) You picked it up with your bare hands and granted it freedom in the yard.

6. How did you react the last time you saw blood?
(a) You fainted or felt queasy and turned away.
b) You felt a bit weird so you got someone else to sort out the problem.
(c) You took action by tending to the wound.

7. How did you react the last time you were hurt by a mean comment?
(a) You burst into tears on the spot.
(b) You bit your lip but then cried when you were out of sight or on your own.
(c) You felt it roll off your back—no big deal.

8. Last time you were picked on or bullied, did you
(a) get upset and give them what they wanted without a fight?
(b) take all their abuse but refuse to give them what they wanted?
(c) stand up for yourself and give it right back?

9. How did you react last time you heard strange noises at night?
(a) You told your parents and got them to do a thorough search of the house, including the closet in your bedroom.
(b) You worried about the noises and kept listening until you were satisfied that it was the radiators and not an ax murderer.
(c) You ignored them and went back to sleep.

Now add up your scores: a = 3, b = 2, c = 1

21–27: You're a big softy, which isn't a bad thing, although you should learn to stand up for yourself a little more and face up to some of your fears.

15–20: You're pretty relaxed, but in touch with your feelings. You have a good balance of sensitivity and levelheadedness.

9–14: You're a tough nut, but one day your toughness may upset someone or get you into trouble. You don't always have to be the brave one. It's good to open up and share feelings.

At the same time you could master these **Things to Know**:
2: What Is DNA (and Are We All That Different from Chimps)? • 34: What Is the World's Favorite Pet? • 77: Why Do People Kiss (and Animals Don't)?

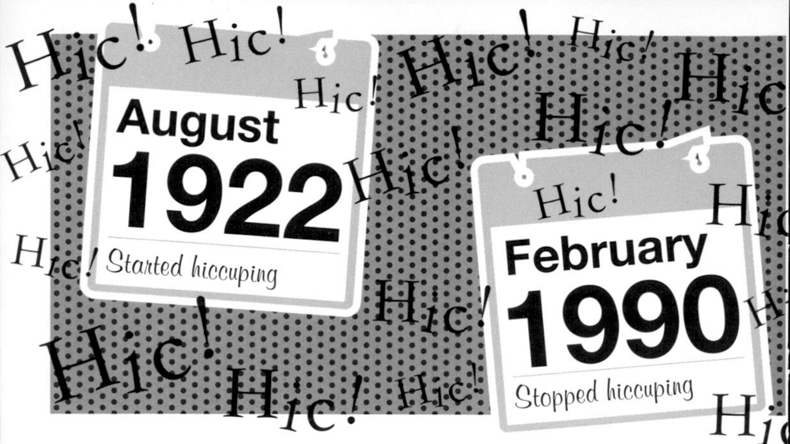

Why Do We Get Hiccups?

Unlike burping, sneezing, or farting, hiccuping doesn't seem to serve any useful purpose at all. It just really gets on your nerves.

Hic . . . Hic . . . Hic . . .

Hiccups can be caused by eating or drinking too fast, drinking carbonated drinks or alcohol, or being nervous, but often they seem to start for no reason at all.

When you hiccup, your diaphragm (the muscle that helps you breathe) contracts, which makes you gulp air suddenly. When the air hits your voice box, you make the *hic* sound.

Sometimes there can be a medical problem that irritates the diaphragm, but usually the cause is a mystery. The best we can do is to say that hiccups are caused by something irritating the diaphragm.

If you hiccup more than seven times you're likely to go on hiccuping for a while. If you're really unlucky you could end up like the world-record hiccuper, Charles Osborne from Iowa, who started hiccuping in 1922 and didn't stop until 1990. That's 68 years!

Some Strange Cures for Hiccups

There are hundreds of cures for hiccups. You've probably heard of quite a few, but what about these strange ones:

1. Think about pineapples.
2. Jump out of a plane (note: make sure you're wearing a parachute).
3. Make yourself sneeze.
4. Pull your tongue.
5. Eat sugar.

But remember that nothing worked for Charles Osborne.

A small hiccup. Babies hiccup even before they're born—ultrasound scans often detect hiccups earlier than breathing movements! And the babies' mothers usually feel them too—it's just as well women tend to hiccup less while they're pregnant!

Why Do We Get Hiccups? **Form**

Once you have mastered this **Thing to Know**, stick your Achieved Star here and fill in the form

Achieved

HICCUPING REMEDIES

How many times do you usually hiccup in a row?

1–20 | 21–40 | 41–60 | 61–80 | 80+

How do you usually stop yourself from hiccuping?

TRY THESE REMEDIES

REMEDY 1: Try to hold your breath for as long as possible.

Did this remedy work? y/n

If no, how much longer did you hiccup for? hours mins

Do you think this remedy is just an old wives' tale? y/n

REMEDY 2: Drink water from the wrong side of the glass.

Did this remedy work? y/n

If no, how much longer did you hiccup for? hours mins

Do you think this remedy is just an old wives' tale? y/n

REMEDY 3: Suck an ice cube.

Did this remedy work? y/n

If no, how much longer did you hiccup for? hours mins

Do you think this remedy is just an old wives' tale? y/n

REMEDY 4: Eat a spoonful of sugar by letting it dissolve on the tongue.

Did this remedy work? y/n

If no, how much longer did you hiccup for? hours mins

Do you think this remedy is just an old wives' tale? y/n

REMEDY 5: Block your ears and nostrils and drink a glass of water.

Did this remedy work? y/n

If no, how much longer did you hiccup for? hours mins

Do you think this remedy is just an old wives' tale? y/n

REMEDY 6: Blow up a balloon.

Did this remedy work? y/n

If no, how much longer did you hiccup for? hours mins

Do you think this remedy is just an old wives' tale? y/n

IF YOU WANT TO HICCUP

If you need an excuse to skip class, you can make yourself hiccup by swallowing air. **WARNING:** it doesn't work for everyone, and you may end up feeling sick instead.

Did this tip work for you? y/n

If yes, how long did you hiccup for? hours mins

At the same time you could master these **Things to Know**:
1: What Was the Biggest Bang Ever? • 14: Will Your Stomach Explode if You Eat Too Much? • 37: Can You Sneeze with Your Eyes Open? • 64: Do Animals Cry?

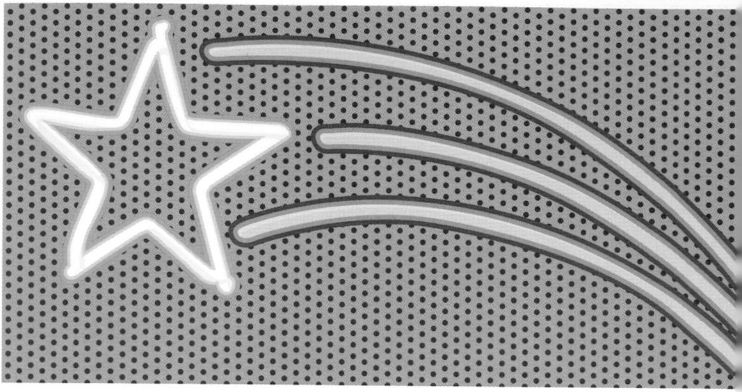

Why Do Stars Twinkle?

Stars are massive balls of gas, just like our Sun, burning in space billions of miles away. They probably support solar systems and planets just like our own too. So when you're feeling down, look up and see them all winking at you, and remember you're not alone.

Up Above the World So High

Stars twinkle because of the Earth's atmosphere. When we look up into the night sky, we're looking through layers of moving air. We see stars as tiny points of light because they're so far away. But the light is refracted (bent) in different directions as it travels through pockets of hot and cold air, and that's why stars seem to twinkle.

- Stars closer to the horizon twinkle more than ones overhead. That's because the light from stars nearer to the horizon has more atmosphere to get through before it reaches your eyes.
- If you could look at the stars from space, or from the Moon, they wouldn't twinkle, as their light wouldn't have any atmosphere to travel through.
- The twinkling of stars is one way of telling them apart from planets. Planets look very much like stars when they're seen from Earth, but they don't usually twinkle because they're closer than stars.

Over thousands of years, astronomers have divided up the stars into constellations to make the night sky easier to map. There are 88 official constellations, but most would be hard to identify from just their names.

Star spotting: most of the constellations were named thousands of years ago after characters and animals from mythology. Some were named in the 1700s and don't have nearly as good names, e.g., the Drafting Compass and the Air Pump.

Why Do Stars Twinkle? **Form**

Once you have mastered this **Thing to Know**,
stick your Achieved Star here and fill in the form

Achieved

THE PLANETS

Of all the planets in our solar system you can see only five of them with the naked eye. Go out one clear night and see if you can spot them. You'll get a better view if you use binoculars or a telescope.

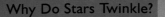

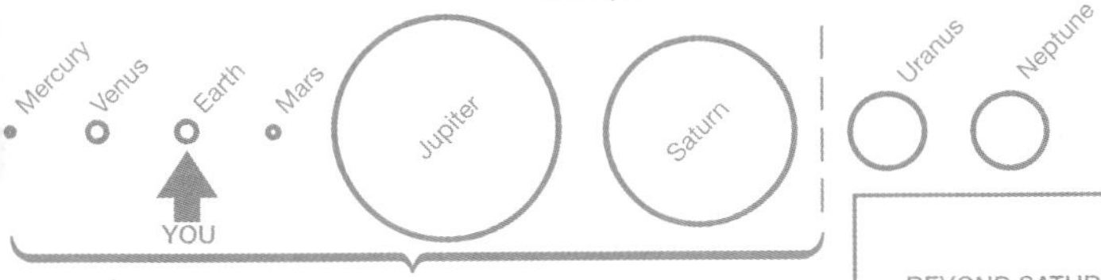

These are the planets you can see with the naked eye.

ASTRONOMY

Have you seen Mercury with the naked eye?	y/n	Have you seen Mercury through a telescope?	y/n
Have you seen Venus with the naked eye?	y/n	Have you seen Venus through a telescope?	y/n
Have you seen Mars with the naked eye?	y/n	Have you seen Mars through a telescope?	y/n
Have you seen Jupiter with the naked eye?	y/n	Have you seen Jupiter through a telescope?	y/n
Have you seen Saturn with the naked eye?	y/n	Have you seen Saturn through a telescope?	y/n

What color did each planet appear to be?

Mercury		Jupiter	
Venus		Saturn	
Mars			

To find the current position of the planets, go to www.heavens-above.com

Put the planets in order. Which was the easiest planet to find (1) and which was the hardest (5)?

Mercury ☐ Venus ☐ Mars ☐ Jupiter ☐ Saturn ☐

BEYOND SATURN

Uranus (discovered in 1781) can be spotted with a telescope if you know where to look. Neptune is incredibly hard to see even with a telescope. It took until 1846 and 1930, respectively, to find them.

In 2006 the solar system as we knew it officially changed. The long-running debate whether Pluto was a planet came to an end, and Pluto was downgraded to a dwarf planet.

There are a lot more potential dwarf planets out there within the boundaries of our solar system waiting to be recognized. Within the next few years we could see our solar system double in size.

MOON COUNT

Earth: 1 • Mars: 2
Jupiter: 39+ • Saturn: 25+
Uranus: 21+ • Neptune: 11+

At the same time you could master these **Things to Know**:
20: Which Way Is North? • 21: What Is the Solar System (and Could It Fit in Your Yard)? • 25: If Light Is Invisible, How Can We See? • 29: How Long Is a Light-Year?

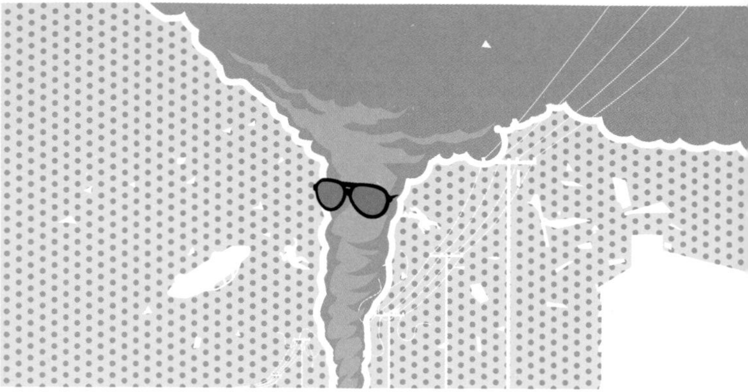

Do Storms Have Eyes?

Do you remember the story about the Cyclops—that mythical Greek giant with one eye in the middle of his forehead? Odysseus and his men blinded the Cyclops in order to escape him. So what's all this got to do with storms? Well, storms are a little like blinded raging giants. They have one eye, right in the middle, but it's really more of a hole than an eye.

Cooking Up a Storm

Storms are an especially scary kind of weather and can bring thunder, lightning, rain, hail, and high winds. If wind speeds are higher than 75 mph the storm is classified as a hurricane or typhoon, and really bad ones can uproot trees, throw cars around, and smash houses.

Inside a storm, winds swirl around in a furious circle, but right at the center there's a hole where the air is warmer and the wind is calm. This is the eye of the storm. It's usually about 10% of the total size of the storm—so if a hurricane measured 12 mi across, the eye would be about 1.2 mi across. People sometimes think the bad weather has passed when in fact they're in the eye of the storm and the second half is about to deal them a devastating blow.

At any one time there are about 2,000 thunderstorms raging away on our planet. Thankfully, only a few of them are classified as hurricanes or typhoons.

Storm names: hurricanes are named according to an alphabetical list that rotates every six years. If a hurricane's been especially bad, the name is taken out of circulation—so there'll never be another Hurricane Gilbert, Katrina, or Wilma.

Do Storms Have Eyes? **Form**

Once you have mastered this **Thing to Know**, stick your Achieved Star here and fill in the form

Achieved

BATTLING THE ELEMENTS

You can't escape the weather. If you haven't battled with a gale force wind or driving rain in the height of summer, you definitely will sometime in the future as the world's climate continues to change. Make a record below of the worst weather experiences you've had so far.

What was the date of your worst weather experience?

m m d d y y y y

Where were you at the time?

Check which conditions you experienced

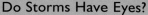

What is the worst weather you've experienced? Write an account of what happened below.

Have you ever . . .

. . . been caught in a torrential downpour without an umbrella?	y/n
. . . had your umbrella turned inside out by the wind?	y/n
. . . been blown over by the wind?	y/n
. . . been hit and hurt by hailstones?	y/n
. . . been caught in a blizzard?	y/n
. . . been struck by lightning?	y/n
. . . slipped on ice?	y/n
. . . been so cold that you thought you were going to freeze?	y/n
. . . been so hot that you thought you would pass out?	y/n
. . . had sunstroke?	y/n
. . . been badly burnt by the Sun?	y/n
. . . walked on a frozen lake?	y/n
. . . seen snow in summer?	y/n
. . . been snowed in?	y/n
. . . been caught in a flood?	y/n

At the same time you could master these **Things to Know**:
26: How Do You Avoid Being Struck by Lightning? • 43: How Do Clouds Stay Up? • 56: What Is the Scariest Thing in the World?

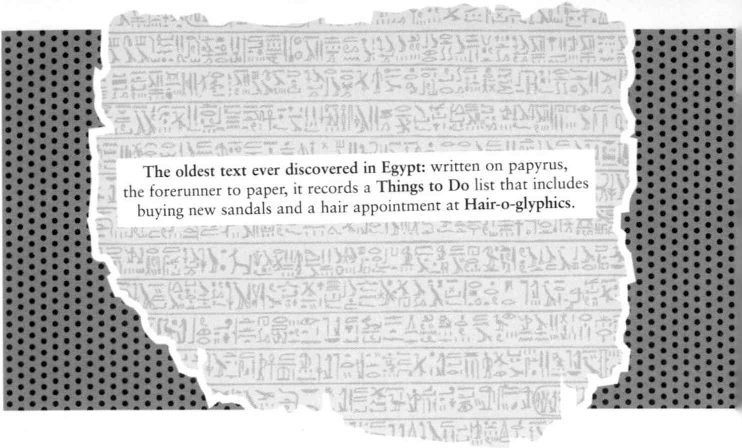

The oldest text ever discovered in Egypt: written on papyrus, the forerunner to paper, it records a Things to Do list that includes buying new sandals and a hair appointment at Hair-o-glyphics.

Who Invented Paper?

Writing has been around for a lot longer than paper. But when paper was invented it made things a whole lot easier—imagine having to gouge away at a lump of clay every time you wanted to take a shopping list to the supermarket.

Pulp Fiction

According to tradition, there was a single inventor of paper: T'sai Lun, a Chinese court official, who came up with the idea in about AD 105. (Recently, though, archaeologists have discovered evidence that probably puts the invention of paper about 200 years earlier than that.) Before paper, the Chinese used to write on silk—which was all well and good, but pretty expensive. The first paper used a type of plant called hemp and a few old rags, which were soaked and beaten to a pulp then spread on a bamboo frame and left to dry. Not only was it cheaper and much easier on the silkworms than using silk, but it was easier to write on too.

This handy new material spread throughout China and eventually to the rest of the world (though it took its time). It had reached Central Asia by about the 8th century, and by the 14th century there were paper mills in Europe. However, it remained something of a luxury until the 19th century when steam-driven paper-making machines made it possible to make paper from the fibers of wood pulp.

We get the word *paper* from . . . the Egyptians, who invented papyrus, made from the papyrus plant—a type of reed also used to make furniture, baskets, rope, and sandals. It was the best alternative to paper and was used until about the 11th century.

Who Invented Paper? **Form**

Once you have mastered this **Thing to Know**,
stick your Achieved Star here and fill in the form

Achieved

MAKE YOUR OWN PAPER

Making your own paper is a fun and very messy thing to do!
It can be a lengthy process, but the results are worth the effort.

WHAT YOU NEED

Junk mail	Hot water	Flower petals	Stapler
Waste paper	Blender or whisk	Glitter	Tea towels
Tissues	Food coloring	Large baking tray	Rolling pin
Bowl	Perfume	Screen	

BUILDING A SCREEN

You can make a screen from an old picture frame, stretching a piece of wire mesh across it. Ask an adult to help you staple the mesh to the frame. If you don't want to make a frame, you can buy ready-made ones from an art shop.

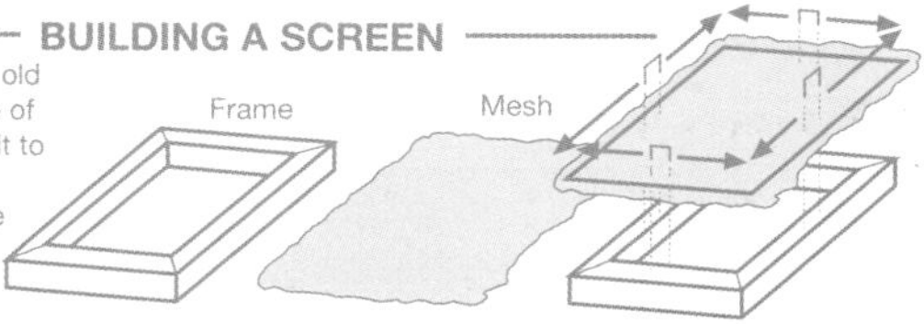

WHAT TO DO

1. Tear the paper and tissues into pieces of about 1 in and place them into a bowl. Add hot water. Make sure all the paper is soaked through.

2. Leave the mixture to stand overnight.

3. When you're happy with the softness of the paper, rip it up into the smallest pieces you can. Blend your mixture into a pulp with the whisk. If you have an electric blender, use it instead, as it is less time-consuming and your mixture will be more even than if you whisk it by hand.

4. If you want to add things to your paper, now is the time. You could add food coloring to give it color, fragrance to give it a nice smell, and flower petals or glitter to make it interesting.

5. Pour water into a large baking tray and add your pulp. Stir the mixture with your hands. The thicker the mixture, the thicker your paper will be.

6. Now you will need the screen. Place your screen into the baking tray and swirl it around to pick up the pulp, using your hands to evenly distribute the mixture across the screen. Lift the screen out and let the excess water drain away. If you find holes in your paper, return it to the mix and add more pulp to fill in the gaps.

7. Lay tea towels on a work surface. When your screen is evenly covered in the pulp, hold it above the towels, flip it over, and gently tap on the top. When you lift the screen away, hopefully the newly formed paper sheet will be left on the towels.

8. Take a rolling pin and gently squeeze out any excess water in your paper sheet. Then take your sheet off the kitchen towels and leave to dry somewhere warm and out of the way.

How do you rate your papermaking skills?

Poor Okay Good Very good Excellent

At the same time you could master these **Things to Know**:
24: When Did Money Start Making the World Go Around? • 92: When Was Writing Invented? • 93: Did People Make Everything from Stone in the Stone Age?

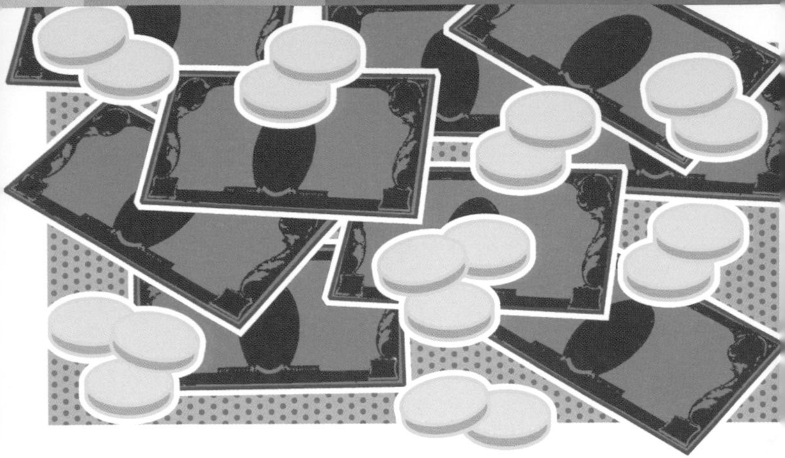

How Can I Win Millions?

It might not put you up there with Bill Gates, but winning the lottery would probably make a big difference to the size of your wardrobe and where you go on your vacations. So how do you do it?

The bad news is that you have to be 18 or over to play the lottery. And the even worse news is that your chances of winning are slim. But you might still want to pay your $1 and take a shot at winning, however remote the chance is. After all, what can a dollar buy you? A chocolate bar? By missing out on the chocolate you *could* win millions of dollars—that's why so many people choose to play despite the odds.

The first modern lottery in the U.S. was established in New Hampshire. Today, lotteries are in 41 states and the District of Columbia.

Some Lottery Tips

- Don't play the lottery more than two days before the draw. This is because you are more likely to die before the results are drawn than you are to win the jackpot.
- Don't go to the beach between buying your ticket and the draw. The chance of being attacked by a shark is 1 in 11 million, which is less than your odds of winning (and this would ruin your big moment).
- Don't go out in a thunderstorm prior to the draw: you're over four times more likely to be struck by lightning than you are to win the jackpot.

You can improve your chances of not having to share the prize money if you do win the jackpot. Avoid popular "lucky" numbers, like 7 and 11, and 1 to 31, which are days of the month and more likely to be picked to match people's birthdays, etc.

How Can I Win Millions? **Form**

Once you have mastered this **Thing to Know**, stick your Achieved Star here and fill in the form

Achieved

I SHOULD BE SO LUCKY

Everyone has a lucky number. What's yours?

Write your lucky number here.

Why is this your lucky number?

When has it been lucky for you?

WHAT ARE THE CHANCES OF THAT?

A coincidence is when two or more things occur at the same time by chance. Life is full of them—some good, some bad, some incredible—e.g., we see a total eclipse because the Moon is 400 times nearer to the Earth than the Sun, which is 400 times bigger than the Moon, and the Moon happens to pass precisely in front of the Sun, blocking it out completely.

Have you ever said the same thing at the same time as someone else?	y/n
Has someone called or visited you just as you were thinking or talking about them?	y/n
Have you ever met someone who shares the same birthday as you?	y/n
Have you ever been on vacation and bumped into someone you know?	y/n
Have you ever wished for something and had it come true in the same week?	y/n
Have you ever met someone who looks like you?	y/n
Have you met someone with your exact same name?	y/n
Have you ever met someone who looks like you AND shares your name?	y/n

What is the most unbelievable coincidence that has happened to you?

What do you think the chances are of the following things happening?

The person you like, liking you	%
You bumping into that person next time you're out	%
Someone filling in this form at the same time as you	%
Rain coming down just as you're about to go outside	%

At the same time you could master these **Things to Know**:
24: When Did Money Start Making the World Go Around? • 47: Who Is the Richest Person in the World? • 84: What Is the Sixth Sense? • 85: Why Do We Dream?

What Is Spontaneous Human Combustion?

Spontaneous human combustion (SHC) is the strange phenomenon of people suddenly bursting into flames for no apparent reason. There are many records of mysterious burned human remains, going back more than 300 years, but no conclusive proof of SHC, whatever it is! Feeling a little hot under the collar?

Smoke Gets in Your Eyes

Among the most famous SHC cases is that of Mary Reeser, a 67-year-old woman from Florida who died in 1951. She'd been sitting in an armchair and all that remained of her was a slippered foot and a shrunken skull. Only the chair and a small circular part of the room had also been burned. Then there was Dr. Irving Bentley of Pennsylvania in 1966. Part of one leg was all that remained of him, and the rest of him had burned a three-foot hole through his bathroom floor.

In both cases, temperatures must have been thousands of degrees to accoun for the damage, and yet the fire was confined to a small area around the person. It all seems very spooky, but it could be that the fires were started accidentally and the unfortunate people burned because there is enough flammable material inside the body to create a "wick effect," like a candle. Experiments using dead pigs have proven that this can happen without setting fire to the surrounding area. And in the case of Mary Reeser, she had taken sleeping pills, was wearing flammable clothing, and had been smoking. But you'll have to decide for yourself if there's a rational explanation or not.

Literary cases: Charles Dickens used SHC to kill off an alcoholic character called Krook in his novel *Bleak House* in 1852. He researched the subject thoroughly and followed current thinking in making a connection between heavy drinking and SHC.

What Is Spontaneous Human Combustion? **Form**
Once you have mastered this **Thing to Know,** stick your Achieved Star here and fill in the form

Achieved

SHC CASES

Search the Internet and libraries for articles about suspected cases of SHC, and fill in the questions below.

FIRESTARTER

How many cases did you find? 0,0,0 cases

Did any occur in the same place? y/n

What were the three most unusual cases?

Case One

Case Two

Case Three

If no, list where the SHC cases occurred.

Case One

Case Two

Case Three

Where there more women or men? 0,0 male 0,0 female

In which country did SHC cases occur the most?

FIRESTOPPER

In case you do encounter someone who bursts into flames, or any other type of fire, it's a good idea to learn how to use a fire extinguisher. Please see directions below.

Remember **PASS**!

Pull the pin.

Aim the hose at the base of the fire.

Squeeze the lever to release the foam.

Sweep the hose from side to side until the fire is extinguished.

At the same time you could master these **Things to Know:**
14: Will Your Stomach Explode if You Eat Too Much? • 26: How Do You Avoid Being Struck by Lightning? • 75: How Can Birds Stand on Electric Wires and Not Be Toasted?

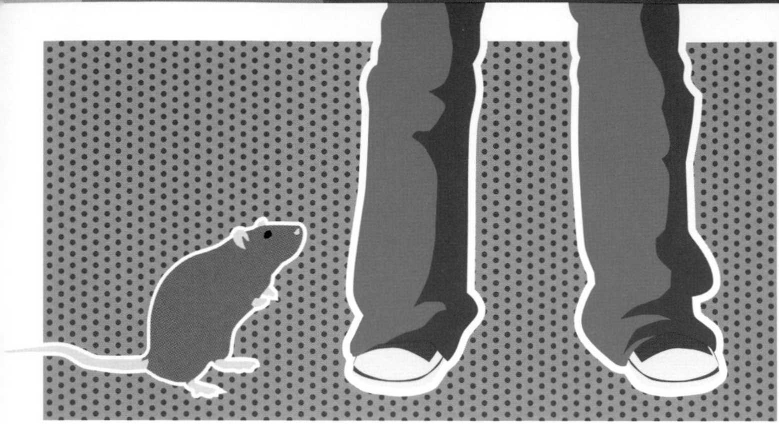

Are You Only Ever a Few Feet from a Rat in a Big City?

Like cockroaches, rats are adaptable creatures and reproduce quickly, which means there are a lot of them around. This is bad news for us because they carry more than thirty diseases, some of them serious (e.g., hantavirus pulmonary syndrome (HPS), leptospirosis, and salmonellosis), that they can spread to humans. They also contaminate and eat human food, and can destroy pipes and insulation and cause a risk of fire. So rats may be furry, but they're not our friends. Call the Pied Piper . . . or pest control if you see one.

You Dirty Rat

There are about 49 species of rat. The most common type found in the wild in the United States is the brown rat, or Norwegian rat, and it's most common wherever humans live (because they live on our trash)—i.e., in big cities. In the U.S., there are an estimated 150–175 million rats. But rat populations vary from place to place—a rat is more likely to survive a mild winter than a severe one, so there are likely to be more rats in, for example, Miami than in Minneapolis.

If you want to deter rats, the best thing you can do is make sure you don't leave any trash lying around uncovered. On the opposite page you'll find some signs to look out for in case rats are at work in an area near you.

Rats' bad rep: some people blame rats for the Black Death, but the disease was actually carried by the fleas that lived on them. Only when there weren't any juicy rats around (because they'd all died of the plague) did the fleas start biting people.

Are You Only Ever a Few Feet
from a Rat in a Big City? **Form**
Once you have mastered this **Thing to Know**,
stick your Achieved Star here and fill in the form

Achieved

AMAZING RAT FACTS

Test your knowledge of rats with this quiz. Once you've done the quiz, memorize the correct facts, then impress your friends to earn your star.

1. **What length can a fully grown brown rat grow to (including the tail)?**

(a) 6 in
(b) 12 in
(c) 18 in
(d) 24 in

2. **How small a hole can a fully grown brown rat squeeze through?**

(a) 0.6 in wide
(b) 1.4 in wide
(c) 2.2 in wide
(d) 3.8 in wide

3. **How many babies can a single female rat reproduce in one year?**

(a) About 25
(b) About 50
(c) About 75
(d) 100+

4. **What can't a rat do?**

(a) Vomit
(b) Burp
(c) See very well
(d) All of the above

5. **What is a group of rats called?**

(a) A mischief
(b) A gathering
(c) A meeting
(d) A rabble

6. **Which of these statements is false?**

(a) Rats have belly buttons.
(b) Rats are very clean animals.
(c) Rats have thumbs.
(d) A baby rat is a called a kitten.

7. **What part of their bodies do rats sweat through?**

(a) Ears
(b) Tail
(c) Feet
(d) Nose

8. **If a rat is caught out in open water, how long can it swim before it dies?**

(a) Three minutes
(b) Three hours
(c) Three days
(d) Three weeks

Answers at the back of the book.

Rats! I have rats. DO you? Here are some signs to look out for . . .

- Rat droppings. An adult rat's dropping is about a half inch long.
- Pattering or squeaking sounds at night (rats are nocturnal creatures).
- Gnawed wood or food.
- An unusual smell—both rats and mice have a pungent odor.
- Burrows outside—the entrance to a rat burrow is about 3–5 in across and might be found under tree roots.

At the same time you could master these **Things to Know**:
56: What Is the Scariest Thing in the World? • 64: Do Animals Cry? • 90: What Is the World's Most Poisonous Creature? • 97: What Is the World's Deadliest Disease?

Who Was the Most Bloodthirsty Pirate Ever?

Pirates specialized in being bloodthirsty. After all, if they didn't have fearsome reputations, no one would be afraid of them and give up their ships and treasure. So the competition for the most bloodthirsty pirate is pretty stiff.

The Scurviest Dog

The pirate who has gone down in history as the worst of the lot is Edward Teach, or Blackbeard to his friends. Here are some of the reasons:

- His appearance was designed to alarm: he had an extravagant black beard, carried six pistols, and stuck lighted cannon fuses under his hat so that he appeared in a cloud of black smoke.
- He kept his crew fearful with random acts of cruelty, e.g., he set fires below decks and forced his crew to stay there until he decided to let them out (he said it was to show them what hell was like), and he shot his second-in-command in the kneecap, crippling him, for no reason.
- He liked to drink. His favorite drink was a cocktail of rum and gunpowder.
- He was utterly ruthless with his victims. When one man refused to give up his diamond ring, Blackbeard simply sliced off his finger with his sword.

Blackbeard was finally killed when he was attacked by British troops. Supposedly, he was wounded 25 times before he died. His head was cut off and stuck on the bow of his ship. Legend has it that his headless body swam around his ship three times before it sank.

Organized crime on the high seas: there are still pirates around today—armed and dangerous—especially in South and Southeast Asia. They tend to prey on smaller ships and attack hundreds every year.

Who Was the Most Bloodthirsty
Pirate Ever? **Form**
Once you have mastered this **Thing to Know**,
stick your Achieved Star here and fill in the form

Achieved

BE A PIRATE FOR A DAY

International Talk Like a Pirate Day is September 19. Act and speak like a pirate for a whole day—on the official holiday or any other time! Here are tips to help you achieve your star.

PIRATE JARGON

KEY PIRATE WORDS

aye—yes

bounty—reward

cackle fruit—eggs

clap of thunder—a powerful drink

Davy Jones's locker—where dead pirates end up

duffle—everything you own

dungbie—rear end

ensign—flag

grog—drink

head—toilet

hornswoggle—to cheat

in Davy's grip—close to death

Jack o' Coins—your boss

lassie/wench—girl

league—3 miles

nipperkin—a small drink

pieces of eight—money

salmagundi—a meat dish

KEY PIRATE PHRASES

"All hands on deck!"—"Everyone ready for action!"

"Arrrr!"—say this a lot between words

"Avast!"—"Check this out!"

" 'Ave ye?"—"Have you?"

"Clap him in irons!"—"Put him in handcuffs!"

"Me 'arties!"—"My friends!"

"Shiver me timbers!"—an expression of shock

"There be . . ."—"There is . . ."

"You've got the Davies!"—"You're scared!"

USE THESE WORDS AS INSULTS

Drivelswigger!

Freebooter!

Landlubber!

Picaroon!

Powder monkey!

WARDROBE

a beard • an eye patch • a hat with three corners • a big belt • a bandana • clothes that don't match • a wooden leg • a hook for a hand • earrings • a parrot • a cutlass (a short curved sword)

Place a photograph of your pirate outfit here

PIRATE FLAG

Every pirate needs a flag to spread fear into the hearts of their victims. Draw your pirate flag below.

At the same time you could master these **Things to Know**:
30: What Is at the Bottom of the Ocean? • 47: Who Is the Richest Person in the World? • 56: What Is the Scariest Thing in the World? • 69: How Can I Win Millions?

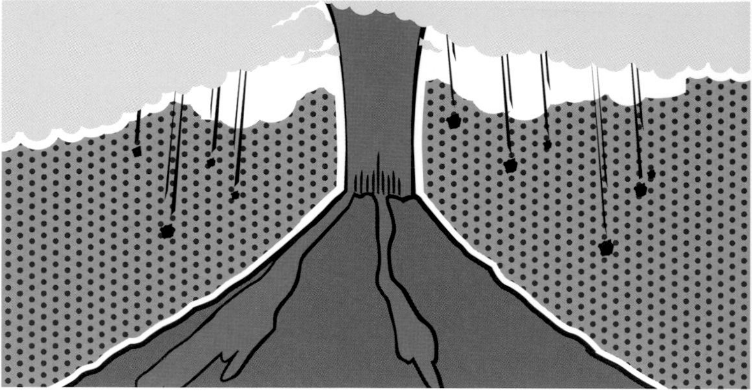

Pus—What Is It Good For?

It's gooey, it's gross, but if you've ever picked a scab or squeezed a rather juicy pimple, you'll have discovered the strangely satisfying ooze of pus.

To Squeeze or Not to Squeeze?

Just so we're clear, pus is the thick, runny stuff you find in pimples and wounds, usually whitish or yellowish in color. It's a response to bacteria, tiny organisms that can cause infections, disease, and all kinds of other horrors, such as especially smelly farts.

In your blood there are white cells called polymorphonuclear cells. These cells kill bacteria and send out a message to other white blood cells to join in the attack. The oozing white pus you see is made up of lots of dead polymorphonuclear cells and dead tissue. It's a sign that a wound is badly infected, but the body is fighting back. Try to see it as a good thing.

If you have a wound filled with pus, take it as your cue to clean it with an antiseptic and give your polymorphonuclear cells a helping hand.

How to Avoid a Pus-Filled Wound

1. Clean the wound *immediately* with soap and water.

2. Make sure you've gotten rid of any small bits of dirt or debris.

3. Apply an antiseptic cream.

4. If the wound is more painful a day later, it's probably infected and you might need to see a doctor.

Go to a doctor or emergency room immediately if you have a wound that seems deep, might have something in it that you can't remove, is more than about a half inch long, or won't stop bleeding.

Suppurating pustules! One more reason why pus is to be praised—it's responsible for some great words. Something that is producing pus is "suppurating" or "purulent." And a pus-filled pimple is called a "pustule." Now add a bit of class to your insults.

Pus—What Is It Good For? **Form**

Once you have mastered this **Thing to Know**, stick your Achieved Star here and fill in the form

Achieved

Accidents are inevitable. Write below how you received your best scars . . .

Where is your first scar?

Does it still hurt? y/n

How did you get it?

Did you pick the scab? y/n

If yes, was the wound full of pus? y/n

Where is your second scar?

Does it still hurt? y/n

How did you get it?

Did you pick the scab? y/n

If yes, was the wound full of pus? y/n

Where is your third scar?

Does it still hurt? y/n

How did you get it?

Did you pick the scab? y/n

If yes, was the scab full of pus? y/n

Your Scar Chart

Mark on the diagram below where your scars are, and in the space provided write how you got them.

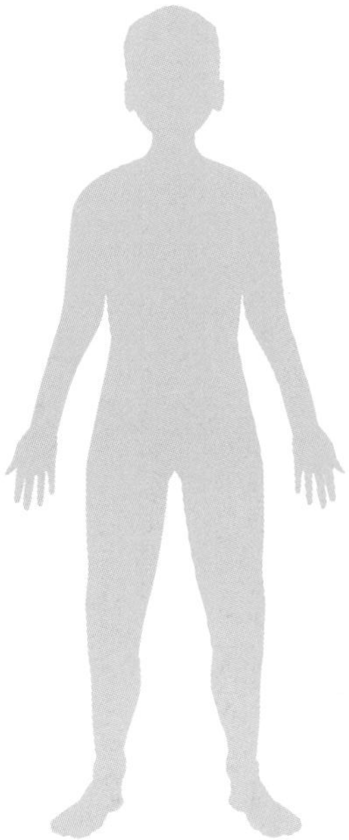

At the same time you could master these **Things to Know**:

5: Why Is Our Blood Red? • 37: Can You Sneeze with Your Eyes Open?

48: What Makes Farts So Smelly? • 98: Nails—What Are They Good For?

How Dangerous Is Quicksand?

Quicksand has a reputation of being like a monster, slowly devouring anything that comes close—many villains in films have met their end this way. But is this the real picture? What on earth is quicksand anyway?

It Sucks

Quicksand is just very wet sand, clay, or silt. It often looks just like ordinary sand. It's made by underground springs pushing water up into sand or silt, and it's found in most parts of the world and in all kinds of places—riverbanks, dry riverbeds, beaches, and hilly country. Earthquakes can cause quicksand too: the vibrations increase the pressure on water in the ground, causing it to mix with sand and soil. This is called liquefaction, and if it happens under a building, that building may sink or tip up. Now that's dangerous.

It might surprise you to know, however, that quicksand *can't* suck you down. In fact, it's pretty difficult to drown in a patch of quicksand—much more difficult than in ordinary water because the particles in quicksand help you to float. Nor is quicksand bottomless; in fact, it's not usually very deep at all—if you should find yourself in a patch you'll probably be able to touch the bottom and walk slowly to the nearest edge. If it is deeper, take off anything heavy, float on your back, and direct yourself toward the edge using your arms. If you struggle you'll sink deeper. Quicksand is only dangerous if you panic and start swallowing the sandy water.

Bogged down: if you were unlucky enough to fall into a bog and drown, your body would be preserved for centuries. The tannin in peat bogs kills the bacteria that would otherwise cause decay. The oldest bog body ever found is about 10,000 years old.

How Dangerous Is Quicksand? **Form**

Once you have mastered this **Thing to Know**, stick your Achieved Star here and fill in the form

Achieved

HOW TO MAKE QUICKSAND

The easiest place to make quicksand is on the beach close to the ocean (but not too close). Pick a spot to dig a hole. Before digging the hole you need to collect a pile of slightly moist sand. Don't go for the wet sand nearest to the sea, but scrape off the top level of dry sand further back and you should find some slightly darker colored sand underneath.

Next to your pile of moist sand, start digging a hole. Your hole needs to be about one and a half feet wide and deep.

As you dig down, the sides of the hole will start to cave in, so you need to dig fast! As soon as the walls begin to crack and sea seeps in, you must fill the hole up with the moist sand you prepared earlier.

When you've totally filled in the hole, level off the sand but don't compress it. Place a sign saying DANGER! next to your hole to warn people not to go near it. After some minutes the surface should start to darken as the sand becomes saturated with water. It's time to try out your quicksand! Are you brave enough to step in it?

At the same time you could master these **Things to Know**:
38: Why Is the Ocean Salty? • 51: How Do You Survive on a Desert Island? • 62: How Do You Survive an Earthquake? • 72: Who Was the Most Bloodthirsty Pirate Ever?

How Can Birds Stand on Electric Wires and Not Be Toasted?

You have to admit, it's a good trick. Is it because birds have special electricity-resistant legs?

Bird on a Wire

If you were able to float up to a power line without touching anything, you'd be able to stand on it as well (although you might not be very comfortable). This is because an electrical current always follows the path of least resistance: when the current reaches the legs of the bird it *could* flow up the bird's legs, but it will always continue to flow along the metal cable because metal is a very good conductor of electricity, whereas a bird's legs are more resistant.

If the bird were somehow able to hold a very long pole in its beak and touch it to the ground, or lean its wing against a nearby tree or the power-line pole it would be toasted instantly. Electrical current will always flow to the earth, so if the bird is touching something that provides a path to the ground, the electricity will flow through it. Luckily, birds very seldom carry long poles.

But the same could happen to you if you were to provide a path between a live electrical wire and the ground. So never fly kites, balloons, or model airplanes near power lines, and don't climb trees near them either. In fact, the safest thing to do is stay away from power poles and lines altogether!

Birdbrained: birds of prey do get killed by power lines. They have such a big wingspan that they sometimes touch the pole top (which is grounded) at the same time as they touch the wire.

How Can Birds Stand on Electric Wires and Not Be Toasted? **Form**

Once you have mastered this **Thing to Know**, stick your Achieved Star here and fill in the form

Achieved

CREATE YOUR OWN ELECTRICITY

You can create your own electricity with the simplest of items and a little effort. An electric charge can be produced through friction: this buildup is called static electricity. Static electricity can be transmitted from one object to another. Try the experiments below.

EXPERIMENT ONE—CREATING STATIC

You can make a balloon stick to the wall by rubbing the balloon on a wool sweater. The balloon has a negative charge whereas the sweater has a positive charge. Positive electrons are transferred to the balloon, and static is created. You can also use your hair if you don't have a sweater.

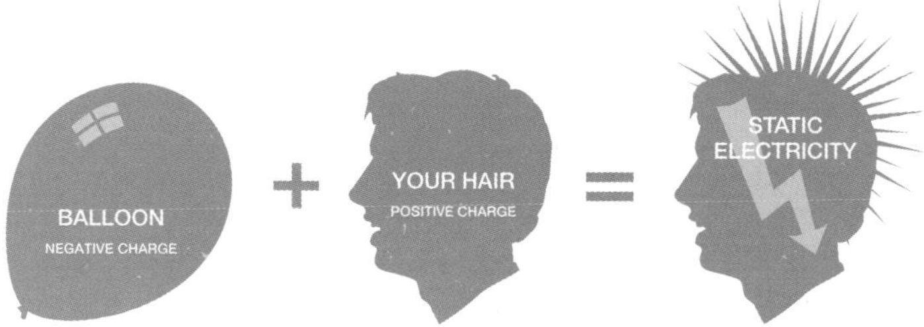

EXPERIMENT TWO—CREATING SPARKS

You can also create a spark of "lightning" with static electricity.

1. Rub your shoe soles vigorously on a nylon carpet, then go touch something. You should see a spark (an electrostatic discharge or ESD) jump from you to the object. You'll probably feel a tingle too!

2. You can create static with other items too. Polyester clothing can create sparks. Wear such an item of clothing all day, then, just before you go to bed, turn off the light and take off the item quickly. You should see sparks.

At the same time you could master these **Things to Know**:
**26: How Do You Avoid Being Struck by Lightning? • 54: Are Bats Really Blind?
63: How Many People Are Flying Through the Air at Any One Time?**

How Do You Survive an Avalanche?

If you plan on skiing, snowboarding, or hiking in the mountains, this is something you need to know.

'Snow Joke

An avalanche is a huge mass of snow rushing down a mountain at up to 80 mph. If it's powdery snow, it isn't usually dangerous. But a "slab avalanche" (when a big chunk of heavy snow breaks away from weaker snow underneath it) can be bad news. Afterward, the snow quickly sets like concrete. Heavy snowfalls or sudden changes in temperature can make snow unstable.

Check avalanche reports, look out for cracks in the snow, and avoid steep slopes. But if you're still unlucky enough to get caught in an avalanche . . .

1. Always carry your phone and an avalanche beacon (or "transceiver"), which will tell rescuers where you are.
2. Let go of your skis and poles.
3. Try using swimming motions to keep close to the surface of the snow.
4. Try to make an air space in front of your face with your hands as the avalanche slows down.
5. If you end up near the surface, try to stick out an arm or a leg so that rescuers can find you quickly.
6. Only shout out when you think a rescuer is nearby: you don't want to waste precious air, and you won't be heard unless someone's close anyway.

The worst-ever avalanche happened in Yungay, Peru, in 1970. An earthquake caused tons of ice, rock, and snow to come crashing down the highest mountain in Peru, destroying the city and killing nearly all of its 20,000 inhabitants.

How Do You Survive an Avalanche? **Form**

Once you have mastered this **Thing to Know**, stick your Achieved Star here and fill in the form

Achieved

THAT'S ONE BIG SNOWMAN!

Next time it snows, try to make the biggest snowman you can!

How tall was your snowman? 0 0 ft

Date you built your snowman

m m d d y y y y

How cold was it as you built your snowman? °F

Where did you build him?

Who helped you to build him?

How many times taller than you was your snowman? 0 0 . 0 times

World's tallest snowman: his name was Angus, King of the Mountain, and he measured more than 113 ft. He took 14 days to build, in February 1999, in the town of Bethel, Maine. Tires were used for his eyes and instead of twigs for arms, he had trees!

At the same time you could master these **Things to Know**:
16: How Do Mountains Grow? • 32: What Is an Ice Age (and When Are We Due for Another One)? • 62: How Do You Survive an Earthquake?

Why Do People Kiss (and Animals Don't)?

When you think about it, puckering up and pressing your mouth against someone else's, exchanging spit (and plenty of bacteria), is a pretty odd thing to do. Whoever thought of it must have gotten quite a reaction the first time they tried it out!

Love and Kisses

In parts of the South Pacific and Africa people only learned about kissing from European visitors in the 1700s. So someone somewhere must have started doing it, decided it was a great idea, and passed it on to almost everyone else in the world. We don't know who that person was, but the first references to it are from India, around 1500 BC. The Greeks and Romans enthusiastically took it up—the Romans even invented a whole kissing vocabulary: a polite peck was an *osculum*, a full lip kiss was a *basium*, and a really big smooch was a *saviolum*. Before long everyone was doing it.

Kissing may have started from the practice of nose rubbing or sniffing one another's faces (you can tell a surprising amount from someone's scent, apparently, including whether they're genetically different enough to produce healthy offspring). Once people had discovered it, they probably kept going because the lips and tongue are among the most sensitive parts of our bodies, and feel-good chemicals are released during a good kiss. It could also be that chemicals in saliva are part of the reason we're attracted to one another (or not).

We aren't the only animals who kiss. Chimps and gorillas kiss as a sign of affection or part of mating too. But most animals have other ways to express the way they feel, e.g., displaying tail feathers, glowing in the dark, or performing elaborate dances.

Why Do People Kiss
(and Animals Don't)? **Form**
Once you have mastered this **Thing to Know**,
stick your Achieved Star here and fill in the form

Achieved

CUSTOMS AND TRADITIONS

Test your knowledge of customs and traditions with this quiz. Once you've done the quiz, memorize the correct facts, then impress your friends to earn your star.

1. **In Western cultures we kiss or shake hands when we meet. How do people greet each other in Inuit society?**

(a) With a pat on the back
(b) By rubbing noses
(c) With a snowball in the face
(d) By hitting each other with a fish

2. **In Thailand, what is it rude to do?**

(a) Touch a person on the head
(b) Point your foot toward someone
(c) Shout
(d) All of the above

3. **In which of the following countries do you NOT have to take off your shoes when you enter someone's house?**

(a) Egypt
(b) Korea
(c) China
(d) Japan

4. **When introduced to someone in China, what will you be given?**

(a) A handshake
(b) A gift
(c) A big smile
(d) A business card

5. **Which of the following is a British regional custom?**

(a) Rolling cheese down a hill
(b) Parading a giant straw bear around town
(c) Men dancing with reindeer antlers
(d) All of the above

6. **How long could a traditional wedding in Iceland take?**

(a) 1 hour
(b) 1 day
(c) 1 week
(d) 1 month

7. **In which country did the tradition of "wearing something blue" at a wedding originate?**

(a) Israel
(b) Venezuela
(c) Chile
(d) Egypt

8. **Where is it considered rude to open a gift as soon as you get it?**

(a) Russia
(b) India
(c) Korea
(d) Japan

9. **When should you bow in Japan?**

(a) When saying hello and good-bye
(b) When thanking and apologizing
(c) When congratulating
(d) All of the above

10. **Which of the following statements is NOT true. By way of greeting, it is customary in the Middle East for . . .**

(a) . . . men and women to shake hands
(b) . . . men to kiss each other on the cheeks
(c) . . . men to kiss women on the cheeks, providing they are related by blood
(d) . . . women to kiss each other on the cheeks

Answers at the back of the book.

At the same time you could master these **Things to Know**:
2: What Is DNA (and Are We All That Different from Chimps)?
61: Were All Romans from Rome? • 64: Do Animals Cry?

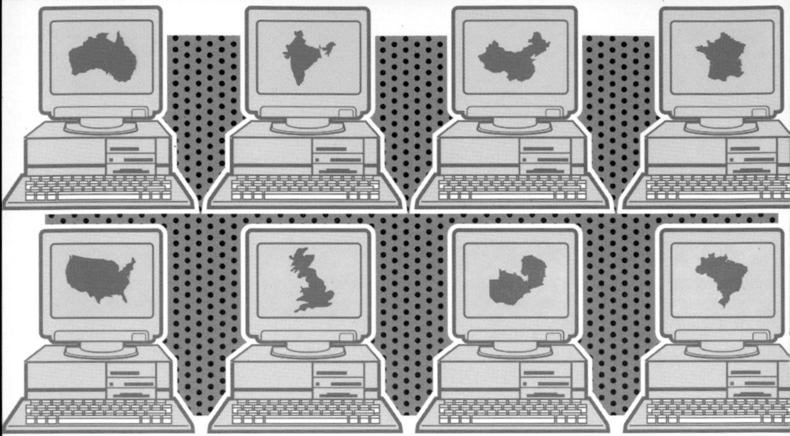

Who Invented the Internet?

It would be nice to imagine someone playing around on a computer one day and exclaiming, "Eureka! A global network of millions of computers and computer networks, allowing instant communication and sharing of information! I'll call it the Internet!" But it didn't quite happen that way.

Networking

The Internet started out as a computer network in the United States Department of Defense called ARPAnet (after the Advanced Research Projects Agency). Rather scarily, the idea was to make a network that would allow the military to communicate effectively in the event of a nuclear war. The network had to be designed so that it could operate even if parts of it disappeared in a terrifying nuclear apocalypse. It was cleverly designed as lots of different networks that could communicate with one another in various ways. It was so successful that the idea eventually became the Internet we know and love, although we don't have any one person to thank for it.

So how did it become so popular? Well, the Internet really took off with the development of e-mail (which actually predates the Internet) and the birth of the World Wide Web—an interactive world of shared information accessible via the Internet. We can thank Tim Berners-Lee, a computer scientist working for the European Centre for Nuclear Research, for inventing the World Wide Web—which is how most of us use the Internet.

How big is the Web? Enormous. There are literally billions of Web sites. Just one search engine, Google, has indexed more than 8 billion Web pages—and there are many more being created each day. Do you have one yet?

Who Invented the Internet? **Form**

Once you have mastered this **Thing to Know**,
stick your Achieved Star here and fill in the form

Achieved

INTERNET

The Internet is an excellent tool for finding out anything you want at the touch of a button.
See if the Internet can help you complete the tasks and questions below.

Type your name into the Internet.

How many other people with your name did you find? 0 0 0

Find out about the origin of your last name.

If you have a Web cam, use it to talk to a friend in another country. Whom did you contact?

Find a blog you like. What is it called?

Send an e-mail to everyone you know and ask them to send it on to everyone they know. See how long it takes before you get the same e-mail back. How long did it take?

hours · days · weeks · months · years · you never got it back

Find three great facts about the town you live in.

What are your top five Web sites?

1.
2.
3.
4.
5.

Find 3 famous people who share your birthday.

1.
2.
3.

Look up your family tree. Find out about your great-great-grandparents. What were their names?

Your great-great-grandad's name here

0 0 0 0 < born died > 0 0 0 0

Your great-great-grandma's name here

0 0 0 0 < born died > 0 0 0 0

If you have your own Web site, what is on it?

At the same time you could master these **Things to Know**:
47: Who Is the Richest Person in the World? • 69: How Can I Win Millions?
87: Who Was the Smartest Person Ever?

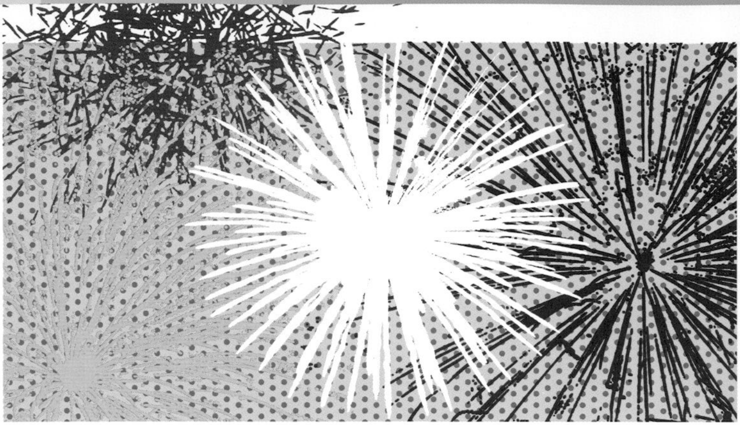

How Does a Firework Work?

Everyone loves going "oooooh" and "aaaaah" at fireworks displays, but how many spectators know how they actually work? Invented in China over 2,000 years ago, fireworks have been around awhile, so the basic structure is pretty simple.

Going with a Bang

A firework starts its journey into the night sky with someone lighting the fuse to a lifting charge. This sits underneath the main part of the firework, called the "shell." The lifting charge sends the shell flying up into the sky and lights the fuse to the shell at the same time. The shell is made up of the following:

- **A container**—usually made from paper or cardboard.
- **"Stars"**—the parts of the firework that will provide the bursts of light and color. They're formed into small shapes and contain iron, steel, aluminum, or zinc powder to make the sparkly parts.
- **A charge**—usually gunpowder, or something similar, to make the firework explode and set fire to the stars.
- **A fuse**—lit by the lifting charge. It takes some time for the fuse to burn down to the shell, so that it explodes when it's high up in the sky.

Modern-day fireworks can get incredibly complicated—they can burst in different phases and colors, and with different noises. They can have shells within shells within shells, so that just when you think the firework is over, it makes the biggest bang and brightest flash of all.

Snap, crackle, and bang! You can have daytime fireworks as well, popular in some parts of Spain. They consist of fewer flashes of light, which are hard to see during the day, but lots more noise and smoke.

How Does a Firework Work? **Form**

Once you have mastered this **Thing to Know,**
stick your Achieved Star here and fill in the form

Achieved

FIREWORK TYPES

Fireworks are becoming more and more elaborate, and louder and louder! Here are some of the types of firework you're likely to see at a public fireworks display. Have you seen them all?

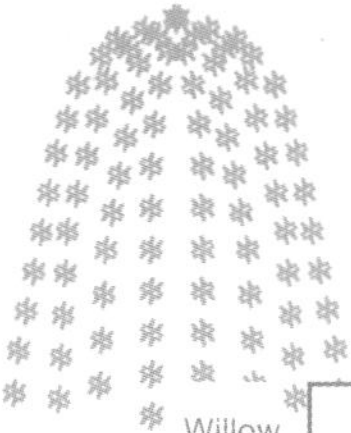

Willow ☐

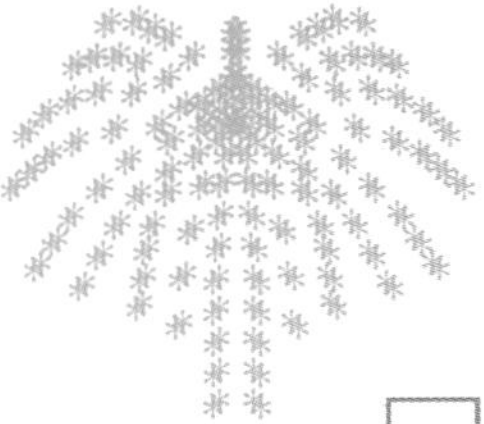

Chrysanthemum ☐

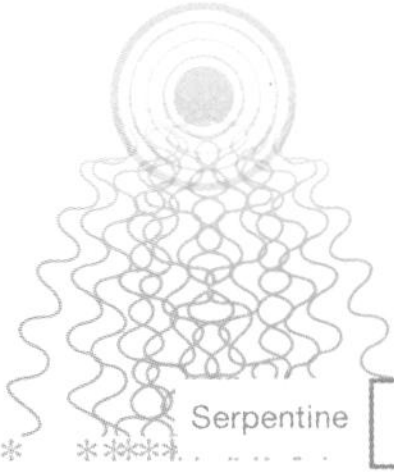

Serpentine ☐

Palm ☐

Ring ☐

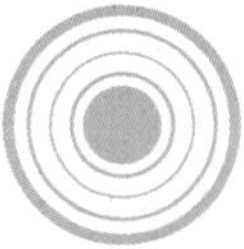

Maroon (a flash and a loud explosion) ☐

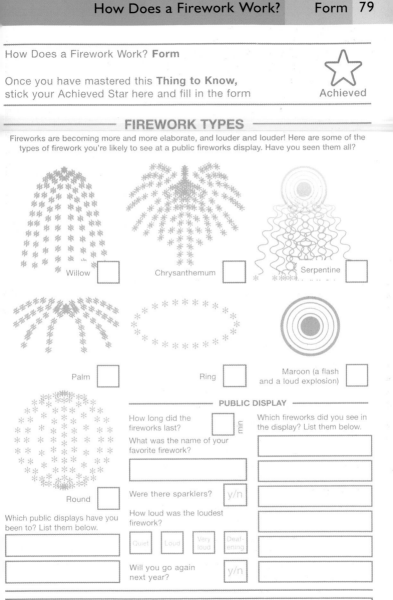

Round ☐

Which public displays have you been to? List them below.

☐

☐

PUBLIC DISPLAY

How long did the fireworks last? ☐ min

What was the name of your favorite firework?

☐

Were there sparklers? y/n

How loud was the loudest firework?

Quiet | Loud | Very loud | Deafening

Will you go again next year? y/n

Which fireworks did you see in the display? List them below.

☐

☐

☐

☐

☐

☐

At the same time you could master these **Things to Know**:
25: If Light Is Invisible, How Can We See? • 70: What Is Spontaneous Human Combustion? • 83: Where Is the Night Sky Multicolored?

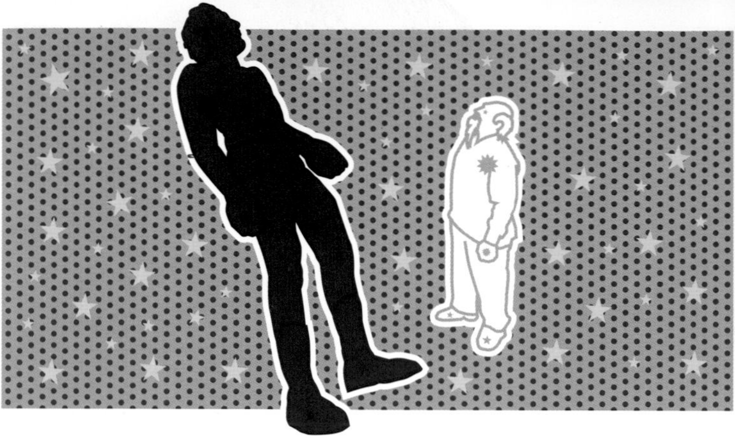

Where Can You Find Red Giants and White Dwarves?

No, not in fairy tales—in space! White dwarves and red giants are both types of stars and perhaps two of the strangest things in the universe.

Starlight, Star Bright

All stars convert hydrogen to helium to make light and heat. A red giant is a star reaching the end of its life.

- Over time, the hydrogen "fuel" inside a star runs out, leaving helium in the center. As the star starts to cool and contract, the outer layers collapse in, making the pressure and temperature rise until the helium starts to burn—and this makes the star expand, bigger and bigger. It becomes a giant!
- The lower temperature at the surface of red giants gives them their color. You can see a red giant in the night sky: Betelgeuse in the constellation of Orion.

A white dwarf is what's left of a small- to medium-sized star after its phase as a red giant.

- The star sheds its outer layers, leaving a core made up mostly of carbon.
- The core becomes very dense—so dense that a teaspoonful of white dwarf would weigh as much as an elephant.
- It also becomes very hot, which gives it its white color.
- Eventually, after billions of years, white dwarves gradually cool to become black dwarves (which don't give out any light).

In about five billion years our Sun will become a red giant, which means it could extend as far as the orbit of Mars (good-bye Earth!), but it would generate less heat—about a third of its present heat. Eventually it would become a white dwarf.

Where Can You Find Red Giants and White Dwarves? **Form**

Once you have mastered this **Thing to Know,** stick your Achieved Star here and fill in the form

Achieved

THE LIFE EXPECTANCY OF OUR SUN

OUR SOLAR SYSTEM

This is our solar system at present. Our Sun is approximately 5 billion years old and is halfway through its life.

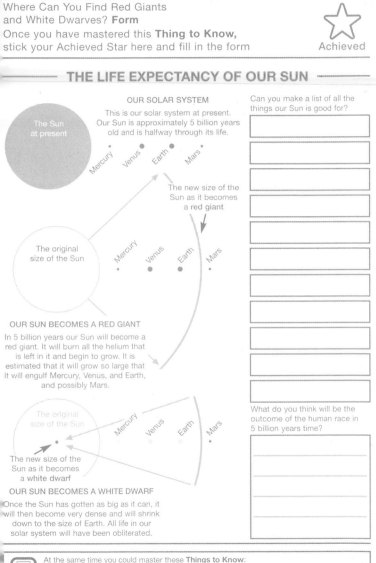

OUR SUN BECOMES A RED GIANT

In 5 billion years our Sun will become a red giant. It will burn all the helium that is left in it and begin to grow. It is estimated that it will grow so large that it will engulf Mercury, Venus, and Earth, and possibly Mars.

OUR SUN BECOMES A WHITE DWARF

Once the Sun has gotten as big as it can, it will then become very dense and will shrink down to the size of Earth. All life in our solar system will have been obliterated.

Can you make a list of all the things our Sun is good for?

What do you think will be the outcome of the human race in 5 billion years time?

At the same time you could master these **Things to Know**:
8: Is Time Travel Possible? • 12: How Big Is the Universe? • 21: What Is the Solar System (and Could It Fit in Your Yard)? • 101: What Would Happen to You in a Black Hole?

Why Do Camels Have Humps?

Camels have a bad reputation and are said to spit a lot. But what's the truth about their bad tempers, their bad habits—and their humps?

Grumpy and Humpy

All camels have humps. A Bactrian (or Asian) camel has two humps, and a dromedary (or Arabian camel) has one. But the humps aren't for storing water as many people think: camels store fat in their humps and use it as a source of energy when there's no food. A camel's hump (or humps) shrinks when it hasn't eaten for a while.

It's true that camels spit when they're angry. Like cows, they have four separate parts to their stomach and can regurgitate undigested food. When they're annoyed, they can spit their foul-smelling stomach contents at whatever is bothering them, but they rarely spit at people. Like most animals, if they're treated well, they're generally pretty good-natured. Some of their bad reputation might come from the fact that they make all sorts of grumpy-sounding grunting noises when they get up—but it doesn't mean that they're in a bad mood.

Clever Camels

Camels have adapted to living in the desert. For example . . .

Camels don't pant and hardly sweat, and the moisture in their breath trickles down a groove back into the mouth to be recycled.

They can close their nostrils between breaths to stop sand from getting in.

Camels walk on soft pads specially adapted to travel on sand.

There are other ways in which camels are well adapted to desert life. The quiz on the opposite page will test you on these and other desert facts.

Camels were brought to Australia from the Middle East in the 1800s to help with transportation across the vast deserts there. Now Australia is one of the only places left in the world with herds of wild camels. Some of them are exported to the Middle East.

Why Do Camels Have Humps? **Form**

Once you have mastered this **Thing to Know**, stick your Achieved Star here and fill in the form

Achieved

DESERT LIFE QUIZ

Test your knowledge of camels and the desert with this quiz. Once you've done the quiz, memorize the correct facts, then impress your friends to earn your star.

1. The Sahara desert is the largest subtropical desert in the world. How big is it?

(a) Almost 400,000 square mi
(b) Over 1 million square mi
(c) About 2 million square mi
(d) Over 3 million square mi

2. What do camels have three of?

(a) Big toes
(b) Bladders
(c) Nostrils
(d) Eyelids

3. How many gallons of water can a camel drink in just ten minutes?

(a) 9
(b) 18
(c) 27
(d) 36

4. Where hasn't it rained for 400 years?

(a) Atacama desert, Chile
(b) Gobi desert, Mongolia
(c) Sahara desert, Africa
(d) Tanami desert, Australia

5. Up to roughly what age can camels live?

(a) 25
(b) 50
(c) 75
(d) 100

6. By what name are camels also known?

(a) Trucks of the desert
(b) Ships of the desert
(c) Vans of the desert
(d) Tanks of the desert

7. The camel is one of the earliest animals to be domesticated by humans. Roughly how long ago did this happen?

(a) 500 years ago
(b) 1,000 years ago
(c) 5,000 years ago
(d) 10,000 years ago

8. What is the highest temperature ever reached in the Sahara desert region?

(a) 115°F
(b) 122°F
(c) 129°F
(d) 136°F

9. What use have people found for camel dung?

(a) Warding off evil spirits
(b) Annoying the tourists
(c) Keeping the flies away
(d) Making a fire

10. For roughly how long can a camel go without water?

(a) 10 days
(b) 20 days
(c) 1 month
(d) 2 months

Answers at the back of the book.

At the same time you could master these **Things to Know**:
3: Why Don't Fish Drown? • 40: How Did the Ancient Egyptians Make the Pyramids? 50: Where on Earth Is the Coldest Place? • 74: How Dangerous Is Quicksand?

Why Are There 60 Seconds in a Minute?

It's easy to see how days were divided into days and nights—what with the rising and setting of the Sun—but why then divide them up into units of 24 hours, etc.?

Time Out

It could all have been much less complicated if time were divided in a simpler way, using multiples of 10. The ancient Babylonians are to blame. Unlike our number system, which is based on 10, they adapted a system from the ancient Sumerians before them, based on 60—a useful number that is divisible by lots of other numbers, such as 5, 6, 12, 30, etc. The number 12 was particularly good for counting because, if you look at your palm, you'll see that each of your four fingers is divided into three segments—and you can use your thumb to count them. This sort of trick was pretty useful in the days before cash registers. You won't be surprised to know that as well as time, we have the Babylonians to thank for the 12 signs of the zodiac, 360 degrees in a circle, and 12 inches in a foot.

We don't know exactly how it was figured out, but maybe the Babylonians started by basing the smallest measurement of a second on a heartbeat (a resting heartbeat is about one second), then made 60 seconds a minute (since they were so fond of the number 60) and 60 minutes an hour. 60 hours isn't a particularly useful period of time, but 24 hours is a day, and, handily for the Babylonians, it's 2 x 12. And that can be used to divide the day into two equal parts of 12.

The French tried out decimal time during the French Revolution in 1793, dividing the day, hours, and minutes into ten parts. Midnight was at ten o'clock and midday at five. It didn't catch on, so they tried again in 1897, only to abandon the idea in 1900.

Why Are There 60
Seconds in a Minute? **Form**
Once you have mastered this **Thing to Know,**
stick your Achieved Star here and fill in the form

Achieved

GONE IN 60 SECONDS

Here are four games that you can play in just one minute!

HOLD YOUR BREATH

Get your friends together and see who can hold their breath the longest. Be sure to breathe when you need to so you won't pass out! Who is the best at this game?

And who is the worst?

What was the winning time? 0 0 . 0 secs

What was your best time? 0 0 . 0 secs

Why did you stop?

Ran out of breath ☐ Someone made you laugh ☐

CRACKER CHALLENGE

Can you eat more than three crackers in one minute? This task is harder than it sounds! There is only one rule: you're not allowed any liquid to help wash the crackers down!

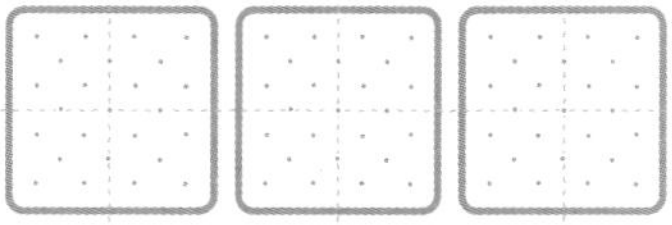

On the crackers above, color in the amount you managed to finish. If it was a bad attempt, keep trying until you eat at least two crackers.

Who did the best? Write the winner's name here.

YES AND NO GAME

The Yes and No game is a very simple idea, but it can be really difficult to win. All you have to do is avoid saying yes or no for a minute while someone else asks you lots of questions. If you make it through a minute, you win. If your opponent tricks you into saying yes or no, they win.

Who is the best at this game?

And who is the worst?

If you don't stop the clock after a minute, what's the longest time you can keep going without saying yes or no? 0 0 . 0 mins

What was the quickest time you got caught out in? 0 0 . 0 mins

JUST A MINUTE!

The object of this game is to speak for one minute on a chosen subject without hesitation (which includes ums and ers), repetition, or deviation (going off the subject). The minute is paused every time someone is challenged for breaking the rules, and if the challenge is fair, play passes to the person who made the challenge.

POINTS: You score 3 points for talking for the whole minute without interruption, 1 point for each correct challenge, and 2 points if you're the person talking when the full minute is up.

Who is the best at this game?

And who is the worst?

What was the hardest subject to talk about?

At the same time you could master these **Things to Know**:
29: How Long Is a Light-year? • 53: Where Does the Sun Go at Night?
100: When Was the First Leap Year and Why Do We Need Them?

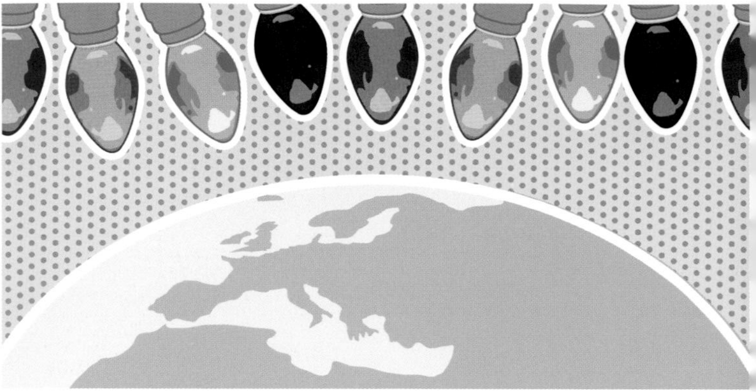

Where Is the Night Sky Multicolored?

You'd have to travel to the ends of the Earth to find colors in the night sky. Ever heard of the northern lights? Do you know what they are or where to find them?

The Light Fantastic

The northern lights, or aurora borealis, are a natural display of colored lights moving across the sky. They can be seen in areas close to the North Pole (but can sometimes be seen as far south as Scotland), and there's a southern version too—the aurora australis, which can be seen near the South Pole.

Although most visible at night, northern lights are actually the work of the Sun. The Sun is not a calm place, and when huge explosions and flares happen on the surface, a stream of particles are ejected and go hurtling through space at speeds up to 620 mi per second! This is called "solar wind," and because the Earth is surrounded by a magnetic field, some of the electrically charged particles of solar wind are captured and head to the magnetic North and South Poles, where they collide with the molecules in the atmosphere and release their energy as light.

If you want to see the northern lights, the best time to go north is September to March. The light display can be unpredictable and can only be seen on clear, dark nights. You'll need to go to the northernmost parts of Scandinavia, Canada, Siberia, or Greenland, but it'll be worth it—the lights are spectacular.

Other auroras: Earth isn't the only planet to experience auroras. Images taken by the Hubble Space Telescope reveal circles of auroral light at the poles on Jupiter and Saturn, but sadly there's no one around to enjoy them.

Where Is the Night Sky Multicolored? **Form**

Once you have mastered this **Thing to Know**, stick your Achieved Star here and fill in the form

Achieved

— THE ATMOSPHERE —

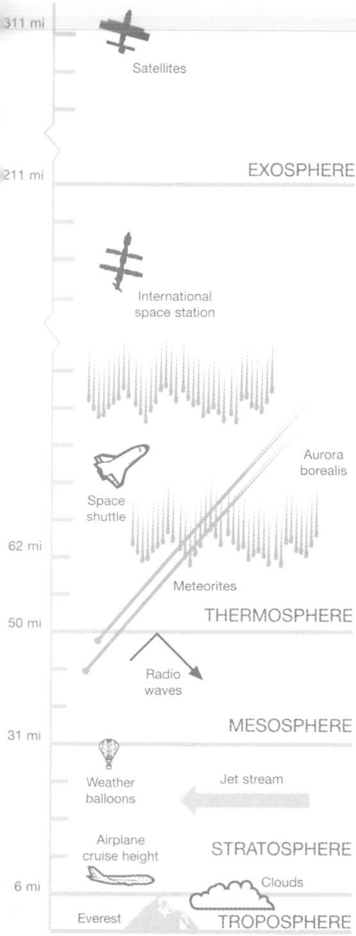

The atmosphere is made up of various layers that get thinner and thinner until they join space. If you travel higher than 50 mi you can be classed as an astronaut.

EXOSPHERE

This is the uppermost layer of the atmosphere. The height of the exosphere goes up to 6,214 mi. This is the area that satellites orbit in.

THERMOSPHERE

The thermosphere is where the aurora borealis (or northern lights) appear. This phenomenon occurs at a height of 62 mi in the Earth's atmosphere. Solar activity in this layer can cause temperatures of up to 3,632°F.

MESOSPHERE

Meteors burn up in this part of the atmosphere (see **Thing to Know** No. 52). The temperatures in the mesophere layer can reach –148°F.

STRATOSPHERE

You travel through the Earth's stratosphere when you're in a plane above the clouds. The stratosphere contains the jet stream, which is fast flowing air currents that flow west to east. If a plane catches a jet stream it can go faster and may arrive at its destination earlier. On the other hand, it may arrive late going the other way.

TROPOSPHERE

The troposhere contains approximately 85% of the air we breathe. This is the area where most of the weather occurs and where clouds form.

On the diagram opposite, draw lines to indicate (a) how high you've been in the atmosphere so far, and (b) how high you'd like to travel into the atmosphere.

At the same time you could master these **Things to Know**:
20: Which Way Is North? • 25: If Light Is Invisible, How Can We See?
52: Could a Rock Destroy Our Planet? • 79: How Does a Firework Work?

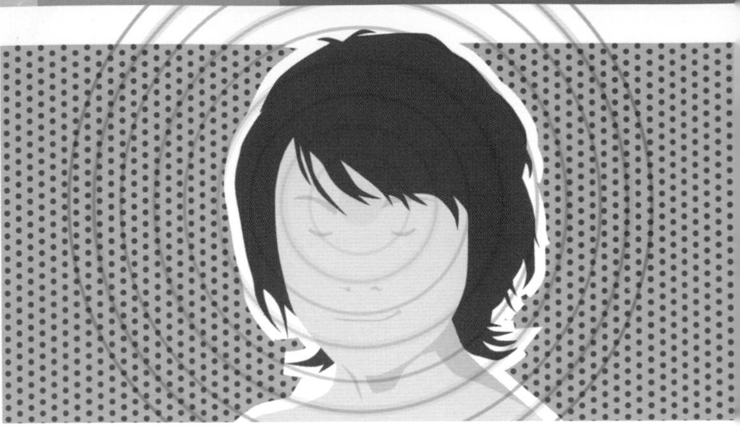

What Is the Sixth Sense?

Sight, hearing, smell, touch, taste, and . . . Hold on, where's the sixth one?

Sensational!

It's difficult to be exact about it, but when people talk about a "sixth sense," they usually mean an ability to perceive things without using any of the five senses, and therefore in a spooky sort of way. This might involve the following

- Sensing that something specific is about to happen
- Sensing that someone you can't see or hear is experiencing a specific thing
- Sensing that a particular thing happened in a particular place in the past

Let's say you experienced a strange feeling of foreboding and decided not to get on an amusement park ride, then all the passengers on the ride were thrown off and injured—you might feel that your "sixth sense" had saved yo from being thrown into the cotton-candy stall. Someone who didn't believe in such things might argue that you had a sense of foreboding because you'd noticed the ride looked ancient and had just seen someone working on it with a wrench.

There are usually rational explanations for this sort of thing: subconsciously we're always thinking and coming to conclusions based on our observations c objects or body language. Or some experiences may simply be coincidence. Various experiments have been devised to try and work out whether people have a sixth sense, but none have proven anything conclusively yet.

In the movie *The Sixth Sense*, the main character had the ability to see dead people when others could not. Spooky!

What Is the Sixth Sense? **Form**

Once you have mastered this **Thing to Know**,
stick your Achieved Star here and fill in the form

Achieved

HOW TELEPATHIC ARE YOU?

THINK OF A NUMBER

This is an easy mind-reading trick because you're not reading minds at all—but try to convince your friends that you are! Ask a friend to think of a number (in the equation below, their number is represented by *x*). Ask them to add 12, subtract 10, subtract 4, add 17, subtract 6, and then subtract the number they first thought of. After a few moments of pretend concentration, tell them that the number they have in their head is 9. The thing is, the answer is always 9! Try it.

$$x + 12 - 10 - 4 + 17 - 6 - x = 9$$

Make up your own equation. Make sure the numbers between the *x*'s add up to the same number you choose as the answer!

$$x + \_\_ - \_\_ - \_\_ + \_\_ - \_\_ - x = \_\_$$

TELEPATHY TEST

In scientific telepathy tests, five symbols on cards are used to discover if the subject has a sixth sense. The cards feature a star, a square, a circle, a plus sign, and wavy lines. The cards are shuffled and pulled out one by one at random. With the back of the card facing the subject, they are asked to say what they think is on the card. This is repeated 20 times and at the end their score is added up.The average score is 25% correct answers (in this case, 5 out of 20). Any more than that and the subject could be telepathic! Get together with a friend and test each other. You can make your own cards or you could use a pack of playing cards and try to guess the suit.

PREMONITIONS

Have you ever had a strong feeling that something specific was going to happen? y/n

Did it come true? y/n

If yes, what was it?

If yes, what's your explanation for this?

DÉJÀ VU

Have you ever felt like you've done something before even though you know you haven't? y/n

Was it just a case of bad memory? y/n

If yes, describe one occasion.

If no, what's your explanation for this?

At the same time you could master these **Things to Know**:
17: Is Your Teacher an Alien? • 58: What Is the Quietest Sound We Can Hear?
69: How Can I Win Millions? • 85: Why Do We Dream?

Why Do We Dream?

If you didn't dream, you might never get to sprout wings and fly, run naked down the street, or kiss your favorite movie star.

Your Wildest Dreams

No one really knows why we dream. There are lots of theories though:

- Dreams happen for no reason at all. Your brain just clicks while you're asleep and random things come out, but they don't mean anything.
- Dreams express emotions you've been bottling up and figure out problems for you—or at least try to.
- Dreams are the gods speaking to you. Many ancient peoples believed that the answers to their questions would come to them in a dream, especially on the night before something important, like a battle.
- The famous psychoanalyst Sigmund Freud thought that dreams are an expression of what we secretly wish for, even if we pretend we don't, and they're full of symbols with hidden meanings.

Whatever the reason, we all dream every night. Most, if not all, of our dreaming happens in a stage of sleep known as rapid eye movement (REM), when our eyeballs move around even though the lids are closed. We might have about an hour and a half of REM sleep each night, but we forget most of what we dream about. Experiments have shown that people become more anxious if they're deprived of REM sleep, suggesting we actually need to dream.

Let sleeping babies lie. Babies dream much more than adults because they sleep a lot more—they have up to eight hours of REM sleep every day. What a pity they can't tell us what they're dreaming about!

Why Do We Dream? **Form**

Once you have mastered this **Thing to Know**,
stick your Achieved Star here and fill in the form

Achieved

Describe the best dream you've had.	What do you think it meant?

Describe a recurring dream you've had.	What do you think it meant?

Describe the worst nightmare you've had.	What do you think it meant?

At the same time you could master these **Things to Know**:
8: Is Time Travel Possible? • 69: How Can I Win Millions?
84: What Is the Sixth Sense?

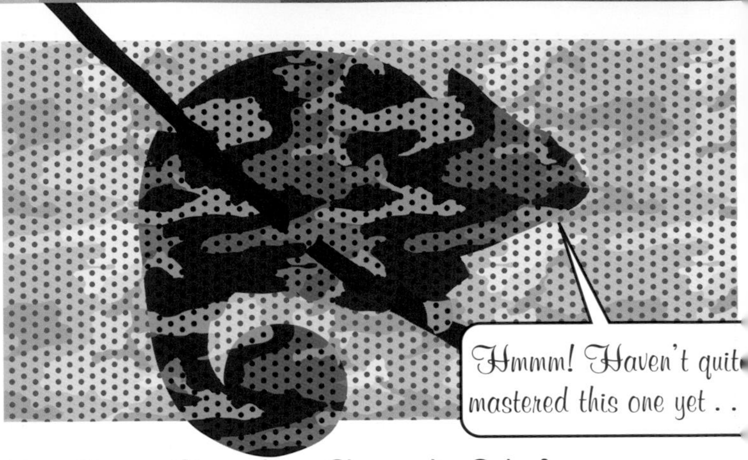
Hmmm! Haven't quit
mastered this one yet . .

How Does a Chameleon Change Its Color?

It would be very useful to be able to change color whenever you felt like it—perhaps to blend into the background or to match your shoes. But sadly we don't have special skin cells like chameleons do.

Chameleoflage

Underneath a chameleon's outer skin are three layers of special cells. The top layer contains yellow pigment. Underneath that, the next layer contains tiny particles that reflect blue light. The third layer of cells contains a dark pigment called melanin (which gives human skin its different colors). These cells are especially unusual because the melanin can move around within them: the chameleon can make the melanin gather together in a clump or spread out within the cell. The melanin layer also has branches so that the dark color can move up and affect the color of the yellow and blue layers. This means that the chameleon can change color and also create different patterns on its skin.

Chameleons change their color for different reasons:

- To camouflage themselves to hide from predators or prey.
- To heat up or cool down—if it's hot, a lighter pigment means that heat from the Sun is more easily reflected away. If it's cold, a darker pigment allows the chameleon to absorb more heat.
- To signal the animal's mood—e.g., when a male chameleon is in the mood for love, he displays particular colors and patterns to attract a mate.

Smart lizards. Chameleons can rotate their eyes independently so that they can watch things without moving their heads. Their tongues can flick in and out to grab prey in one-sixteenth of a second.

How Does a Chameleon
Change Its Color? **Form**

Once you have mastered this **Thing to Know**, stick your Achieved Star here and fill in the form

Achieved

CAMOUFLAGE

Most animals use a form of camouflage to hide themselves from their predators or prey. Take a look around your local area for creatures that use camouflage, and draw them below.

Type of creature	Type of creature	Type of creature
Type of creature	Type of creature	Type of creature
Type of creature	Type of creature	Type of creature

At the same time you could master these **Things to Know**:
25: If Light Is Invisible, How Can We See? • 45: Why Do Some Animals Shed Their Skin? • 95: Are Cats and Dogs Color-Blind (and How Do We Know)?

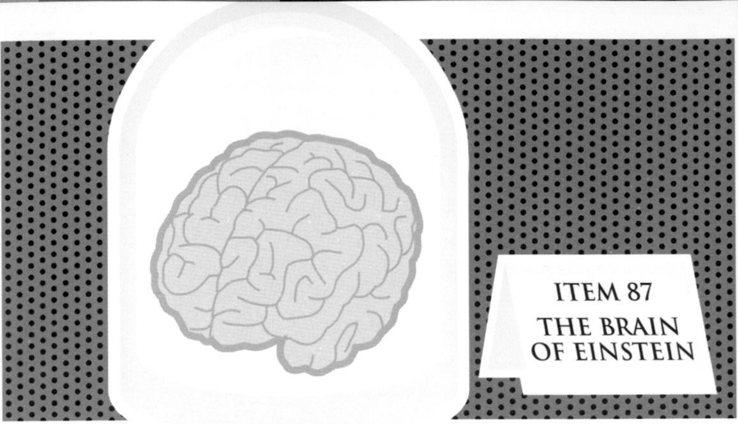

Who Was the Smartest Person Ever?

Do you have plans to claim this title for yourself? If so, it's going to be pretty challenging to manage it.

Smarty-Pants

How do you define smartness or intelligence, and how do you measure it? It's a matter for heated debate, but the most common way of measuring intelligence is with an IQ (Intelligence Quotient) test. The test isn't about what you know, but rather measures math and language skills, memory, and the ability to visualize shapes—most people score about the same in each category. You're supposed to be of average intelligence if you score between 85 and 115 on an IQ test. If you score 130 or above: congratulations, you're exceptionally intelligent. You're not supposed to be able to improve your IQ score—it stays the same however much you practice.

However, IQ tests don't measure many things that could be associated with intelligence, like social skills and creativity, and they seem to favor people from particular cultures. Some argue that they're not a very good gauge of real intelligence . . . but no one's been able to come up with a definition of intelligence that everyone accepts. So it's impossible to say who is (or was) the smartest person ever. What do you think? A scientist, like Stephen Hawking or Albert Einstein? A composer, like Mozart? An inventor, like Archimedes, or an artist, like Michelangelo? Or someone who's a bit of both, like Leonardo?

Einstein's IQ is unknown, but his brain was removed after he died to see whether it was different from anyone else's. Scientists discovered that one part—thought to be related to mathematical reasoning—*was* a bit bigger than most people's.

Who Was the Smartest Person Ever? **Form**

Once you have mastered this **Thing to Know**, stick your Achieved Star here and fill in the form

Achieved

IQ TEST

Try the IQ test below to see how smart you are. You must solve the problems in your head—do not use pen and paper. If you answer the questions correctly in 7 minutes, you're a genius! If it takes you 9, you're extremely gifted. For every 2 minutes that pass, your IQ rating drops a place.

1. If Carl is taller than Simon and Richard is taller than Carl, this means Simon is the shortest. T/F
2. If a clock hanging upside down reads twenty-five past nine, it is really five to three. T/F
3. Helen would like to buy an MP3 player costing $135 but she only has $62. If she borrows $49 from Tania and $22 from Becky, she can afford it. T/F
4. Two badgers, a kangaroo, a cat, and a three-legged dog have a total of 18 legs. T/F
5. Rob watches three horror films. Their lengths are 120 mins, 90 mins, and 150 mins. The total duration for all three movies is six hours. T/F
6. Three of the following numbers can be subtracted from each other to equal 2: 1, 4, 5, 9, 12 T/F
7. The words "twin, square, unlucky, day" correspond to this sequence of numbers: "2, 4, 13, 24." T/F
8. "Was it a bar or a bat I saw?" reads the same forward as it does backward. T/F
9. If the word *sky* can mean *sea* and *land* means *see*, this sentence reads correctly: "Looking out to sky, I could sky a ship on the land." T/F
10. The eighteenth consonant in this sentence is the letter *H*. T/F
11. The sum of six times seven and fourteen times three equal the same amount. T/F
12. *H* is exactly ten letters before *R* in the alphabet. T/F
13. It takes forty minutes to walk into town. If I get the bus, it takes five minutes to reach the bus stop and then twenty-one minutes on the bus to town. If I walk the whole way into town, it is fourteen minutes slower. T/F
14. 22 minutes before four o'clock is 18 minutes past three o'clock. T/F
15. Rick eats 135 nuts, Jane eats 115, and Ruby eats 60. Two of them together have eaten 200 nuts. T/F
16. The word *computer* is spelled by using the first letters of the words in the following sentence: Clever, organized monkeys packed up twelve expensive robots. T/F
17. Jim cooked dinner. Jim ate all his meal but Holly left an eighth, Ed left four-sixteenths, and Clare left five-eighths. With what was left over they could have invited Helen for dinner after all. T/F
18. Ten seconds out of a minute is the same as two months out of a year. T/F
19. Written backward, the number nine thousand, two hundred thirty-two would be written two thousand, three hundred twenty-nine. T/F
20. The figure that replaces *x* is 7: 1, 2, 3, 5, *x*, 13 T/F

Answers at the back of the book.

At the same time you could master these **Things to Know**:
2: What Is DNA (and Are We All That Different from Chimps)?
17: Is Your Teacher an Alien? • 78: Who Invented the Internet?

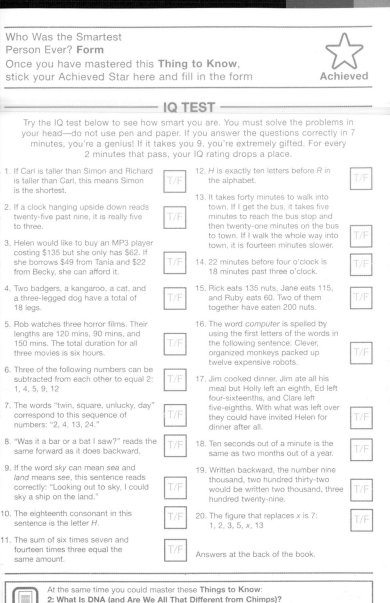

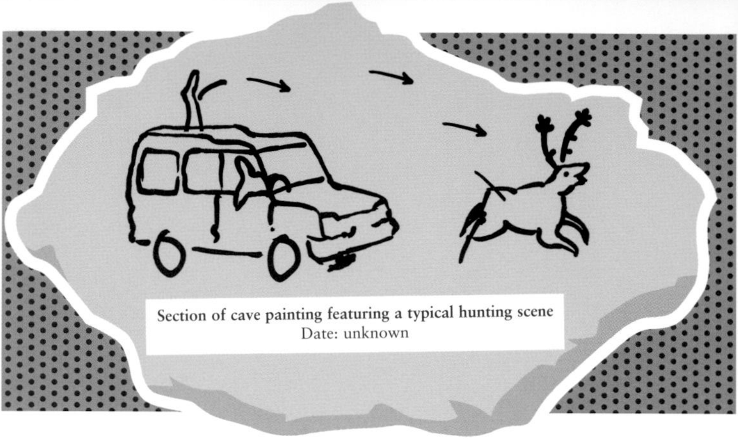

Section of cave painting featuring a typical hunting scene
Date: unknown

Who Invented the Wheel?

The oldest wheel ever found is thought to be more than 5,500 years old. So th person who invented it isn't famous—we don't even know who he or she was!

The Wheel Deal

Wheels seem like such obvious things that it's easy to miss why they're so ingenious.

- Over time, people realized that transporting heavy or awkward items was easier if they were rolled along on something round, like a log.
- Sleds were invented when people figured out that it was easier to drag things on runners. Then sleds were put on top of rollers: as the sled was pulled, rollers were moved from the back to the front to take the load
- The sleds eventually made grooves in the rollers. It was soon realized that these grooves actually made things easier.
- The rollers were replaced by long poles with round parts at the ends—wheels, in fact!
- Improvements continued to be made over time—the axles became separate from the wheels, spokes were made (instead of having heavy, solic wheels), and eventually rubber tires made life a lot less bumpy.

Archaeologists think wheels may have existed as long ago as 10,000 years, in Asia. The oldest one that's been found is from Mesopotamia (modern-day Iraq). It hasn't been possible to pinpoint a precise date, but either way, we have our Stone Age ancestors to thank for making life so much easier.

Running in circles: the civilizations of South America got by without the wheel until it arrived with the Spanish conquerors in the 16th century. In some remote parts of Africa, the wheel was unknown right up until the 19th century.

Who Invented the Wheel? **Form**

Once you have mastered this **Thing to Know**, stick your Achieved Star here and fill in the form

Achieved

WITHOUT WHEELS

There aren't many ways to travel without wheels these days. Here are some of them. Have you traveled on any of these modes of transport?

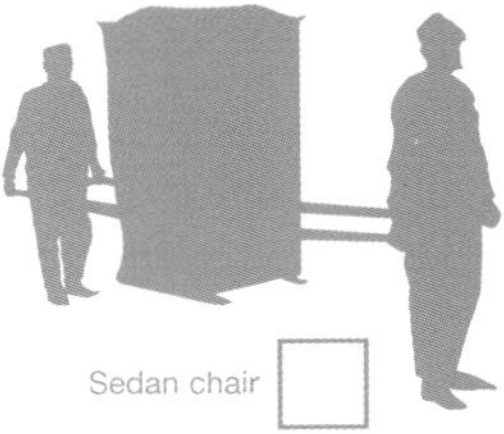

Sedan chair ☐

Sleigh ☐

High-speed train ☐

Hovercraft ☐

Horseback ☐

Can you think of any other modes of transport without wheels? If yes, draw them below.

At the same time you could master these **Things to Know**:

89: How Do You Do a Wheelie on a Bike?
93: Did People Make Everything from Stone in the Stone Age?

How Do You Do a Wheelie on a Bike?

This stunt involves balancing on the rear wheel of your bike, with the front wheel in the air. It looks impressive, so it's essential to learn how to do it.

Wheelie Difficult

This is a hard trick to do, so be prepared to put in some time and effort.

1. Put on a helmet, knee pads, elbow pads, and any other padding you can lay your hands on (not that anything's going to go wrong . . .).
2. Put the bike seat at its lowest setting—it helps to have a low center of gravity.
3. Start pedaling until you get to about 5 mph.
4. Crouch forward over the handlebars and pull them up—keep pedaling.
5. Quickly lean back—it's important not to keep your weight over the handlebars once the wheel is in the air.
6. Sit on the back edge of the seat.
7. Keep pedaling and use your back brake to keep you upright (this will take practice, but be careful not to fall over backward).

You'll find doing a wheelie much easier on a BMX-style bike than on a mountain or road bike, but whatever kind of bike you've got, it'll take lots of practice. It's a good idea to get used to jumping off the back of the bike. And when you're learning the trick, try it out on a soft surface like grass first.

Wheelie long: Kurt Osburn did a wheelie on his bike all the way from California to Florida, between April and June 1999, setting a world record for the longest wheelie ever.

How Do You Do a
Wheelie on a Bike? **Form**
Once you have mastered this **Thing to Know**,
stick your Achieved Star here and fill in the form

Achieved

BIKE TRICKS

Can you do a wheelie? y/n

Did you have a witness for the stunt? y/n

If yes, who was it?

How do you rate your skills?

Can you do a bunnyhop? y/n

Did you have a witness for the stunt? y/n

If yes, who was it?

How do you rate your skills?

Can you do an endo? y/n

Did you have a witness for the stunt? y/n

If yes, who was it?

How do you rate your skills?

Can you do an XUP? y/n

Did you have a witness for the stunt? y/n

If yes, who was it?

How do you rate your skills?

Have you jumped off a ramp? y/n

Did you have a witness for the stunt? y/n

If yes, who was it?

How do you rate your skills?

DRAW YOUR STUNT HERE.

Name of stunt

Did you have a witness for the stunt? y/n

If yes, who was it?

How do you rate your skills?

At the same time you could master these **Things to Know**:
9: Who Would Win the Animal Olympic 100-Meter Race?
10: How Do You Do an Ollie on a Skateboard? • 88: Who Invented the Wheel?

What Is the World's Most Poisonous Creature?

There's a difference between poisonous animals and venomous ones. Venomous creatures inject poison into their victims by biting them, while poisonous ones have poison on their bodies that kill predators when they eat or touch them. Not that it makes much difference to you once you've been poisoned, of course.

Small but Deadly

The most poisonous creature in the world (at least, that we know about so far) is the golden poison frog (*Phyllobates terribilis*, if you want to be scientific about it). This tiny creature contains only about a milligram of poison, but it's enough to kill between ten and twenty adults. So while the frog is very pretty to look at, you'd be well advised not to go anywhere near it. Its poison is stored in skin glands—if you touch the frog the poison could easily get into your bloodstream and kill you. Anything that eats the frog dies—apart from one type of snake, but even that will get very sick if it eats one. In South America, where the frog comes from, some tribespeople smear its poison on the darts they use for hunting.

But golden poison frogs are a bit of a mystery. In captivity, they aren't poisonous, and scientists have discovered that they get their poison from eating another creature. But no one knows what that creature is. It could be a tiny insect—which should really win "the world's most poisonous creature" title.

Deadliest poisons: there's debate about which poisons are the deadliest—they're tested in laboratories but scientists can't be sure what effect different poisons have on humans without testing them out! Any volunteers?

What Is the World's Most Poisonous Creature? **Form**

Once you have mastered this **Thing to Know**, stick your Achieved Star here and fill in the form

Achieved

POISONOUS CREATURES LIST

On your travels abroad, keep your eyes open for the world's most poisonous creatures.

SOUTH AMERICA

WORLD'S MOST POISONOUS CREATURE

1. Golden poison frog

WORLD'S MOST POISONOUS SPIDERS

2. Brazilian wandering spider and the Sydney funnel web spider

AFRICA & THE MIDDLE EAST

WORLD'S MOST POISONOUS SCORPION

3. Death stalker scorpion

AUSTRALIA

WORLD'S MOST POISONOUS SNAKE

4. Inland taipan

PACIFIC OCEAN

WORLD'S MOST POISONOUS OCTOPUS

5. Blue-ringed octopus

WORLD'S MOST POISONOUS SNAIL

6. Marbled cone snail

WORLD'S MOST POISONOUS FISH

7. Stonefish

WORLD'S MOST POISONOUS JELLYFISH

8. Box jellyfish

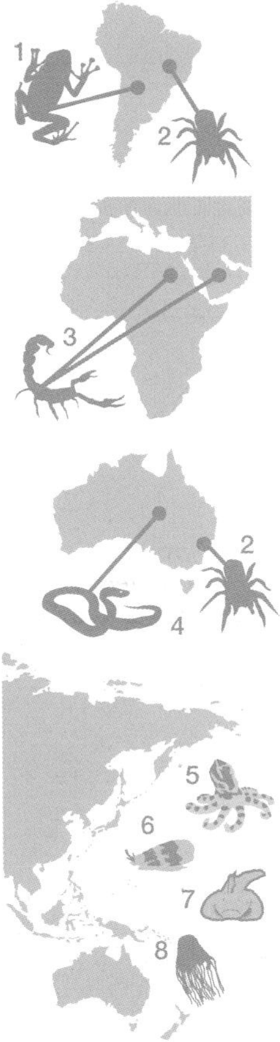

Have you ever been bitten or stung by a creature? y/n

If yes, what bit/stung you?

Where were you bitten/stung?

Did you swell up? y/n

Did it hurt? y/n

Did you have an allergic reaction? y/n

Why do you think it bit/stung you?

How long did it take for the swelling to disappear?

weeks ☐ days ☐ hours ☐

At the same time you could master these **Things to Know**:
23: How Does a Snake Swallow Things Bigger Than Its Own Head? • 41: What Is the World's Most Dangerous Shark? • 56: What Is the Scariest Thing in the World?

How Do Bees Make Honey?

Most people like honey, but do you think they'd like it as much if they knew that it's basically bee spit?

Buzz Off

Honeybees travel thousands of miles every year in their search for nectar, the sugary substance found in flowers, which they make into honey in an interesting process:

- Honeybees suck nectar out of flowers using their long, hollow tongues. Then they store it in special sacs inside their bodies.
- The bees return to the hive when their honey sacs are full and regurgitate the nectar into the mouths of "house" bees, which stay in the hive.
- The house bees then chew the nectar to mix it with a chemical in their bodies, which turns it into honey.
- The honey is then spread across honeycomb cells so that it loses any excess moisture.
- Once the honey is gooey enough, the bees seal off the cell of the honeycomb with a plug of wax.

The bees need the honey to live on during the winter. An average hive needs about 22 lb of honey to see it through the winter months, but the bees are capable of making much more than this. Beekeepers encourage them to make as much honey as possible, so that there's plenty left over for us.

Time is honey: honey can be kept for a very long time. A three-thousand-year-old honeycomb has been found in the tombs of Egyptian pharaohs . . . and, apparently, it was *still* edible.

How Do Bees Make Honey? **Form**

Once you have mastered this **Thing to Know**, stick your Achieved Star here and fill in the form

Achieved

HONEY: WAYS TO ENJOY IT

There are lots of ways to use honey. Try the ideas below and rate them according to how much you enjoyed them.

Spread it on toast	out of 10	Mix it into hot cereal	out of 10	Put it in tea instead of sugar	out of 10
Drizzle it on your cereal	out of 10	Drizzle it on pancakes	out of 10	Mix with plain yogurt	out of 10
Use it to make a marinade for meat (soy sauce and ginger or mustard and lemon juice work well with it)	out of 10			Drizzle it on a slice of melon or over a fruit salad	out of 10
Use it in a smoothie or milkshake (e.g., honey, milk, vanilla ice cream, and banana)	out of 10			Use it in a salad dressing with oil, mustard, and lemon juice or vinegar	out of 10

SANDWICH COMBINATIONS

Rate them on a scale of 1 to 10.

Peanut butter and honey	out of 10	Cheese and honey	out of 10	Banana and honey	out of 10

Make your own combinations and record them below.

Combination one	Did it taste good?	y/n	Combination two	Did it taste good?	y/n

HEALTHY HONEY

A spoonful of honey acts as an energizer for when you're feeling tired	out of 10	It's great for soothing a sore throat—mix it in hot water with lemon juice	out of 10	It can even help if you're feeling a bit constipated!	out of 10

TYPES OF HONEY

There are hundreds of different types of honey. The taste varies depending on which flower the nectar was harvested from by the bees. Here is a list of some of the different types of honey. Have you tried them? What did you think?

Acacia	out of 10	Orange blossom	out of 10	Manuka	out of 10	Heather	out of 10	Eucalyptus	out of 10
Clover	out of 10	Chestnut	out of 10	Sunflower	out of 10	Pine	out of 10	Leatherwood	out of 10
Alfalfa	out of 10	Wild thyme	out of 10	Cherry blossom	out of 10	Lavender	out of 10	Ulmo blossom	out of 10

How many have you tried?		Could you tell the difference?	y/n	If yes, which was your favorite?	

At the same time you could master these **Things to Know**:
11: Who Were the First Chocoholics? • 14: Will Your Stomach Explode if You Eat Too Much? • 34: What Is the World's Favorite Pet? • 57: How Do Oysters Make Pearls?

When Was Writing Invented?

Archaeologists keep turning up examples of early writing in different areas of the world. Dating the artifacts can be hard, as is determining whether the markings are really part of a writing system or just pictures and random symbols!

Write at the Start

It's widely believed that the first ever writing was developed by the Sumerian people of Mesopotamia (part of modern-day Iraq). Tokens inscribed with symbols date back thousands of years before this civilization, but etched clay tablets from around 3200 BC show how these may have led to an early Sumerian system for keeping records and accounts. By about 3100 BC, symbols representing the sounds of speech were imprinted on clay slabs and used for many purposes, including storytelling. This type of writing, known as cuneiform, looks like a series of triangular marks.

The Egyptians developed hieroglyphs around the same time as the Sumerians, so there is debate as to who got the idea from whom (they are known to have traded with one another). Clay tablets etched with primitive words and dating back to 3300 BC were found in the tomb of a pharaoh named Scorpion.

And then there's the Chinese. . . . Archaeologists recently unearthed tortoiseshells carved with signs dating back to 6600 BC! They believe there are links between some of the symbols and signs used in later ancient Chinese script.

Gobbledygook: inscribed pieces of pottery unearthed from other ancient civilizations, like the Indus (modern-day India and Pakistan) and Vinča (southeast Europe), also predate cuneiform, but so far no one's been able to decipher the symbols on them!

When Was Writing Invented? **Form**

Once you have mastered this **Thing to Know**,
stick your Achieved Star here and fill in the form

Achieved

HANDWRITING ANALYSIS

Graphology is the study of handwriting. A lot can be determined about a person through their handwriting. In the space provided, write a few sentences for analysis.

Here are some of the basic elements you can determine from your handwriting. Does it give an accurate assessment of your personality? The list below isn't definitive, as there are other factors to consider as well as different opinions.

SLANT

If your handwriting slants to the right, this indicates that you are expressive, caring, and outgoing. You tend to act on your emotions.

If your handwriting slants to the left, this indicates that you can be self-centered and selfish. You are more likely to be artistic and defiant.

If your handwriting is upright, this indicates that you're self-reliant. You tend to act with your head and not your heart.

SIZE

If your handwriting is large, this indicates that you're likely to be an extrovert and have a wide range of interests.

If your handwriting is small, this indicates that you're more likely to be an introvert. You have few interests but you're passionate about them.

PRESSURE

If you press lightly, this indicates you can be sensitive and submissive. You prefer to follow than to lead.

If you press hard, this indicates commitment and that you take things seriously. You're self-determined and forceful. You prefer to lead than to follow.

If you press excessively hard, you get uptight, act first, and ask questions later, and see things as criticism.

UPPER LOOPS

If these letters (b, d, f, h, k & l) are tall, this indicates that you're ambitious. If they're really tall, this shows that your ambitions are unrealistic.

If these letters are loopy, this indicates a sensible, imaginative thought process. If they're really loopy, then your ideas will be overconsidered.

LOWER LOOPS

If the loops in these letters (f, g, j, p, q & y) are fat, this indicates an appetite for material wealth.

If there are no loops in your handwriting, this indicates impatience.

At the same time you could master these **Things to Know**:
24: When Did Money Start Making the World Go Around?
68: Who Invented Paper? • 87: Who Was the Smartest Person Ever?

Did People Make Everything from Stone in the Stone Age?

You've probably figured out that people didn't drive stone cars like they do on *The Flintstones*. So what's with the name? This may seem odd, but the Stone Age is more precisely defined as the time before people started using metal (although they did use some metal for part of it, just to be confusing). It lasted a couple of *million* years, and it started before humans like us even existed.

Stone-Age Mummy

Although people in the Stone Age used stone tools, they used all kinds of other materials too. Most of them have rotted away, but a 5,000-year-old mummy known as Otzi the Iceman has preserved some of the materials. His frozen body was discovered in the Alps, along with . . .

- a flint dagger, a wooden bow, and arrows with flint tips;
- a copper ax (this was before people discovered bronze and later iron, which were much more useful than copper);
- a wooden-framed backpack and containers made from birch bark; and
- a fur cap, a cape of woven grass, and snowshoes with bearskin soles.

Stone Age people used lots of materials from the animals they killed for food: bones and antlers for digging tools, ligaments for thread, leather for clothes, and animal stomachs made good (but gruesome) bags. Still wondering why it's called the Stone Age? Well, it's better than Animal Stomach Age!

Mossy rocker: Otzi the Iceman was also carrying some moss, which archaeologists think was the Stone Age version of toilet paper. Otzi was also covered in tattoos—no one's sure why, but they might have been magic charms to cure his arthritis.

Did People Make Everything
from Stone in the Stone Age? **Form**
Once you have mastered this **Thing to Know**,
stick your Achieved Star here and fill in the form

Achieved

STONE ART

Painting stones is fun, and they make great gifts (cheap too!). Search the yard for stones whose shapes resemble something, and turn them into works of art.

Turn this plain stone . . .

. . . into a fabulous paperweight!

Place pictures of your favorite painted stones here.

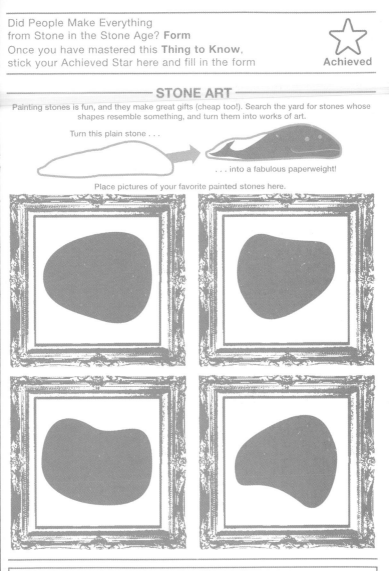

At the same time you could master these **Things to Know**:
32: What Is an Ice Age (and When Are We Due for Another One)? • 46: Who Built Stonehenge, How and Why? • 52: Could a Rock Destroy Our Planet?

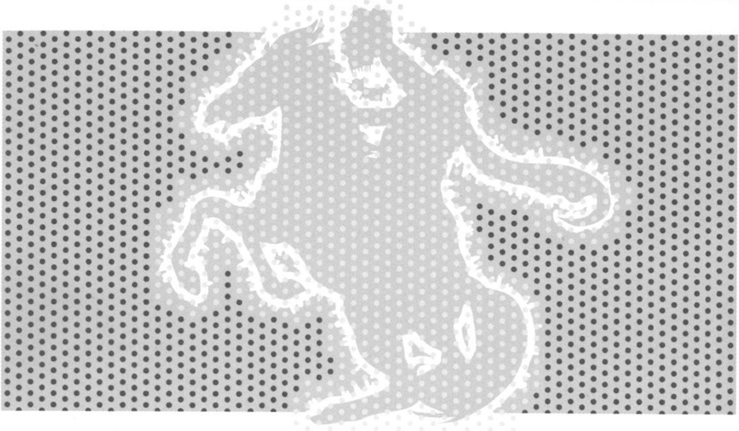

What Makes Things Glow in the Dark?

Have you ever had glowing stars on your bedroom wall, waved a glow stick, or worn luminous paint or clothing? Ever wondered what makes them glow?

Here We Glow

The answer is chemicals called phosphors. The ones that are used most often are zinc sulfide and strontium aluminate, which are made in labs. Phosphors work because when they're exposed to light they become excited and their electrons start jiggling around crazily. When the light source is taken away, the electrons release the energy as light of their own—and that's why they glow in the dark. Eventually the energy runs out, but it usually takes a few hours.

Some things glow in the dark without man-made chemicals:

- Sometimes the ocean glows at night when the water is disturbed. This is caused by tiny single-celled organisms called Noctiluca (or sea sparkle!)—a type of algae. These creatures have special substances called luciferin and luciferase in their bodies that react in the presence of oxygen and water. This effect is often known as "phosphorescence" (although it doesn't have anything to do with phosphors) or "bioluminescence."
- Lots of sea creatures glow in the dark: marine worms, jellyfish, even one type of shark. Insects like glowworms and fireflies light up at night too. As far as we know, all animals and plants that glow in the dark do so because of luciferin and luciferase.

Radioactive glow: until the 1950s, radium was used to make things glow, especially watch dials. Unfortunately, because it's radioactive, radium can cause cancer, and many of the workers who handled this dangerous substance died as a result of their exposure.

What Makes Things
Glow in the Dark? **Form**
Once you have mastered this **Thing to Know,**
stick your Achieved Star here and fill in the form

Achieved

THINGS THAT GLOW BUMP IN THE NIGHT

Some creatures and organisms naturally glow in the dark. How many have you seen? And where? You will probably have to travel to many different parts of the world to see them all.

ALGAE

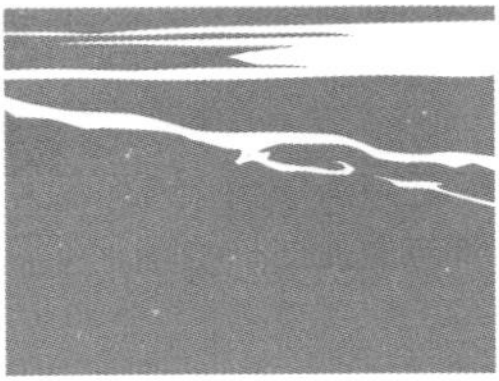

Have you ever seen algae glow in the sea? y/n

If yes, where?

MUSHROOMS

Have you ever seen a mushroom glow? (e.g., Jack O'Lantern mushroom or the honey fungus) y/n

If yes, where?

JELLYFISH

Have you ever seen a jellyfish glow? (e.g., crystal and pelagia jellyfish) y/n

If yes, where?

SQUID

Have you ever seen a squid glow? (e.g., bobtail squid) y/n

If yes, where?

FIREFLIES

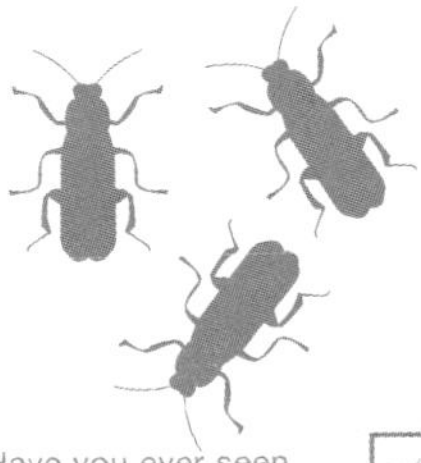

Have you ever seen a firefly glow? y/n

If yes, where?

GLOWWORMS

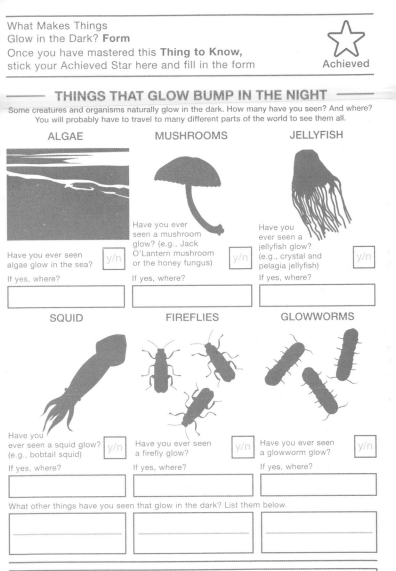

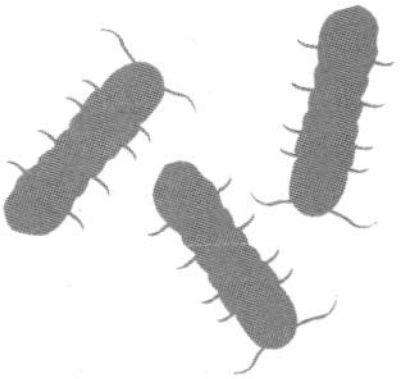

Have you ever seen a glowworm glow? y/n

If yes, where?

What other things have you seen that glow in the dark? List them below.

At the same time you could master these **Things to Know**:
3: Why Don't Fish Drown? • 25: If Light Is Invisible, How Can We See? • 30: What Is at the Bottom of the Ocean? • 86: How Does a Chameleon Change Its Color?

Are Cats and Dogs Color-Blind (and How Do We Know)?

Life without color would not only be pretty dull, but quite hard—for us humans at least. Scientists used to think that dogs and cats were completely color-blind, but now they think they were wrong—at least, partly.

Eye-Opener

The reason we're able to see is because of two types of light receptors in the retina at the back of our eyes. "Rods" allow us to see in dim light but don't pick up colors. "Cones" let us see colors and fine details. We need three different types of cones to see all the colors of the rainbow, each kind specializing in one range of colors: red, green, or blue. (About 9% of people have a problem with one or more types of cones, making them color-blind.)

As well as examining the animals' eyes, one of the main ways scientists test the ability of cats and dogs to see color is to reward the animals for picking out colors by giving them their favorite thing in the world—food. After years of experiments they've come to the conclusion that cats can see colors, but their sensitivity is not as good as ours, and they have particular difficulty with reds and greens. Dogs have a similar problem. They appear to have only two different types of cones instead of the three needed to see all the colors of the rainbow. The green type cones are the missing ones—dogs can tell the difference between red and blue, and even between blue and violet, but are confused about other colors (so don't expect them to obey traffic lights).

Human color vision is among the best, but some creatures can see colors we can't: insects, birds, and spiders can see ultraviolet light (below the violet end of the spectrum), and snakes can see infrared light (beyond the red end of the spectrum).

Are Cats and Dogs Color-Blind (and How Do We Know)? **Form**

Once you have mastered this **Thing to Know**, stick your Achieved Star here and fill in the form

Achieved

COLOR TEST

Do you see the same colors as everyone else? Take a look at these colors and write the name you think best describes them below. Is the first color "autumn leaves" or is it more of a "sunshine yellow"? When you've decided on the colors' names, try them on your friends to see if they agree.

your color name here	your color name here	your color name here	your color name here

your color name here	your color name here	your color name here	your color name here

your color name here	your color name here	your color name here	your color name here

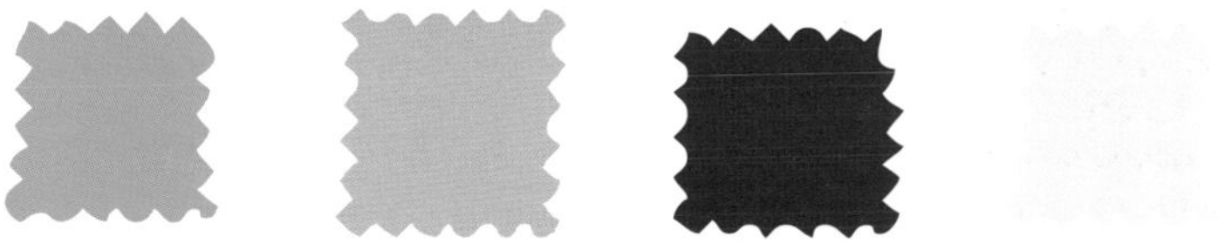

your color name here	your color name here	your color name here	your color name here

At the same time you could master these **Things to Know**:
25: If Light Is Invisible, How Can We See? • 34: What Is the World's Favorite Pet? 54: Are Bats Really Blind? • 86: How Does a Chameleon Change Its Color?

Where Are the Most Haunted Houses in the World?

Built in 1857 by Thomas Whaley, the Whaley House of San Diego, California, embraces the title of "most haunted house in the U.S." Destined for ghoul inhabitance, this stately house was built on land that was once a cemetery. Th earliest recognized ghost at the Whaley House was "Yankee Jim," or James Robinson—convicted of attempted grand larceny in 1852. His clunking footste can be heard near the stairs on which he was killed. The ghost of Thomas Whaley himself is sometimes spotted resting in the parlor or standing on the upper landing.

The White House, Washington, D.C.

1600 Pennsylvania Avenue is home to both living and departed presidents, as the paranormal world would have it. On your next visit, take notice of the Oval Office and the ghoul inside of it:

- Andrew Jackson is rumored to stroll through the halls of the White House night, supposedly muttering indecencies to himself.
- Legend states that Dolley Madison paid the White House a visit in her afterlife, coming back during the Wilson Administration when Mrs. Wilson was making plans to dig up the rose garden. Dolley's ghost materialized an advised that the garden be left as it was. Her roses are still blooming.
- Abe Lincoln is known to have shown up at visitors' doors in the night, though he is sometimes glimpsed standing stoically in the Oval Office.

Most haunted house in . . . Germany is the Babenhausen Barracks, haunted by ghosts of German soldiers. In the U.K. it was Borley Rectory, until it mysteriously burned down. In Australia, it is Monte Cristo, New South Wales, built in 1884 and haunted by old Mrs. Crawley, a maid, and a baby girl.

Where Are the Most Haunted
Houses in the World? **Form**
Once you have mastered this **Thing to Know**,
stick your Achieved Star here and fill in the form

Achieved

I SEE DEAD PEOPLE

A lot of people believe in the existence of ghosts. Have you ever seen anything out
of the ordinary? If yes, record your experience here. If not, quick—get ghost hunting!

Have you ever heard unexplained noises? `y/n`

What kind of noises?

Have you ever felt a ghostly presence? `y/n`

What did you feel?

Cold	Creepy	Someone watching you	Something touching you	Your hair standing on end	Other
☐	☐	☐	☐	☐	☐

If other, please specify.

Rate how scared you were.

☆ ☆ ☆ ☆ ☆
Not at all / Sweating / Shaking / Frozen with fear / Ran from the scene screaming

Have you ever seen an actual ghost? `y/n`

Was it a friendly ghost? `y/n`

Did it speak? If yes, what did it say?

Draw what the ghost looked like in the space below.

How long did it stick around for?

It was gone in the blink of an eye	A few seconds	Longer than a minute	Ages	It's always hanging around	Other
☐	☐	☐	☐	☐	☐

If other, please specify.

Did you hunt for the ghost or was it luck?

Hunted for the ghost		Just lucky		Just unlucky	
☐		☐		☐	

If you hunted, how many attempts did it take to see something? `0 , 0`

At the same time you could master these **Things to Know**:
8: Is Time Travel Possible? • **56: What Is the Scariest Thing in the World?**
58: What Is the Quietest Sound We Can Hear? • **84: What Is the Sixth Sense?**

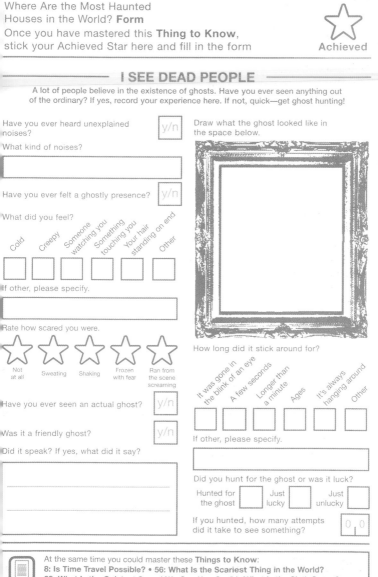

What Is the World's Deadliest Disease?

It's handy to know the answer to this question so that you can put some effort into avoiding it.

Catch!

You'll be relieved to know that the disease that kills most people every year isn't contagious. It's heart disease, which kills about 7 million people per year worldwide. You can avoid it by getting lots of exercise, eating healthily, and making sure you don't become overweight—it's best to start now before it's too late.

But don't feel too safe: about one in every eight deaths in the world is caused by an infectious disease. If you're going to die of an infectious disease it's very likely to be one of a handful, including HIV/AIDS (which affects the immune system), tuberculosis (a lung disease), malaria (spread by mosquito bites), and diseases that cause diarrhea, like dysentery and cholera. Whether you're at risk of catching any of them depends quite heavily on where in the world you live—e.g., HIV and AIDS are most common in Africa.

The single deadliest disease event in history was an outbreak of flu. It started in 1918 and spread all around the world, killing 40 million people. Most of the people who died were young and otherwise healthy. The pandemic happened just after the First World War and killed even more people than died in the war

It wasn't the cough that carried her off . . . Tuberculosis (TB) has been around for ages. It's been found in the skulls and spinal cords of 3,000-year-old Egyptian mummies. Now curable, it's estimated that between the years 1700 and 1900, TB killed over a billion people.

What Is the World's Deadliest Disease **Form**

Once you have mastered this **Thing to Know**, stick your Achieved Star here and fill in the form

Achieved

YOUR ILLNESSES

Which of these common illnesses have you had?

Chicken pox ☐ Measles ☐ Rubella (German measles) ☐ Mumps ☐ Common cold ☐ Flu ☐

What other illnesses have you had?

Which was the worst illness?

On a scale of 1 to 5 (5 being the worst), how bad did you feel?

1 2 3 4 5

What is the longest number of days you've been ill for? 0 0 0

How many days were you absent from school? 0 0 0

Did you have to take bad-tasting medicine? y/n

Did you have to go to the doctor? y/n

Did you have to be hospitalized at any point? y/n

Are you better now? y/n

What Were Your Symptoms?

On the diagram below, mark the areas affected by your worst illness and tell how they were affected.

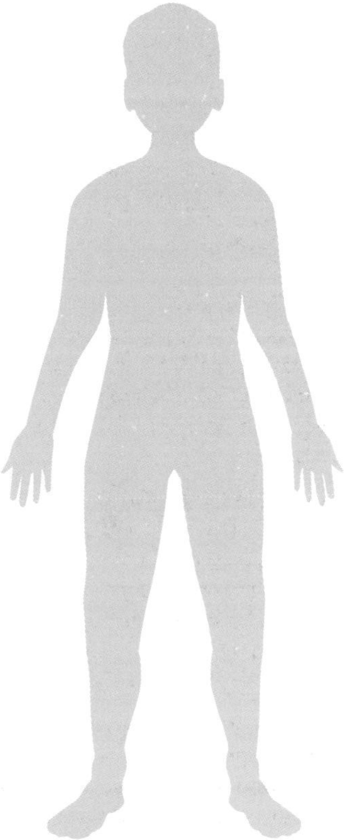

At the same time you could master these **Things to Know**:
37: Can You Sneeze with Your Eyes Open? • 55: What Wiped Out Nearly Half the Population of Europe? • 71: Are You Only Ever a Few Feet from a Rat in a Big City?

Nails—What Are They Good For?

The nails on your fingers can sometimes come in handy for picking off labels and scratching your back, but other than that, they're not all that useful. And toenails are of no use at all. So why do we have them?

Hard as Nails

Your fingernails might only be useful to you every so often, but imagine how much you'd rely on them if you didn't have any other tools—like knives, tweezers, and back scratchers. Millions of years ago, before humans walked on two legs or had any interest in manicures, our fingernails were extremely useful for picking fleas out of one another's fur, breaking open fruit, and that kind of thing. Nowadays, instead of using our nails to groom, we groom our nails to make us more attractive.

Toenails are harder to justify. Even when we spent most of our lives climbing trees and making grunting noises, toenails stood out as one part of the early human body that didn't really do too much. Maybe they were there to protect our toes before we found out how to make shoes. It's probably more likely that toenails are just an evolutionary leftover: all mammals have some kind of hard covering at the ends of their limbs—like hooves or claws—and apes' and humans' claws developed into nails. Millions of years later, we're still stuck with them. Try painting yours bright red and be glad you don't still have hooves instead.

Toe-tally amazing: Louise Hollis holds the record for the world's longest toenails. When they were officially measured in 1991, the combined length of her ten toenails was more than seven feet!

Nails—What Are They Good For? **Form**

Once you have mastered this **Thing to Know**, stick your Achieved Star here and fill in the form

Achieved

YOUR NAILS

In the boxes provided on the diagram below, draw your nails. Draw the length and shape. What is the longest they've ever been? Chart the growth rate of your nails using the ruler provided.

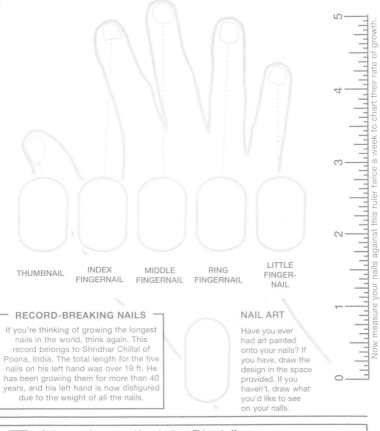

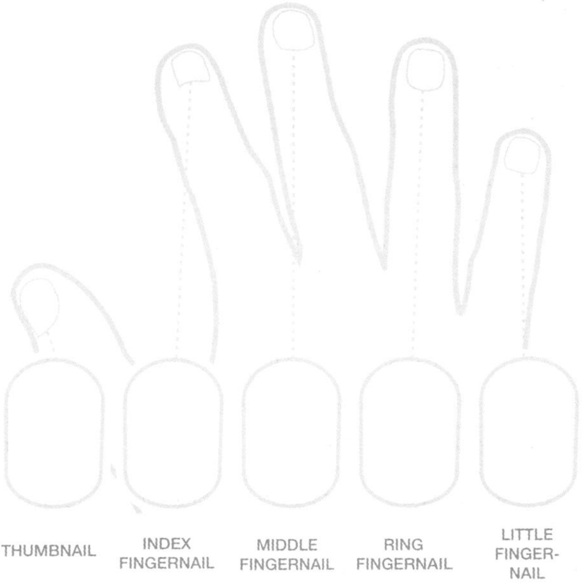

RECORD-BREAKING NAILS

If you're thinking of growing the longest nails in the world, think again. This record belongs to Shridhar Chillal of Poona, India. The total length for the five nails on his left hand was over 19 ft. He has been growing them for more than 40 years, and his left hand is now disfigured due to the weight of all the nails.

NAIL ART

Have you ever had art painted onto your nails? If you have, draw the design in the space provided. If you haven't, draw what you'd like to see on your nails.

At the same time you could master these **Things to Know**:
2: What Is DNA (and Are We All That Different from Chimps)? • 73: Pus—What Is It Good For? • 93: Did People Make Everything from Stone in the Stone Age?

Who Was the Greatest Conqueror of All Time?

No one's ever really managed to conquer the world. But one ruthless warrior did come pretty close.

Khan the Conqueror

Genghis Khan conquered the Mongol Empire. It wasn't the biggest empire there's ever been—that was the British Empire—but it was the second largest and pretty impressive by anybody's standards. And Genghis did it by himself (well, with the help of his rampaging hordes of fearless warriors), pushing the boundaries of his empire farther and farther outward until it was huge.

Genghis Khan, the son of a Mongol chieftain, was born in the 1160s. He was originally called Temujin but was later given the name Genghis Khan, which means Emperor of Emperors. It took years of political maneuvering and smart military campaigns to unite all the Mongol tribes under his leadership in 1206. Then he started conquering in a really big way. When he died in 1227, Genghis Khan's empire stretched from Southeast Asia to eastern Europe, and you don't get an empire that size without being a brilliant leader, a military genius, and utterly ruthless—all qualifications that make Genghis probably the greatest conqueror of all time. When he died, Genghis Khan passed his empire on to his sons, and the Mongol Empire eventually grew to its maximum size of almost 13 million square miles (and 100 million people).

The British Empire covered an area of almost 14 million square miles. Unlike Khan's, it wasn't continuous and it wasn't amassed in one long conquering spree: it was spread out in bits and pieces all over the world and grew over a much longer time period.

Who Was the Greatest
Conqueror of All Time? **Form**
Once you have mastered this **Thing to Know**,
stick your Achieved Star here and fill in the form

Achieved

HEROES AND VILLAINS QUIZ

Test your knowledge of historical heroes and villains with this quiz. Once you've done the quiz, memorize the correct facts, then impress your friends to earn your star.

1. Al Capone was a famous gangster, but what did his business card claim his job was?

(a) Cleaner
(b) Furniture dealer
(c) Banker
(d) Taxi driver

2. What did Julius Caesar's friend Marcus Brutus do?

(a) Denounce him
(b) Crown him
(c) Assassinate him
(d) Die for him

3. Where was Captain Cook born?

(a) Stratford-upon-Avon
(b) Marton in Middlesbrough
(c) Stoke-on-Trent
(d) Berwick-upon-Tweed

4. On his deathbed, what did Nelson allegedly ask for from the captain of HMS *Victory*, Thomas Hardy?

(a) A handkerchief
(b) A kiss
(c) His blessing
(d) A beer

5. In what year did Columbus land in America?

(a) 1249
(b) 1294
(c) 1492
(d) 1942

6. How many women is Jack the Ripper thought to have killed?

(a) 1
(b) 5
(c) 8
(d) 12

7. Who was Dick Turpin?

(a) A king
(b) A pirate
(c) A zookeeper
(d) A highwayman

8. Divorced, beheaded, died, divorced, beheaded, survived: whose wives suffered this fate?

(a) Henry VIII
(b) Charles I
(c) James II
(d) Richard III

9. What did Guy Fawkes attempt to do?

(a) Burn down London with a great fire
(b) Blow up the Houses of Parliament
(c) Destroy the Church
(d) Defeat the Spanish

10. What did Abraham Lincoln abolish?

(a) Alcohol production
(b) Taxes
(c) Slavery
(d) Dancing

Answers at the back of the book.

At the same time you could master these **Things to Know**:
27: What Is the Deadliest Martial Art? • 61: Were All Romans from Rome?
72: Who Was the Most Bloodthirsty Pirate Ever?

When Was the First Leap Year and Why Do We Need Them?

If your birthday is on February 29, you may be cursing the need for leap years The problem is that the calendar isn't in perfect alignment with the Earth's orbit around the Sun. It takes the Earth 365.2422 days to make one revolutio around the Sun, but this would be very inconvenient on a calendar. So once every four years (or thereabouts—see below) we add an extra day to make up the difference of four times 0.2422 of a day. It's still not perfect, but it'll d

One Giant Leap

Most modern countries follow the Gregorian calendar, which was devised by Aloysius Lilius and introduced by Pope Gregory XIII in 1582 (so blame them if you have a leap-year birthday). Leap years are figured out like this:

- Every year divisible by four is a leap year . . .
- BUT every year divisible by 100 is NOT a leap year . . .
- UNLESS it's also divisible by 400—in which case it IS a leap year

So the years 2004, 2008, 2012, etc., are all leap years, the year 2000 is a leap year, but the years 1900 and 2100 are not leap years. If you live until the year 2104, you will experience the thrill of a rare eight-year gap between leap years.

The Gregorian calendar was adapted from the Julian calendar (named after the Roman leader Julius Caesar), which was a bit too long and eventually made spring arrive at the wrong time in the calendar, confusing everyone.

One small leap for man . . . Some years contain one or two leap seconds (which can be added or taken away). The last one was added on: one leap second was added at midnight on December 31, 2005—it was the first leap second in seven years.

When Was the First Leap Year and
Why Do We Need Them? **Form**
Once you have mastered this **Thing to Know**,
stick your Achieved Star here and fill in the form

Achieved

YOU FORGOT MY BIRTHDAY!

Make sure you never forget anyone's birthday again. Write the most important birthdays below, but most important to earn your star, REMEMBER WHEN THEY ARE!

At the same time you could master these **Things to Know**:
8: Is Time Travel Possible? • 60: Why Does the Moon Change Shape?
82: Why Are There 60 Seconds in a Minute?

What Would Happen to You in a Black Hole?

Next time you're traveling in space, beware! You can't see a black hole—nothing, not even light, can escape from it—but you may be able to see the effect it has on its surroundings. So read up and find out why it's wise to avoid them.

Lost in Space

- A black hole is formed when a large star runs out of fuel and can no longer support its own weight. The layers of hydrogen that make up the star are forced to become smaller and smaller, until they're even tinier than an atom (which is extremely tiny—see **Thing to Know** No. 42). All of the mass of the original star is now concentrated into this one point.
- If you make something smaller by forcing it into a smaller space (e.g., if you squash up a bath sponge), its gravity gets stronger. So the star's gravity becomes enormously strong. The star is now a "singularity," and forms the center of a black hole.

Because black holes are areas of space with extremely strong gravity, anything that comes near them is swallowed. This includes comets, meteors, light . . . and you. It would be like being drawn into the center of a whirlpool (except not so wet and a lot hotter), and, as the gravity increased, you'd be stretched. As you got closer to the center of the black hole, the temperature would increase. One hopes the end would be quick, but you'd either be pulled apart by the strong gravity or cooked by the temperature.

A word of warning: astronomers think there's a huge black hole at the center of our own galaxy. So, next time you're up there, it's probably best to avoid the middle of the Milky Way.

What Would Happen to
You in a Black Hole? **Form**

Once you have mastered this **Thing to Know**,
stick your Achieved Star here and fill in the form

Achieved

UNIVERSE QUIZ

Test your knowledge of the universe with this quiz. Once you've done the quiz, memorize the correct facts, then impress your friends to earn your star.

1. What is the study of the universe called?

(a) Cardiology
(b) Cereology
(c) Climatology
(d) Cosmology

2. How old is the universe?

(a) 13.7 thousand years
(b) 13.7 million years
(c) 13.7 billion years
(d) 13.7 million billion years

3. What theories exist about the fate of our universe?

(a) It will keep expanding forever
(b) It will collapse in on itself
(c) It will become too cold
(d) All of the above

4. What type of galaxy is the Milky Way?

(a) A spiral galaxy
(b) An elliptical galaxy
(c) An irregular galaxy
(d) A dwarf galaxy

5. How many Earths would fit into the Sun?

(a) 100,000
(b) 250,000
(c) 500,000
(d) 1 million

6. What percentage of the universe do scientists believe is dark matter—something no one has ever seen?

(a) 10
(b) 35
(c) 50
(d) 90

7. Which is the largest planet in our solar system?

(a) Saturn
(b) Jupiter
(c) Neptune
(d) Earth

8. What kind of animal, named Laika, was sent into space?

(a) A mouse
(b) A dog
(c) A monkey
(d) A pigeon

9. On April 12, 1961, which historic event happened?

(a) Albert Einstein died
(b) Black holes were discovered
(c) Yuri Gagarin became the first human to go into space
(d) The space shuttle *Challenger* blew up

10. Who was the first man on the Moon?

(a) Neil Armstrong
(b) Neil Diamond
(c) Neil Gaiman
(d) Sam Neill

Answers at the back of the book.

At the same time you could master these **Things to Know**:
8: Is Time Travel Possible? • 12: How Big Is the Universe? • 25: If Light Is Invisible, How Can We See? • 80: Where Can You Find Red Giants and White Dwarves?

Your Things to Know

List the **Things** you'd like **to Know** the answers to that weren't mentioned in the book

Thing to Know 1

Thing to Know 2

Thing to Know 3

Thing to Know 4

Thing to Know 5

Thing to Know 6

Thing to Know 7

Thing to Know 8

Thing to Know 9

Thing to Know 10

How will you attempt to master these **Things**? Do you know any smart people or experts who can help you? If not, try a library or the Internet—or find out for yourself by conducting some experiments with friends. Don't do anything dangerous, though!

Answers Page

Hey! **No cheating!**

THING TO KNOW NO. 5
WHY IS OUR BLOOD RED?

1. b / 2. c / 3. d / 4. c / 5. c / 6. b

THING TO KNOW NO. 7
WHAT IS THE DIFFERENCE BETWEEN A FRUIT AND A VEGETABLE?

Technically speaking, these are **all** vegetables, as they are all grown to eat. However, only carrot, broccoli, peas, cabbage, lettuce, and brussels sprouts are **only** vegetables. All the others can be classed as fruits too—although, out of them, only apple, banana, orange, and watermelon are generally known as fruits.

THING TO KNOW NO. 14
WILL YOUR STOMACH EXPLODE IF YOU EAT TOO MUCH?

1. Liver / 2. Kidneys / 3. Stomach
4. Rectum / 5. Duodenum / 6. Lungs
7. Pancreas / 8. Large intestine / 9. Anus
10. Small intestine / 11. Esophagus
12. Gallbladder / 13. Appendix / 14. Heart
15. Bladder

THING TO KNOW NO. 18
WHAT ARE THE BIGGEST AND SMALLEST ANIMALS IN THE WORLD?

Isn't it funny how many enormous creatures feed on such small things? Thus they have to eat a lot of those small things to satisfy their appetites.

Blue whales (1) eat the minute shrimplike creatures **krill** (D).

Argentinosaurus (2) was a herbivore and ate **plants** (C).

Colossal and giant squid (3)—the answer is **unknown** (B). Very little is known about these creatures, as they have rarely been observed in their natural habitat. However, it is thought they prey on fish, small marine mammals, squid, and plankton.

Sperm whales (4) eat **octopus and squid (including colossal and giant squid)** (F). The massive tentacles and beaks of these squid have been found inside sperm whales' stomachs.

Great white sharks (5) eat **sharks, seals, and dolphins** (A) and occasionally humans!

Elephants (6) mostly eat **grass** (G).

Humans (7) eat pretty much **everything** (E)!

Kitti's hog-nosed bats (8) eat **beetles** (H).

THING TO KNOW NO. 23
HOW DOES A SNAKE SWALLOW THINGS BIGGER THAN ITS OWN HEAD?

1. a / 2. b / 3. c / 4. c / 5. a
6. d / 7. c / 8. d / 9. a / 10. b

THING TO KNOW NO. 29
HOW LONG IS A LIGHT-YEAR?

1. 53.68 times

2. 7.48 times

3. 1.28 light seconds

4. 8.32 minutes

5. 96.51 years!

6. 5.47 hours

7. 5.78 days

THING TO KNOW NO. 31
CAN A COCKROACH REALLY LIVE FOR A WEEK WITHOUT ITS HEAD?

1. c / 2. d / 3. d / 4. b / 5. b
6. b / 7. c / 8. b / 9. b / 10. d

THING TO KNOW NO. 42
HOW BIG IS AN ATOM?

1. d / 2. c / 3. a / 4. a / 5. d
6. c / 7. c / 8. c / 9. b / 10. a

THING TO KNOW NO. 45
WHY DO SOME ANIMALS SHED THEIR SKIN?

1. TRUE
2. TRUE
3. **FALSE:** Your skin makes up 15% of your entire body weight.
4. TRUE
5. **FALSE:** You have about 650 sweat glands per square in of skin.

Answers Continued

Hey! **No cheating!**

6. **FALSE:** The outer layer is called the epidermis and the inner layer is called the dermis.

7. **TRUE** / 8. **TRUE** / 9. **TRUE**
10. **FALSE:** You lose 40,000 dead skin cells every minute!
11. **TRUE**

THING TO KNOW NO. 54
ARE BATS REALLY BLIND?

THING TO KNOW NO. 55
WHAT WIPED OUT NEARLY HALF THE POPULATION OF EUROPE?

1. b / 2. c / 3. a / 4. a / 5. c
6. a / 7. d / 8. a / 9. b / 10. d

THING TO KNOW NO. 57
HOW DO OYSTERS MAKE PEARLS?

JANUARY
Garnet—usually red, but comes in almost any color except blue

FEBRUARY
Amethyst—Purple

MARCH
Aquamarine—pale greenish blue or bluish green
Bloodstone—green with red bloodlike spots

APRIL
Diamond—usually clear, but comes in many colors

MAY
Emerald—Green

JUNE
Pearl—usually white, cream, or pinkish (black is rare and precious), but cultured pearls can be almost any pale color
Moonstone—usually whitish blue, but available in many colors
Alexandrite—usually appears green in natural light and reddish purple in artificial light

JULY
Ruby—Red

AUGUST
Peridot—usually yellowish green
Sardonyx—usually white and brownish red

SEPTEMBER
Sapphire—usually blue, but can be almost any color

OCTOBER
Opal and **Tourmaline**—come in almost any color and are often multicolored

NOVEMBER
Topaz—usually golden brown or yellow, but comes in a wide range of colors
Citrine—yellow or orange

DECEMBER
Turquoise—usually sky blue or greenish
Blue topaz—clear blue
Zircon—usually brown or green

THING TO KNOW NO. 58
WHAT IS THE QUIETEST SOUND WE CAN HEAR?

10 dB—Rustling leaves

20 dB—Your bedroom at night

30 dB—Forest

40 dB—Whisper/Library

50 dB—Electric toothbrush/Rainfall

Answers Continued

Hey! **No cheating!**

60 dB—Normal conversation
70 dB—Busy street traffic
80 dB—Vacuum cleaner/Alarm clock
90 dB—Average factory
100 dB—Walkman on at highest volume
110 dB—Front row of a rock concert
120 dB—Jet aircraft taking off/Thunder
130 dB—Gunshot
150 dB—Professional fireworks show
160 dB—Instant perforation of eardrum/Glass breaks
180 dB—A rocket firing from a launching pad
190 dB—Blue whale singing
210 dB—Sonic boom created by a jet aircraft
220 dB—Space shuttle taking off
230 dB—Large nonnuclear explosion
240 dB—Tornado, Fujitsu scale 5
250 dB—Atomic bomb—Hiroshima and Nagasaki
320 dB—Volcanic eruption

THING TO KNOW NO. 71
ARE YOU ONLY EVER A FEW FEET FROM A RAT IN A BIG CITY?

1. c / 2. a / 3. d / 4. d
5. a / 6. c / 7. c / 8. c

THING TO KNOW NO. 77
WHY DO PEOPLE KISS (AND ANIMALS DON'T)?

1. b / 2. d / 3. c / 4. d / 5. d / 6. c
7. a / 8. d / 9. d / 10. The answer is a, but you also get half a point for choosing c, as, strictly speaking, men should only kiss female relatives they are not allowed to marry.

THING TO KNOW NO. 81
WHY DO CAMELS HAVE HUMPS?

1. d / 2. d / 3. c / 4. a / 5. b
6. b / 7. c / 8. d / 9. d / 10. a

THING TO KNOW NO. 87
WHO WAS THE SMARTEST PERSON EVER?

1. TRUE
2. TRUE
3. **FALSE:** Helen is $2 short
4. **FALSE:** They have a total of 17 legs
5. TRUE
6. TRUE
7. TRUE
8. TRUE
9. **FALSE:** It reads "Looking out to sea, I could sea a ship on the see."
10. **FALSE:** The 18th consonant is *S*
11. TRUE
12. TRUE
13. TRUE
14. **FALSE:** 22 minutes before four = 3:38 and 18 minutes past three = 3:18
15. **FALSE:** Rick and Ruby's nuts together = 195; Jane and Ruby's nuts = 175; Rick and Jane's nuts = 250
16. TRUE
17. TRUE
18. TRUE
19. TRUE
20. **FALSE:** The figure that replaces *x* is 8 (1+2=3, 2+3=5, 3+5=8, 5+8=13)

GENUINE IQ Ratings:
40–55 Severely challenged
55–70 Challenged
70–85 Below average
85–115 Average
115–130 Above average
130–145 Gifted
145–160 Extremely gifted
160+ Genius

THING TO KNOW NO. 99
WHO WAS THE GREATEST CONQUEROR OF ALL TIME?

1. b / 2. c / 3. b / 4. b / 5. c
6. b / 7. d / 8. a / 9. b / 10. c

THING TO KNOW NO. 101
WHAT WOULD HAPPEN TO YOU IN A BLACK HOLE?

1. d / 2. c / 3. d / 4. a / 5. d
6. d / 7. b / 8. b / 9. c / 10. a

How to Use Your Pocket-Sized Checklist

Use the following instructions to keep track of the **Things to Know** you've mastered and pass on your knowledge at a moment's notice.

Cut out the list . . .

. . . and keep it with you at all times.

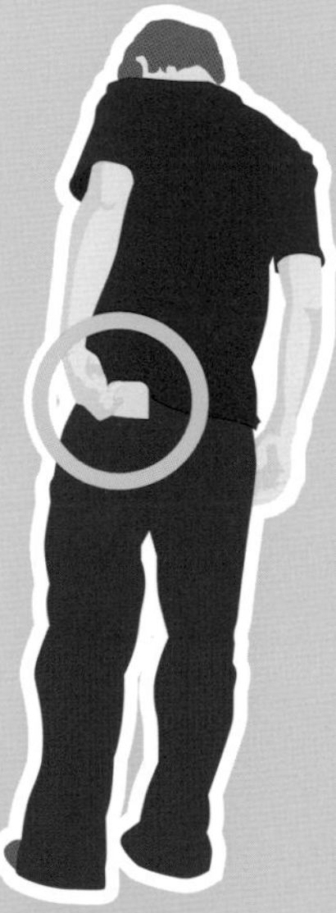

When you've mastered a **Thing to Know** . . .

. . . check it off on the list.

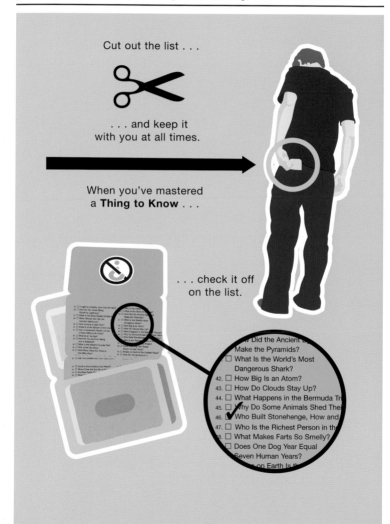

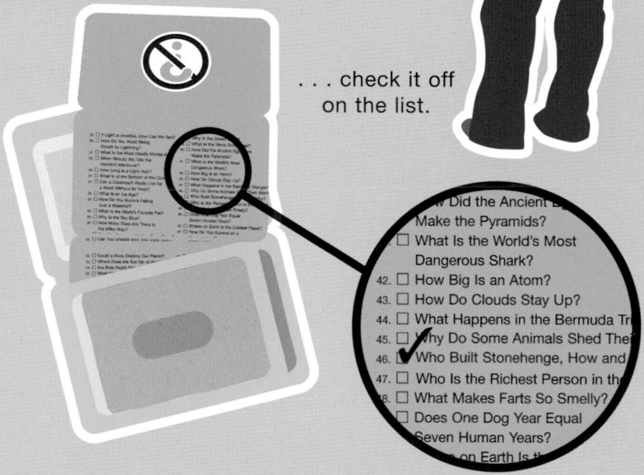

Fold — Fold

Fold — Fold

Small print: keep this list with you at all times. Use every opportunity to master the **Things to Know** on this list and pass on the knowledge.

1. ☐ What Was the Biggest Bang Ever?
2. ☐ What Is DNA (and Are We All That Different from Chimps)?
3. ☐ Why Don't Fish Drown?
4. ☐ What Were the Seven Wonders of the World?
5. ☐ Why Is Our Blood Red?
6. ☐ What Is the Oldest Living Thing?
7. ☐ What Is the Difference Between a Fruit and a Vegetable?
8. ☐ Is Time Travel Possible?
9. ☐ Who Would Win the Animal Olympic 100-Meter Race?
10. ☐ How Do You Do an Ollie on a Skateboard?
11. ☐ Who Were the First Chocoholics?
12. ☐ How Big Is the Universe?
13. ☐ Did Cannibals Really Exist?
14. ☐ Will Your Stomach Explode if You Eat Too Much?
15. ☐ When Was It Possible to Walk from London to New York?
16. ☐ How Do Mountains Grow?
17. ☐ Is Your Teacher an Alien?
18. ☐ What Are the Biggest and Smallest Animals in the World?
19. ☐ How Much Does the Earth Weigh?
20. ☐ Which Way Is North?
21. ☐ What Is the Solar System?
22. ☐ Why Don't We Fall Off the Earth?
23. ☐ How Does a Snake Swallow Things Bigger Than Its Own Head?
24. ☐ When Did Money Start Making the World Go Around?

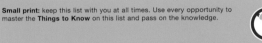

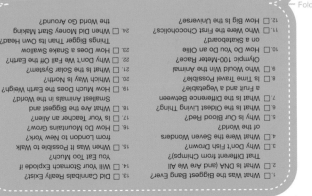

Checklist

25. ☐ If Light Is Invisible, How Can We See?
26. ☐ How Do You Avoid Being Struck by Lightning?
27. ☐ What Is the Deadliest Martial Art?
28. ☐ When Should You Use the Heimlich Maneuver?
29. ☐ How Long Is a Light-Year?
30. ☐ What Is at the Bottom of the Ocean?
31. ☐ Can a Cockroach Really Live for a Week Without Its Head?
32. ☐ What Is an Ice Age?
33. ☐ How Do You Survive Falling over a Waterfall?
34. ☐ What Is the World's Favorite Pet?
35. ☐ Why Is the Sky Blue?
36. ☐ How Many Stars Are There in the Milky Way?
37. ☐ Can You Sneeze with Your Eyes Open?
38. ☐ Why Is the Ocean Salty?
39. ☐ What Is the Worst Smell Ever?
40. ☐ How Did the Ancient Egyptians Make the Pyramids?
41. ☐ What Is the World's Most Dangerous Shark?
42. ☐ How Big Is an Atom?
43. ☐ How Do Clouds Stay Up?
44. ☐ What Happens in the Bermuda Triangle?
45. ☐ Why Do Some Animals Shed Their Skin?
46. ☐ Who Built Stonehenge, How and Why?
47. ☐ Who Is the Richest Person in the World?
48. ☐ What Makes Farts So Smelly?
49. ☐ Does One Dog Year Equal Seven Human Years?
50. ☐ Where on Earth Is the Coldest Place?
51. ☐ How Do You Survive on a Desert Island?

52. ☐ Could a Rock Destroy Our Planet?
53. ☐ Where Does the Sun Go at Night?
54. ☐ Are Bats Really Blind?
55. ☐ What Wiped Out Nearly Half the Population of Europe?
56. ☐ What Is the Scariest Thing in the World?
57. ☐ How Do Oysters Make Pearls?
58. ☐ What Is the Quietest Sound We Can Hear?
59. ☐ How Do Planes Get into the Air—and Stay There?
60. ☐ Why Does the Moon Change Shape?
61. ☐ Were All Romans from Rome?
62. ☐ How Do You Survive an Earthquake?
63. ☐ How Many People Are Flying Through the Air at Any One Time?
64. ☐ Do Animals Cry?
65. ☐ Why Do We Get Hiccups?
66. ☐ Why Do Stars Twinkle?
67. ☐ Do Storms Have Eyes?
68. ☐ Who Invented Paper?
69. ☐ How Can I Win Millions?
70. ☐ What Is Spontaneous Human Combustion?
71. ☐ Are You Only Ever a Few Feet from a Rat in a Big City?
72. ☐ Who Was the Most Bloodthirsty Pirate Ever?
73. ☐ Pus—What Is It Good For?
74. ☐ How Dangerous Is Quicksand?
75. ☐ How Can Birds Stand on Electric Wires and Not Be Toasted?
76. ☐ How Do You Survive an Avalanche?
77. ☐ Why Do People Kiss (and Animals Don't)?
78. ☐ Who Invented the Internet?

79. ☐ How Does a Firework Work?
80. ☐ Where Can You Find Red Giants and White Dwarves?
81. ☐ Why Do Camels Have Humps?
82. ☐ Why Are There 60 Seconds in a Minute?
83. ☐ Where Is the Night Sky Multicolored?
84. ☐ What Is the Sixth Sense?
85. ☐ Why Do We Dream?
86. ☐ How Does a Chameleon Change Its Color?
87. ☐ Who Was the Smartest Person Ever?
88. ☐ Who Invented the Wheel?
89. ☐ How Do You Do a Wheelie on a Bike?
90. ☐ What Is the World's Most Poisonous Creature?
91. ☐ How Do Bees Make Honey?
92. ☐ When Was Writing Invented?
93. ☐ Did People Make Everything from Stone in the Stone Age?
94. ☐ What Makes Things Glow in the Dark?
95. ☐ Are Cats and Dogs Color-Blind?
96. ☐ Where Are the Most Haunted Houses in the World?
97. ☐ What Is the World's Deadliest Disease?
98. ☐ Nails—What Are They Good For?
99. ☐ Who Was the Greatest Conqueror of All Time?
100. ☐ When Was the First Leap Year and Why Do We Need Them?
101. ☐ What Would Happen to You in a Black Hole?

Write the name of the **Thing to Know** title here.

Cut here

Cut here

Extra Paper

Write the name of the **Thing to Know** title here.

Cut here

Cut here

Thank-Yous and Noteworthy Acknowledgments

Write your own acknowledgments
over the example below

The biggest thank you goes to Helen Szirtes, the behind-the-scenes hero of this book, for her brilliant touches and attention to detail. The book wouldn't be this good without you and your fine-tooth comb.

Thanks to Tracey Turner for her appetite for useful (and useless) facts and her talent for explaining them, Ele Fountain for making this book happen and for laughing in the right places, and Helena Coryndon in production.

Thanks to Jane & Rick, Mom & Dad, Rob & Karly, Jim & Holly, Jan & Carl, Allison, Katy, Stephen & Amanda, Hackett, Ed & Clare, and all the others for their suggestions for Things they really Needed to Know—I hope we answered the questions for you.

Thanks also goes to Dr. Lisa Conlan for showing me where my kidneys are and Simon & Charlotte for their amazing snowman-building talents.

About the Authors

Write your details over the top of the example below

Richard Horne is an illustrator and designer of album covers, book covers, Web sites, and greeting cards. A self-confessed risk taker and left-hander, this is his third book, following the success of ***101 Things to Do Before You Die*** and ***101 Things to Do Before You're Old and Boring***. He lives in London, England.

Tracey Turner is a writer for children and adults. A lifetime of finding herself in dire circumstances and in desperate want of essential information has made her only too aware of the need for this book. She now hopes to be ready for anything, including avalanches, black holes, and time travel. She lives in London, England.